P9-DGJ-258

DOUBLEDAY
CELEBRATES
100 YEARS OF
EXCELLENCE

GIFTS *of* Love

Crafts and Presents That Embody the Spirit of Giving

ALICE CHAPIN

Doubleday New York London Toronto Sydney Auckland

OUACHITA TECHNICAL COLLEGE

A MAIN STREET BOOK
PUBLISHED BY DOUBLEDAY
a division of Bantam Doubleday Dell Publishing Group, Inc.
1540 Broadway, New York, New York 10036

MAIN STREET BOOKS, DOUBLEDAY, and the portrayal of a building with a tree are trademarks of Doubleday, a division of Bantam Doubleday Dell Publishing Group, Inc.

Book design by Bonni Leon-Berman

Originally published by Tyndale House Publishers as *The Big Book of Great Gift Ideas*
Scripture quotations are taken from *The Living Bible* copyright © 1971 owned by assignment by KNT Charitable Trust. All rights reserved.

The recipe for "Bath Bag" on page 18 is from *The Scented Room* © 1986 by Barbara M. Ohrback. Used by permission of Crown Publishers, Inc.

"11 Steps to End Family Cold Wars" on page 49 is adapted from the article by James and Mary Kenny in the June 1986 *St. Anthony Messenger*. Used with permission.

The poem "Waiting" on page 126 by Theresa V. Meyer, copyright © 1982, is used with permission of *Signs of the Times*.

Library of Congress Cataloging-in-Publication Data
Chapin, Alice Zillman.
Gifts of love: crafts and presents that embody the spirit of giving / Alice Chapin.
p. cm.
"Main Street books."
1. Handicraft. 2. Gifts.
TT157.C3823 1997
745.45—dc21 97-10152
CIP

ISBN 0-385-49042-9
Copyright © 1991 and 1997 by Alice Chapin
All Rights Reserved
Printed in the United States of America
November 1997
1 3 5 7 9 10 8 6 4 2

TT
157
C3823
1997

ACKNOWLEDGMENTS

SPECIAL THANKS to my many friends, the friends of friends, neighbors, colleagues, relatives, participants in seminars I taught, and other "contributing angels" for sharing, one by one, the wonderfully creative ideas for this book. When folks found out I was a gift-hints pack rat, suggestions came in by mail, during kaffeeklatsches and dinner conversations, from houseguests or jogging companions, people I sat next to on airplane trips, and even by phone from perfect strangers who wanted to be part of the project. Finally, after twenty years of such collecting, *Gifts of Love* was born.

CONTENTS

Introduction 1

1. Great Gifts for Grown-ups to Give Each Other 3

ENCOURAGER JARS 5
A Jar of Love Notes 5
A Jar of Bible Promises 5
A Jar of Smiles 7

TOYS FOR GRANDMA'S HOUSE 7

GREEN GIFTS 8
Forced Bulbs 9
Easy Terrarium 10

HEIRLOOM RECIPE BOOK 11

OLD-TIME CRAFT PATTERN BOOK 12

HIGHLIGHTED PHONE BOOK 13

WISH BOOKS GALORE 13
Clothing Catalogs 14
Gift Catalogs 14
Department Store Catalogs 14
Catalogs for People with Special Needs 15
Gardening Catalogs 15
Miscellaneous Catalogs 15

MAPPING IT OUT 16
Memory Maps 16
Welcome Maps 17

SWEET FRAGRANCES 18

COLLECT-A-GIFTS 19

JUST-A-LITTLE-BOOK GIFTS 20

PHOTO ALBUMS 21

TOLLS APLENTY 21

RERUNS FOR FUN 22

SECONDHAND BRAND-NEW GIFTS 22

PERSONALIZED LIST BOOK 23

IOU CERTIFICATES AND COUPONS 24
IOU Coupons for Specific Services 25
IOU Coupons from Artisans and Professionals 27

SWAP-A-GIFT 29

LETTER GIFTS 29
Birthday or Christmas Letters 29
Thank-You Letters 30
Loving-Memories Letters 31
Journal Letters 32
Family Newsletter Chain 33
Out-of-the-Blue Letters 33
Keepsake Letters 34
Link Letters 34

GIFTS OF GOOD TASTE 35
Special Recipes 35
Cookies 36
Homemade Breads 36
Muffin Pyramid 37
Candy 37
Coconut Cake Wreath 37
Meals 37

HEIRLOOM GIFTS 38
Old Photos 39
Granddad's Old Bible 40
Mementos 41
Heirloom Collections 41

RECYCLED HANDMADE ITEMS 42
Patchwork Pieces 42
Children's Art Pillow 43
Hands-of-Love Quilt 43

FAMILY ROOTS ON TAPE 44

GOODWILL TOWARD ALL: THE BEST OF GIFTS 45
The Gift of a Better Attitude 45
The Gift of Openly Showing Love 46
Making Time for Others 47
Pledges of Personal Change for Another's Sake 48
Mercy Mild: The Gift of Forgiveness 48

THE SILENT GIFT: PRAYER 50

2. Great Gifts for Grown-ups to Give Youngsters 53

COLLECTIONS THAT MAKE GREAT KIDS' GIFTS 55
Coins 55
Inspirational Packet 56
Buttons 56
Paper Dolls Galore 56
Geological Specimens 56
Postage Stamps and Matchbooks 57
Celebrity Autographs 57

ACTIVITY KITS 58
Very, Very Busy Box 58
Bathtub Kit for Preschoolers 60
Nurse's Kit 60
Scientist's Kit 61
Dress-up Kit 61
Do-It-Yourself Baking Kit 61

Fabric Design Kit 62
Manicure Kit 62
Soap Carving Kit 62
Grab Bag Basket 63
Hobby Library 63
Wallets 63

FASCINATING FREEBIES IN THE MAIL 63

ONE BIG THING 64

LITTLE FOLKS EMERGENCY PHONE DIRECTORY 65

PERSONALIZED ADDRESS BOOK 65

COOKIE MESSAGES 65

HEIRLOOM TOYS 67

INSECT HOUSES 67

STICKERS 68

SEW WHAT? 68
Designer Socks 68
Bean Bags 68
Pillowcases 69
Hand Puppets 69
Stuffed Creatures 69
Doll Wardrobe 69
Quilts 70
"Just Like Me" Doll 70
I-Can-Do-It Book 70
ABC Book 71
Christmas Ornaments 71
Banners 71
Christmas Stockings 72
More Ideas from Books 72

SHOP PROJECTS 73
Sources of Toy Ideas 73

GIFTS FOR THE CHILD WHO LIVES FAR AWAY 73
Balloons 74
Cassette Tapes or Videos 74
Family Tales 74
Fantasy Book 75
Special Mail 75
Postcards 76
Film 76

GIFTS OF TIME AND TALK 76
Excursions 77
Mystery Trip 78

PROMISE GIFTS THAT KIDS WILL LOVE 79

PROMISE GIFTS FOR TEENS 82

3. Nifty No-Cost Gifts for Children to Give Grown-ups 85

BOOKS, BOOKS, BOOKS 87

COVERS, COVERS, COVERS 88
Phone Book Covers 89

BOOKMARKS FOR BOOKWORMS 89

TAPED INTERVIEW 90
Love on Tape 90

PARENTS' POSITIVE REPORT CARD 91

HAPPY FAMILY CALENDARS 93

GIVING IT BACK 94

GIFTS FROM DOUGH 94
Clay Cookie People 94
More Dough Projects 95

SILHOUETTE PROFILE 96

DECK THE WALLS 96
Other Things to Frame as Gifts 96

THINGS CHILDREN CAN COLLECT FOR GIFTS 98

GIFTS OF LIFE 100
Sprouts 100
Forced Flower Blooms 101
Dyed Blooms 101
Avocados 102
Other Plants 102

HANDY GARDENING ACCESSORIES 103

UNDERCOVER IDEAS 104

FANCY STATIONERY AND NOTEPAPER 105

HOLIDAY SHELF EDGING 107

TABLE ACCESSORIES 107
Place Mats 108
Napkins 109
Napkin Rings 109

PLANT A FAMILY TREE 109

OTHER IDEAS FOR NO-COST ADULT GIFTS 110

IOU COUPONS 111

4. Nifty No-Cost Gifts for Children to Give Other Children 113

FOR PET LOVERS 115

PASS-THEM-ON GIFTS 116

JIGSAWS 117

MOBILES 117

SPOOL PEOPLE 118

CONE GIFTS 118

TOY BOX 119

PAINTER'S PARTY 119
Easy Easel 119
Painter's Caddy 119

HOMEMADE PLAY DOUGH 120

FOOD FOR THE BIRDS 121
Peanut Butter Cone 121
Feeder for Small Birds 121
Coconut Shell Feeder 122

OTHER EASY THINGS CHILDREN CAN GIVE 122

MY TIME IS YOUR TIME 123

5. Great Gifts for Grandparents 125

PROMISES OF TIME 127

A BOOK OF HAPPY COUPONS 128

HELPS FOR OLDER EYES AND EARS 130
Large Print Hints 130
Many-Colored Threads 130
Self-Esteem Builders 131
News from Friends 131
Good Grooming 132
Daily Calls 132
Special Occasion Calls 132
Search-a-Puzzle 133
Safety Mirror 133

IDEAS FOR SHARING CHRISTMAS ACTIVITIES 134

GREAT LOW-COST GIFTS TO BUY OR PUT TOGETHER 135

GIFTS FOR THE ELDERLY IN A NURSING HOME OR HOSPITAL 139

6. Gifts from Stores and Catalogs for Just About Anybody 143

BABIES AND TODDLERS UNDER THREE YEARS 145
Baby Maybes 145
Toddler Pleasers 145
Preschoolers 146

SIX- TO TWELVE-YEAR-OLDS 147

TEENS 150

ADULTS 153

PEOPLE WITH SPECIAL INTERESTS 157
Seamstresses 157
Other Needlework Enthusiasts 157
Serious Cooks 158
Mostly for Men 159
Parents of Young Children 160
Gardeners 160
Clergy 161

THE WHOLE FAMILY 162

7. Wrap It Up with Imagination and Economy 167

FOCUS ON THE BOX 169

DESIGNER PAPER 169

JUNIOR SMART WRAPS 172

WRAP-UPS FOR PROBLEM PRESENTS 173

A FINAL WORD 175

COUPON EXAMPLES 178

INTRODUCTION

The only gift is a portion of thyself;

Thou must bleed for me.

Therefore the poet brings his poem;

the shepherd his lamb;

the sailor coral and shells;

the painter his picture;

the girl a handkerchief of her own sewing.

—RALPH WALDO EMERSON

COME ALONG THROUGH the following pages and discover great gifts of a different kind. Here you will find hundreds of unique year-round gift suggestions that are far beyond the ordinary. For the most part, they cost nothing or next to it, and they encourage replacing a splurge of money with gifts of time and personal interest in others. They demonstrate the mottoes: "Less is more" and "Giving ourselves away is best of all." These ideas are especially for those who have felt victimized by the whirlwind of advertising during times that should be full of celebration.

No cheap gifts here! The sizable worth of these remembrances comes from the imagination and thoughtful creativity behind them, personal time spent, special kindnesses or talents given, magic memories recycled, experiences shared, ties to family and friends renewed, or promises made to fulfill the recipient's dream. The items here are likely to bless both gifted and giver, and the price is always right!

In many instances, all you pay is maintaining a goodwill attitude that keeps you attuned to another's specific needs and desires. The "just for fun" gifts will bring delighted smiles or guffaws, while others may bring tears of joy. When you give something special that nobody but you can offer, it is a creation of love. For the recipient, it is often an uncommon gift of love that will give deep encouragement and joy long after the gifting occasion.

Browse in leisure through these ideas for uplifting gifting for practically everybody. We have included chapters with ideas for presents that grown-ups can give to other adults and to favorite children. Youngsters can pick and choose from chapters with kids in mind, stocked with plenty of ideas for nifty no-cost personalized presents to both adults and other children. Be sure to take extra time to read the chapter featuring satisfying gifts for older folks because their needs are sometimes misunderstood and they are often most difficult to shop for. One chapter is devoted to ideas that *do* cost a bit of money just because there are times you will need to go out and purchase something. Perhaps the most creative of all is the gift-wrap chapter with ideas for wrapping in novel ways with recycled materials. The recipients on your list will imagine that you spent all day making your packages so dramatic.

My fervent wish is that you will discover the joy of a new kind of gift giving that will gladden hearts as never before. Memories are made of these!

—ALICE CHAPIN

CHAPTER 1

GREAT GIFTS *for* Grown-ups to Give Each Other

YOU MAY DREAD special days if you have a large family that insists on exchanging costly gifts. One year, my husband and I grew tired of January bills left over from an expensive Yule celebration. We had a hunch others did too, since each family unit was spending several hundred dollars to buy presents for fourteen relatives. It took a lot of courage for us to break tradition and suggest that everyone cut back to what we now call "token gifts" costing under three dollars each.

The challenge of buying more for less sent us all scurrying for new ideas. Now we try to locate something just right for everyone. Sometimes, we give things like a white elephant from the knickknack shelf or a beautiful silk tie picked up at a clearance sale. Some gifts are strictly for fun like an absurd, bargain-basement wall hanging that got passed from one to the other, year after year (always disguised in an elegant box) until it has become a tradition to see whose home it will settle into next. Last Christmas, we conspired to load up one daughter's family with thirty-five jars of tongue-tingling hot salsa because the rest of us kid them about "torching" each and every meal at their house with red hot sauce. Can you imagine the fun this kind of creative gifting has added to our celebration? There are lots of guffaws from wisecracking brothers-in-law and giggles from the children and teenagers. The good-natured give-and-take and the anticipation of getting such uncommon presents have added to the thoughtful love and caring of the Christmas season.

This same spirit of giving opens doors for creative, low-cost gifts all year round. Browsing in these pages will touch off a torrent of inspiration so you will feel like a joyful giver at each occasion.

ENCOURAGER JARS

GIFTS OF ENCOURAGEMENT provide an emergency supply of love and self-esteem at just the time they are needed most. An encourager jar is a glass apothecary jar with short messages inside capsules. First, empty and flush away the contents of several pill capsules, or ask the pharmacist for a dozen empty see-through capsules. Type and cut apart tiny messages to your spouse, a beloved friend, or a parent who may need encouragement. Roll and stuff one message in each capsule. Be sure to write the prescription and attach to the jar as follows:

Rx: Take one pill per day while supply lasts, or as needed for a pickup.

A Jar of Love Notes

This kind of encourager jar has messages that tell your love and admiration.

Ideas

You are not only my lover and spouse but also my best friend.
Roses are red; violets are blue; I am glad I married you.
Your hugs are the best when I'm feeling blue.
Thanks for being so patient when Mom was sick. I'll bake you an angel food cake soon.
The thing I most like about you is your integrity.

A Jar of Bible Promises

Fill the jar with Bible promises typed on small cards to lift the spirit.

Ideas

Shall I look to the mountain gods for help? No! My help is from Jehovah who made the mountains! And the heavens too! He will never let me stumble, slip or fall. For he is always watching, never sleeping. Jehovah himself is caring for you! He is your defender. He protects you day and night.

Psalm 121:1–6

Now in your strength I can scale any wall, attack any troop. What a God he is! How perfect in every way! All his promises prove true.

Psalm 18:29–30

I can do everything God asks me to with the help of Christ who gives me the strength and power.

Philippians 4:13

Be bold and strong! Banish fear and doubt! For remember, the Lord your God is with you wherever you go.

Joshua 1:9

God can do what men can't!

Luke 18:27

Others:
Psalm 89:7–13
2 Chronicles 20:15*b*
Isaiah 40:11
Matthew 10:29–31
Psalm 145:18–19
1 Peter 1:6
Hosea 6:1–3
Psalm 43:5

Psalm 34:18–19
Psalm 18:2
Ephesians 1:19–20

A Jar of Smiles

Fill the jar with small fun items for someone going through a hard time. They will show your love and caring and they may bring forth a mind-mending smile or giggle. Examples: Wrap a purse packet of tissues "to catch your tears of crying or laughter," a tube of glue "to help hold things together," a bottle of vitamins "for inner strength and outer glow," a bag of peppermints "because your life needs a little sweetening right now," or a game of jacks "to jack up your spirits."

Send encourager gifts also to loving care givers of chronically ill people who are probably hurting just as much as those suffering with sickness.

7

TOYS FOR GRANDMA'S HOUSE

WHEN THE FAMILY with young children visits an older adult or a grandparent, toys may not be available. I tracked down every garage sale I could find for a month. I haunted friends, neighbors, and relatives who had extra toys and filled a toy chest. After packing it with dozens of playthings just right for my own four children and my sister's, I gave it to Mom. The kids then enjoyed visiting Grandma even more. Mom knew how much time I spent getting the gift together and was very grateful because her occasional baby-sitting was a lot easier.

GREEN GIFTS

PLANTS THAT YOU have nurtured and raised from cuttings make very personal presents because you have invested a small part of your own life in them before giving them away.

Gifts of growing plants nurture happiness all year. The oxygen they produce is a healthy benefit too. Best of all, they are quiet companions. They need us to care for them weekly or even more often. And who doesn't love to be needed?

Make cuttings between two and five inches from your own greenery or ask folks you know for snippets from their hardiest plants about eight weeks before the gift occasion. For best sprouting, cut from *below* the leaf node. Place the cuttings in a colored glass of water in bright but not direct sunlight to root, changing the water every three or four days. Some of the easiest to grow are coleus, wax begonia, wandering Jew, philodendron, and ivy. After four to six weeks, cuttings usually show excellent roots and can then be potted in good soil in containers big enough to allow room for growth. Since it may take more than one attempt to get good rooting, start with several trial cuttings.

After potting, decorate the container in a way that fits the occasion. For example, dress up your Christmas plant gifts by hooking candy canes all around the top of a plastic pot and adding a sprig of holly and a red velvet bow. These terrific red-and-white pots cannot be found in floral shops.

Forced Bulbs

What can make a more dramatic gift than a vivid blooming amaryllis or narcissus to decorate the coffee table or use as a dinner centerpiece? Both are unbelievably easy to grow from bulbs. They do not need a long preliminary rooting period, and the cheerful blooms will eagerly come forth about four to eight weeks after planting. Best of all, they will bloom in the dead of winter.

- *Amaryllis.* Place about one inch of pebbles or broken clay pottery in the bottom of a clay, plastic, or ceramic pot with bottom drainage hole. The container should be at least two inches wider than the bulb's diameter. Fill the pot with several inches of potting soil and center the bulb. Continue adding soil so that two-thirds of the bulb is covered (one-third should remain exposed). Firm up soil around the bulb. Place the container in the sink or on a saucer, water thoroughly, and set it in a cool, bright spot. No fertilizer is needed and only very, very sparse watering until stems begin to appear. After growth shows well, move the plant to a place where there is direct sunlight three or four hours a day, and keep the soil moist. When flowers show (amaryllis often produce two to five spectacular stalks), remove the container to less direct sunlight so blooms will last longer.
- *Paperwhite narcissus.* Gently work three or four narcissus bulbs down into a shallow container half full of pebbles, perlite, vermiculite, or pearl chips. (Paperwhites grow so easily that they do not need soil.) Add more of the medium, leaving the top one-third of each bulb exposed. Carefully add enough water so liquid touches the base of each bulb and place the container in a rather cool, dark place. Roots will develop quickly. When green growth shows, usually after about two weeks, move the pot to a warm, sunny room. Keep the water level so it always

touches the base of the bulbs. Rotate the container so bulbs grow evenly.

• *Bonus idea.* Flower bulbs make good gifts. The receiver will remember you when planting each one and the bulbs can multiply over the years to make a yard full of sweet-smelling blooms. If you know a gardener-seamstress, be clever and tuck bulbs inside a little covered sewing basket with a note, "As ye sow, so shall ye reap."

Easy Terrarium

Terrariums are particularly nice to give during cold winter months when it is difficult to go outside for a daily dose of nature. You will need a glass container with a very wide opening, maybe a brandy snifter, a fishbowl, an aquarium, a bell jar, a water cooler jug, or an institution-sized glass food jar. Plastic scratches easily, and acids from the soil will make it look cloudy.

Find moss in the woods, or buy it already dried in a garden shop. Press a solid layer of moistened moss along the bottom and about a quarter up the side of the glass bowl with the greenest side facing out. Over the moss, spread a thin layer of aquarium gravel, then some finer gravel and crushed charcoal, which discourages bacterial growth. Fill the container about a quarter full with the best potting soil and pack it tightly. Push two- or three-inch cuttings of your favorite green plants into the soil far enough apart to allow room for growth. Plants that do well are ferns, English ivy, spider plant, wild ginger, wild violets, and hepatica. If you create a bog by keeping the terrarium very moist, interesting carnivorous plants like Venus's-flytrap can be included. Water the plants with about two teaspoons of water each. Add several very bright pebbles, small figurines, seashells, and a bit more moss on top for color. Cover the jar as tightly as possible with plastic wrap, and be sure it gets sun at least part of the day. It will take care of itself.

Create a desert terrarium by using mostly sand and planting several varieties of cactus. It should remain uncovered. You can make a cactus windowsill garden by planting cacti in a shallow wooden bowl lined first with charcoal, then with a layer of sandy soil. Water very lightly every few months.

HEIRLOOM RECIPE BOOK

RECIPES FOR A family's favorite foods never seem to get written down. Wonderful gourmet secrets often die when older relatives do. Many good cooks do not realize the treasury of fascinating recipes they have gathered over the years. Some have been forced by circumstances to make terrific collections of meatless menus, low-cholesterol, sugar-free, or high-fiber diet recipes.

You can create a priceless book for each family unit on your gift list by collecting these precious secrets. Begin collecting recipes by sending a photocopied note or E-mail to everybody asking each person to carefully type or write out neatly in longhand a few favorites along with complete instructions, one recipe per page. Include a sample to show the size sheet you have in mind, and emphasize accuracy. And set a date for the reply. Suggest specific dishes you have enjoyed like Mom's lemon pie, Grandma's black walnut cake, Aunt Tillie's red-hot chili, or Dad's Old World spaghetti sauce. Or gather family recipes on a single theme: ethnic, Christmas favorites, desserts, casseroles, or pasta.

When you receive the recipe sheets, photocopy and then staple them into booklets as your gift. An attractive cover and catchy title will make the collection even more memorable. If you have time, accompany the book with a casserole or plate of cookies you have prepared from one of the recipes. Can you imagine the excitement in years to come when a younger niece or nephew finds Aunt Lil's icicle pickle recipe or Grandma's dark fruitcake instructions, especially in her very own handwriting? Sharing recipes is a wonderfully heartwarming way to keep in touch if family members live far apart.

A beloved hand-me-down recipe can be photocopied and shellacked onto a beautiful wall plaque to give brothers and sisters, aunts and uncles. Family members will feel more united seeing this simple reminder while visiting each other's kitchens, especially when the dish is prepared and served at various get-togethers.

Unexpected bonus: Older people who have tenderly tucked away zillions of great ideas will love being asked to share from their wonderful store of old recipes. Being able to pass on such old-time traditions can be especially gratifying for them.

12 OLD-TIME CRAFT PATTERN BOOK

GROWN-UPS OFTEN RECALL wearing favorite hand-knit sweaters, mittens, slippers, and other handcrafted items given them as youngsters by loving adults. You can photocopy or write out in longhand the patterns for these special knitted or crocheted items and others such as afghans, tablecloth edgings, and booties. For quilts and wooden toys, you may cut full-sized paper patterns. Include a note, for example: "Remember when you asked for the pattern to this ski cap that I made for you when you were fifteen? You wore it every day to school. I finally found the pattern in the attic trunk last month. Here it is so you can make one for your Mary Ann. Let me know if you need help. HAPPY VALENTINE'S DAY!"

HIGHLIGHTED PHONE BOOK

FOR SOMEONE WHO lives in your house, highlight every important and often-called number in the white pages of a new phone directory. Keep a yellow marking pen handy, and do the highlighting every time you look up a number. The personalized phone book will save the other's searching up and down long columns over and over for the same numbers all year. See page 89 for directions to make a nifty felt cover.

WISH BOOKS GALORE

WHO DOES NOT enjoy wishing her way through a colorful catalog and turning down corners of the pages with appealing items? Gather up as many specialized catalogs as you can, and match them to the interests of those on your gift list. Hundreds of free or very inexpensive catalogs for tools, toys, home furnishings, vitamins, crafts, and people with special needs make fascinating reading.

The United States Consumer Information Center, P.O. Box 100, Pueblo, CO 81002, offers a catalog featuring booklets on nearly two hundred interesting subjects, many free. Here are a few:

For the Birds; How to attract and feed different species of birds (50¢)

Stars in Your Eyes; Helpful hints on finding the seven best-known constellations ($1.50)

Being an Executor; What an executor is and does to settle an estate (free)

How to Buy a Home with a Low Down Payment; Qualifying for a mortgage (free)

Walking for Exercise and Pleasure ($1)

Clothing Catalogs

CHADWICKS, One Chadwick Place, Box 1600, Brockton, MA 02403-1600

LERNER NEW YORK, P.O. Box 8380, Indianapolis, IN 46283-8380

BEDFORD FAIR, 421 Landmark Drive, Wilmington, NC 28410

ROAMAN'S, P.O. Box 8360, Indianapolis, IN 46283-8360

THE ULTIMATE OUTLET, P.O. Box 182557, Columbus, OH 43218-2557

SHEPLERS, 6501 West Kellogg Drive, Wichita, KS 67209 (Western wear)

NORDSTROM'S, P.O. Box 91018, Seattle, WA 98111-9118

KING-SIZE COMPANY, 2300 Southeastern Avenue, Indianapolis, IN 46283 (large-size men's)

TALBOTS, 175 Beal Street, Hingham, MA 02043

Gift Catalogs

CURRENT GIFTS, The Current Building, Colorado Springs, CO 80941

LILLIAN VERNON, 543 Main Street, New Rochelle, NY 10801

WALTER DRAKE & SONS, 56 Drake Building, Colorado Springs, CO 80940

HARRIET CARTER, Department 16, North Wales, PA 19455

CHARLES KEITH, 1265 Oakbrook Drive, Norcross, GA 30090

Department Store Catalogs ($5–$10)

SPIEGEL, P.O. Box 182563, Columbus, OH 43218-2563

J. C. PENNEY, P.O. Box 2021, Milwaukee, WI 53201-2021

SERVICE MERCHANDISE, P.O. Box 25130, Nashville, TN 37202-5130

Catalogs for People with Special Needs

SEARS HOME HEALTHCARE CATALOG, 9804 Chartwell Drive, Dallas, TX 75243

DR. LEONARD'S HEALTHCARE CATALOG, 42 Mayfield Avenue, Edison, NJ 08818-7821

J. C. PENNEY'S Clothing for People with Special Needs Catalog (1-800-222-6161)

MAXI AIDS, P.O. Box 3209, Farmingdale, NY 11735 (aids for people who are physically challenged)

THE COMFORT CORNER, P.O. Box 649, Nashua, NH 03061 (hard-to-find shoe sizes and widths)

Gardening Catalogs

W. A. BURPEE COMPANY, 300 Park Avenue, Warminster, PA 18974

GURNEY'S SEED & NURSERY, Yankton, SD 57078

STARK BROTHERS NURSERY, Louisiana, MO 63353

JACKSON & PERKINS ROSES, P.O. Box 1028, Medford, OR 97501

WAYSIDE GARDENS, 1 Garden Lane, Hodges, SC 29695-0001

Miscellaneous Catalogs

METROPOLITAN MUSEUM OF ART, 1000 5th Avenue, New York, NY 10028

CABELA'S, 812 Thirteenth Avenue, Sidney, NE 69160 (fishing, boating, and camping equipment)

L. L. BEAN, INC., Freeport, ME 04032-9984 (casual men's and women's clothing and outdoor equipment)

LAND'S END, Dodgeville, WI 53595 (casual men's and women's clothing and outdoor equipment)

SEARS (offers catalogs for big and tall men, tools, athletics, tall women, home). Call 1-800-948-8800.

THE VERMONT COUNTRY STORE, P.O. Box 3000, Manchester Center, VT 05255-3000

BARGAIN BOOKS, Box 15-165, Falls Village, CT 06031

RENOVATORS, P.O. Box 2515, Conway, NH 03818 (bath, lighting, and home decorating essentials)

CRITICS CHOICE VIDEO, P.O. Box 749, Itasca, IL 60143-0749

READER'S DIGEST HOME LIFE CATALOG, P.O. Box 182612, Columbus, OH 43218-2612 (books and items on hobbies, outdoor living, home decor, kid stuff)

MACWAREHOUSE CATALOG, 1720 Oak Street, Lakewood, NJ 08701-5926 (for Macintosh computer owners)

MARY MAXIM, P.O. Box 5019, Port Huron, MI 48061-5019 (needlework and crafts)

GENEVA WOODWORKS, 1502 North Elkhorn Road, Lake Geneva, WI 53147 (supplies for woodworkers)

EDMUND SCIENTIFICS, 101 E. Gloucester Pike, Barrington, NJ 08007-1380 (telescopes, microscopes, magnets, biology and physics supplies)

MAPPING IT OUT

YOU CAN MARK an inexpensive map for a special person or family to make a wonderful connection with a place.

Memory Maps

A map of someone's hometown marked to show nostalgic places stirs many memories. Obtain a map from the chamber of commerce, and mark it to show special places such as Dad's elementary and high school, the cemetery where relatives are buried, the location of the family's church, the important monuments and buildings like City Hall, museums, the library, the house or hospital where the person was born, and the homes of neighbors, friends, and relatives. Cut out simple shapes that symbolize the special house, school, or hospital from colored paper and then attach them to the correct site on the map. Or use brightly colored markers to draw right on the map. The map can be rolled and tied with a ribbon or glued on a decorative piece of wood and coated with polyurethane to hang.

Welcome Maps

Welcome new neighbors with a handy personalized map of the community. First, take note of the family, the ages of any children, their pets, and type of car. Mark off appropriate nearby places like shopping centers, schools, the hospital, post office, medical center, veterinarian, parks and playgrounds, library, community college, bake shop, and other shops on a local map. Add helpful comments along the edge like: "post office open eight to five weekdays except nine to twelve on Wednesdays," or "using back entrance to shopping center helps avoid traffic." Use Post-it Notes to stick on important phone numbers for ordering trash pickup, newspaper subscriptions, telephone and utility service, and dog and car licensing offices. Include your own phone number for further information. Personally deliver this customized map, or sneak it inside the storm door as a warm welcome gift from your family to theirs.

SWEET FRAGRANCES

HOMEMADE LAVENDER AND spice bags create fresh fragrance in drawers and storage chests. You can cover a three-pound coffee can with Con-Tact paper and fill it with a dozen of these sweet-smelling sachet pouches.

For each pouch, cut a pair of three-inch squares from gauze, lace, satin, or some other lovely fabric. Embroider the date on one of the squares. With right sides together, stitch up three edges. Turn right side out. Stuff the bags with flower petals you dried yourself, maybe from Susie's wedding, with lavender flowers, or with good-smelling herbs available in natural food shops. (See page 14 for names of mail-order companies.) Homegrown herbs can be dried between two paper towels in two or three minutes in the microwave on high setting. The pouches can also be filled with crushed pine needles for longer-lasting scent. After stuffing, sew up the fourth side, and trim with as many sequins or yards of lace as you like.

A good book on creating potpourri with flowers, herbs, and spices is *The Scented Room* by Barbara M. Ohrbach (Clarkson Potter, Inc.). Ohrbach includes this recipe for a bath bag to swish around in a hot tub to scent the bathroom with heavenly fragrance. She suggests using unbleached muslin tied with twine and hanging the pouch from the faucet after each use.

Bath Bag

1 ounce rose petals
1 ounce lavender flowers
1 ounce rolled oats (for bulk)
1/2 ounce cut orange peel
1/2 ounce cut lemon peel
2 bay leaves, broken
2 rosemary sprigs, crushed
Yield: 4 ounces, or enough to fill 4 sachet bags

COLLECT-A-GIFTS

WITH A LITTLE forethought and lead time, you can gather articles for giving that will exactly match your favorite person's taste.

• *Devotional quarterlies.* Bundle and tie with a pretty ribbon the back issues. Inspirational reading never gets outdated and is good all year.

• *Flyers.* Collect free craft instruction flyers from store counters. Many are already punched to fit a notebook for a gift to a crafty cousin.

• *Samples.* Ask for cologne, perfume, body lotion, skin refresher, and other personal product samples every time you pass by a cosmetics department. They are often kept under the counter. Wrap a half dozen or so for your best-loved man, woman, or teen.

• *Soaps.* Collect little bars of complimentary soap every time you stay at a motel or conference center. They make an interesting and practical bathroom gift when packed in a covered glass canister jar. The recipient will enjoy reading the label on each bar to find out where it came from and will have opportunity to try many varieties of soap, including some luxury brands.

• *Clippings.* Whatever the person's interest—soccer, auto racing, computers, water aerobics, Atlanta Braves, jokes and riddles, trains, or collie dogs—you can clip and save every photo, news story, or cartoon on the subject for a year. Make them up into a scrapbook for the person's birthday or some other gift occasion. The book will make fascinating reading and let the recipient know that you care about her interests, even if they do not exactly match yours.

• *Bonus idea.* Research library archives for old newspapers and magazines to copy and paste up the articles in a scrapbook of events that happened on the date or year of the person's birth. This marvelously personalized gift is bound to be perused over and over in years to come.

JUST-A-LITTLE-BOOK GIFTS

IT SEEMS THAT every company or agency is publishing free or nearly free bulletins, pamphlets, and flyers these days, so it is easy to order one or more that will match a person's hobby or situation.

If Mom is a chocoholic, write to Hershey Chocolate Company, Hershey, PA 17033, for recipe booklets.

For a person about to install a woodstove, you can write to one of these suppliers for information: Englander Stove Works, P.O. Box 206, Monroe, VA 24574 or Jotul USA, 400 Riverside Street, Portland, ME 04104.

Someone with back trouble might appreciate a book of products designed for back and health comfort from BackSaver Products Company, 53 Jeffrey Avenue, Holliston, MA 01746.

For someone planning a cruise, write for a multitude of free booklets to Caribbean Tourism Association, 20 East Forty-sixth Street, New York, NY 10017-2417.

If you have a close friend who is struggling with a stepfamily situation, write the Stepfamily Association of America, 215 Centennial Mall, Suite 212, Lincoln, NE 68508 for literature outlining their services to make the role of stepparents easier.

If someone you know will be moving soon, remember that most large moving companies offer a myriad of literature to make the job easier, even information about a new town. Look in the yellow pages for the company addresses. Mayflower Transit Company will send a moving kit or a pamphlet titled *Movers' Rights and Responsibilities.* Call your local agent or write: Mayflower Transit Inc., 1 United Drive, Fenton, MO 63026.

For a complete list of more than two hundred free or low-cost government publications, phone your congressional office or write for *Consumer's Resource Handbook,* Consumer Information Center, Pueblo, CO 81002.

PHOTO ALBUMS

CREATE A BOOK titled *A Day in the Life of the Johnsons* (or whoever). Take snapshots of your family from wakeup to bedtime, and paste them in an album for grandparents or other loved ones, especially those who live far away. A real-life book of family scenes—sleepy-eyed Dad rolling over in bed at 6:00 A.M., the family watching television, Mom at the computer, friends who visit often, pets, music practice sessions, or big sister reading to the younger children—will give recipients an opportunity to catch up on family activities and see how everyone has changed. Be sure to identify the people and places in photos. Do not make a big deal of taking perfect pictures. The imperfections will only make them seem more "real-life."

• *Bonus idea.* Send a few photos of a previously given item being used. These make a special gift for someone who helped out in a tough situation. Include a note, for example: "Here are a half dozen photos of Cathy wearing the prom gown you helped sew for her last fall when she needed it in a hurry. Cathy's date said her dress was a real winner, and she and Mike proved it when they were chosen king and queen of the evening."

TOLLS APLENTY

FOR SOMEONE WHO commutes to work or school, toss coins from the bottom of your pockets or purse into a piggy bank all year. Stitch up a tiny drawstring bag of heavy cloth or suede, personalize it by drawing or embroidering the recipient's initials, and fill with nickels, dimes, quarters, or tokens for fares. Make a different colored bag for each person who uses public transportation or toll roads. P.S.—a great idea for a college student needing coins for the laundromat.

RERUNS FOR FUN

VIDEOTAPE APPROPRIATE TELEVISION programs during the year to match someone's special interests, perhaps a woodworking hobby, opera, or World War II. Or, tape your church's Christmas and Easter choral presentations for someone like a shut-in who would enjoy them over and over. To save on costs, tape over old videos.

SECONDHAND BRAND-NEW GIFTS

• *Reading material.* Wrap up a nearly new book you have enjoyed, or locate an out-of-print book or a pile of hobby magazines that might fit a friend's special interest. Be honest about the secondhandedness with a note: "You came to mind when I found these books and magazines on your favorite subject at the church rummage sale. Enjoy!"

• *Furniture and tools.* Perhaps you can part with those three wicker pieces hidden under old sheets in the attic for a gift to somebody who just bought a house with a sun porch, or maybe you can give away an unused set of carving tools to a would-be whittler or handyman. Can you give up that perfectly good dresser in your grown-up daughter's bedroom to somebody who needs extra space to store sewing supplies and gadgets?

• *Canning jars.* What to do with Grandma's antique canning jars? Just fill them with colorful peppermints, butterscotch candies, or homemade fudge, and tie a ribbon around the top for a tasty gift with a nostalgic flair. Blue jars are especially valued and look lovely loaded with cellophane-wrapped ice-blue hard mints. Add a note telling the history and value of these old containers so they will not be tossed aside after being emptied. Suggest that they be used as pretty kitchen canisters to keep bugs out of rice, popcorn, and macaroni.

• *Wall plaques.* Make beautiful wall plaques from tiny flowers picked from the yard or a field and dried. Stain or paint a fine wood piece any color to match decor. Press ferns, leaves, stems, and flowers into glue on the front. Use tweezers to arrange the smallest items.

• *Clothes hangers.* Got too many wood or plastic clothes hangers? Decorate them with tole painting, or spray-paint them a rainbow of pastel colors. If you can sew, why not pad them with foam and cover with satin or other fabric scraps in colors to match someone's closet?

PERSONALIZED LIST BOOK

USE YOUR OWN creativeness to dress up a dime-store notebook with appropriate stickers, a collage of pictures shellacked on, or even lace and ribbon to make a card or gift-list book. Fill in as many names and addresses as you think are useful.

IOU CERTIFICATES AND COUPONS

BUSY FOLKS HAVE dreams of accomplishing this or that, but lack of time makes fulfillment impossible. Perhaps you know someone else's secret longing (or pet peeve) so that you can become the Fabulous Fairy Godmother who makes the wish come true with a redeemable certificate for goodwill services rendered on request. Your own imagination and the other's needs and desires are the only limits here.

For instance: Maybe you heard your working wife say at one time or another, "Someday I'll get rid of all this stuff cluttering the attic and basement." A loving Christmas angel like you could write a promise to arrange a garage sale from beginning to end. A definite date and logistics can be worked out, but your certificate offers to help collect items, do the advertising, act as salesclerk and cashier, and dispose of unsold articles afterward.

You might want to include a book on the topic such as *The Garage Sale Handbook* by Peggy Hitchcock (Pilot Books, 103 Cooper Street, Babylon, NY 11702), a step-by-step manual showing how to use a business approach to preparation, pricing, and displaying merchandise. Another good book available in bookstores is *The Garage Sale Book* by Jeff Groberman and Colin Yardley.

As the Gift Pixie, you might give a whole booklet of certificates for personal services. Pledges of help can be typed neatly, one each in the center of a page, and then stapled together. Include a special page with a removable silver seal that can be cashed in for "emergency services of your choice." Maybe Sis will need help with a new baby so she can catch up on sleep, or perhaps Uncle Joe could use a driver for an unexpected trip. Giving promise certificates to others often takes the embarrassment out of asking for help. The rewards of such a thoughtful gift of service will remain long after the ribbon and tinsel from other gifts are discarded. What needs do your loved ones have that a gifted cherub like you can help fulfill?

IOU Coupons for Specific Services

IOU coupons can offer your help in many ways. For example:

- *Make* and deliver a Christmas wreath by December 15.
- *Install* a ceiling fan.
- *Shop* for sale items in a local department store for someone who works all day, or locate hard-to-find articles for someone who lives in a small town and cannot get to big city shopping malls.
- *Help* a new computer owner get started by showing him or her what you know.
- *Arrange* a car pool for someone in your office who lives nearby but who dreads the daily drive into town alone. Making a few phone calls to the personnel office or speaking to coworkers may be all it takes. For one nurse who works nights at an inner-city hospital, this promise was her finest gift.
- *Drive* a coworker to work daily for a month or so after surgery or after a death in the immediate family.
- *Give* weekly rides to the mall to someone who dislikes driving in congested areas.
- *Plant* a spring garden for a gardener recovering from an illness.
- *Give* a nightly visit and rubdown to someone who has difficulty settling down at bedtime after surgery or an illness.
- *Make* one phone call or have a joint weigh-in a week to encourage a fellow dieter.
- *Pick up* extra entry blanks or rebate coupons from grocery and department stores for a contest lover or smart shopper.

• *Bake* and deliver a dessert to your favorite person each month for a year. Promise a pie a month to elderly parents or a shut-in who does not bake much. Make each choice match the season: February—cherry; May—rhubarb; November—pumpkin; December—mincemeat. What older person do you know who would enjoy a monthly visit from you bearing a warm pie and a friendly smile? (Or if your friend is on a sweet-restricted diet, consider baking bread or fixing a favorite dish!)

• *Donate* a day of your time to a friend's favorite charity or cause. Perhaps she needs a replacement to collect on your street for the March of Dimes, a substitute teacher for her Sunday school class, a pianist in her mother's nursing home, home-baked bread or pies for her church bazaar, or your artistic craft for the PTA festival in her child's school.

Or maybe you could volunteer a day's vacation time to work at the local cancer society office in the name of a friend whose husband is dying of the disease. It could be a meaningful and compassionate gift for others as well as your friend.

• *Teach someone:*
to hook a rug
to quilt
to knit, crochet, or tat (this ancient art is dying!)
to speak a foreign language
to arrange flowers
to appliqué with a sewing machine
to refinish old trunks
to play a musical instrument like a harmonica or guitar
to develop film
to play tennis
to do calligraphy

IOU Coupons from Artisans and Professionals

You may have a skill that has taken years to develop. Make a gift of your time and talent.

- A *lawyer* can promise to draw up a will or carry out some other legal service.
- A *photographer* can promise to photograph a new baby several times during the year or to take pictures of an upcoming graduation, wedding, or ordination. He can enlarge and frame an old family photo or a photo of a building or monument that has special meaning or the house where he and his siblings spent their childhoods. Or he can arrange a secret photo session for his brothers and sisters and their families so portraits can be given to parents.
- A *carpenter* can promise to fix a window; to build shelves, a spice rack, a cookbook holder, a birdhouse; or to deliver wood scraps for a wood stove or sawdust for a garden.
- A *wicker worker* can promise to cane chairs or to make a custom woven basket.
- A *mechanic* can promise to show someone how to change the oil and spark plugs in a car or pledge a free tune-up.
- A *hairdresser* can promise a hairstyling, cut, or perm.
- A *nurse* can promise to visit someone for monthly allergy shots or to check blood pressure.
- A *secretary* can promise a few hours of typing letters or a term paper.
- An *artist* can paint, draw, or do a watercolor sketch of someone's home, child, pet, or favorite scene.
- A *teacher* can promise to tutor someone's young son or daughter who needs extra help in a subject.
- A *gardener* can promise to provide enough tomatoes and cucumbers for fall canning or offer to start extra tomato and cabbage and flower-bed seedlings in the spring.

• *Bonus IOU ideas for a gardener.* "I promise to save a ten-by-twenty-five-foot space in the rear of my garden so you can plant those special muskmelon and cucumber seeds that you never have room for in your own," "I promise use of my garden tiller for six hours during the spring and summer in the coming year," or "I promise to plow up your garden in the spring when you are ready."

• A *seamstress* can promise to shorten pants or a skirt; to take up a waistband; or to make pajamas or a sexy satin nightgown, a Halloween costume, curtains, an extra-large tote bag, or cushion covers to match bedspread and drapes.

• A *cross-stitch hobbyist* can make wall hangings or a table runner, decorate a pair of pillowcases or a T-shirt, or personalize almost anything with initials.

• *Homeowners* have special gifts to share with friends and relatives. If Mom lives in a cramped condo, you could offer your spacious living room to help her entertain a church group when it's her turn. Would your niece appreciate use of your beautiful backyard rose garden for her outdoor graduation party?

Other homeowner pledges:

"I promise one week for you and your family in our beach house (or mountain cabin or ski lodge) whenever you have vacation time and it's available."

"I promise (to out-of-towners) use of our spare bedroom and our second car when you come to visit Atlanta in September." Include brochures of your area's great tourist attractions and maybe even a snapshot of your bedroom.

See pages 178–189 for examples of coupons.

SWAP-A-GIFT

YOU CAN SWAP a service or possession instead of exchanging wrapped presents with someone. Some folks barter "my skill for yours" or "the use of my tools for six months' use of your attic for storage." You could promise your sister the gift of Grandfather's lovely gold antique picture frame if she will stay in your house with a live-in older relative while you spend a few nights at the beach. Or maybe your husband would like to exchange the gift of one winter's use of his new snowblower for the use of a neighbor's riding lawn mower for three months next summer. Do you know a weaving enthusiast who would appreciate one of your patriotic red, white, and blue handmade quilts in exchange for a handcrafted blanket made on her home loom? These unconventional swap gifts can be quite valuable and may satisfy the longing of someone's heart.

LETTER GIFTS

EVERYBODY LIKES TO get mail. A message from a friend or relative, whether handwritten, taped, or by E-mail, is a very personal and wonderful gift. Even a single sentence or paragraph says to the other, "I am thinking about you today."

Birthday or Christmas Letters

A few years ago, I searched my brain for what I could give to a friend of our daughter who had been like a member of our family while our kids were growing up. This pleasant child seemed to stay around our house almost as much as her own. Now in her thirties and living in a distant city while battling multiple sclerosis, she can-

OUACHITA TECHNICAL COLLEGE

not use her trembling hands. After thinking it over, I decided a newsy letter would mean the most to her. I included news from the whole family, now scattered over the face of the earth, as well as news from the home front about my husband's new job, my newest course in computers, our crazy bulldog, Bubba, and my burning the roast in the oven while I talked to neighbors. Her mother told me later on the phone that my letter meant more than any gift I could have bought. Next year I want to record an audiocassette message of comforting Bible passages, poems, and Christmas stories as well as family activities because this beloved friend loves to hear the voices of her "second family."

Maybe you can think of someone who would appreciate a heart-warming letter. You don't have to be a great writer. It's the message that counts. You can write on the back of the kids' artwork or on the most exquisite stationery available. You can roll it and tie it with a slim red ribbon before hanging it on a Christmas tree, or you can send it as birthday mail. Little surprises tucked into the envelope will show that you care lots. If Mom loves herbal tea, stick a new flavor packet in with her letter. Enclose a comforting Bible verse for a recent widow or a pressed flower from a wedding bouquet for a faraway loved one who could not attend the special event.

Thank-You Letters

Every day is a good day to say thank you, but it's especially appropriate on gift occasions to thank those who have given to you in the past.

Write to an elementary or high-school teacher who was especially understanding or a faithful Sunday school teacher, pastor, sports coach, bus driver, police officer, or some other person who has meant much. There is nothing better than being told you have helped somebody. Here are some ways to put such tender sentiments into writing:

• *To a coworker.* Just a note to let you know how very much I have appreciated your help on my new job these past few weeks. Without you, I never would have made it! Who else could I have confided in about my computer fears, or who else would have helped me mop up the can of orange soda I spilled on the new office carpet? You are a kind friend, and I want you to know just how much I appreciate you.

• *To your best buddy.* I have appreciated your letting me share my troubles with you this past year when the days seemed darkest after my divorce. It meant a lot to be able to tell somebody my feelings and to know you would keep them confidential.

• *To the newspaper delivery person.* Not one day this year did you fail to leave the morning paper by 6:00 A.M. Thank you! I would often see your headlights in the road by the mailbox as I looked out my bedroom window the first thing on a rainy or foggy morning. It means so much to be able to read the morning news with coffee before heading out through city traffic. Your faithfulness is much appreciated!

Loving-Memories Letters

What parent wouldn't appreciate a letter of thanks?

Ideas:

To Dad: I am so glad that God chose you to be my dad and for the values of diligence, honesty, and compassion you gave me. You made life smooth for our family even when we were all worried about Mom's auto accident. I remember once when you gave me money for college commuter tokens on a day when *you* needed a new winter coat.

To Mom: Now that I have kids of my own, I appreciate what a great mother you were, and I especially admire your patience. I remember saying to you over and over again whenever I was lonesome as a child, "Let's rock." And you would put aside your yarn and needles and tuck me in beside you in the big antique rocker and put your arm around me. Thank you for this and so much more.

• *Bonus idea.* You can carry on for pages and pages to a sister, brother, or good friend about all the wonderful remembered details of your lives when you were together in earlier years: "Remember our Christmases as kids when we ate so much that we had to walk thirty times around the house before dessert?" or "Remember how we would laugh until we cried sitting three times through Laurel and Hardy movies on Saturday afternoons?" Heartfelt reminiscences draw folks close together even though they are shared across the miles. P.S.: Why not let your own children enjoy the letter before sending it along?

32 Journal Letters

Someone who likes to keep a journal can create a gift for friends and family from a daily log. Keep a loose-leaf mini-diary on the dining room table, jotting down a line or two in free moments here and there. "Beth got her driver's license so now she drives herself to the dentist," or "Grandpa fell and broke his hip but everybody is pitching in to help," or "Jim got a new job as staff accountant for the J. B. Smith Co. so we all went to Arby's to celebrate," or "Jack and Wilma have been married twenty-five years!" About December 1, remove the sheets to be copied off, scribbles and all, and send a copy to each family in a Christmas envelope.

Family Newsletter Chain

Write to every family member (you can use photocopies) suggesting a round-robin as a shared Christmas or birthday gift. Ask who wants to be included, and make an alphabetical list of all who want to participate, with your own name and address at the top. Then write a newsy letter, enclose recent photos and news clips about family events, and send them to the first person who, in turn, will add a page and mail the whole packet to the next in line. Rule: Everybody must write a substantial note (more than just "Hi there!") and send the letters on within seven days.

Your part as organizer is to contact procrastinators who hold up replies and to nudge them to get the chain going again. Each family discards their old letter before inserting a new message to start the robin over. After the chain letter starts, you will be in on all the glorious details in the lives of people you really care about: Jenny's first day at her new job, Fred's new punk hairstyle, or a niece's newest boyfriend. Give a clever name to your family newsletter like "The Haskells' Home News," and let everybody in your house contribute a column such as: "Sportnews from Sally" (the athlete), "Charlie's Corner," "Memos from Merton," "News from Nancy," "December Cartoon from Cathy" (the artist). At Christmas, glue on a bit of red, green, and gold confetti to add a festive touch. Each family will remember your gift of time as the originator and organizer whenever they receive an envelope chock-full of fascinating news.

Out-of-the-Blue Letters

Dig out a photograph of a long-lost college or high school chum wearing the styles of the era (maybe a miniskirt or cheerleader sweater) and posing outside the dorm or gymnasium. Or perhaps you can locate a picture of both of you in prom dresses or band uniforms.

Wouldn't you love to see the surprised look on the face of your friend receiving this gift, especially if you have not been in touch for years? Perhaps she will "gift" you with a return letter outlining how things are in her life. My old buddy I had not seen in twenty-five years did just that!

Keepsake Letters

At Christmas or other special occasions, each member of the family draws a name and, instead of buying a gift, writes a letter to let the person know why he or she is appreciated. Keepsake letters make it easy for folks who love and respect each other to express their positive feelings. The letters to both young and old can be read aloud by the writer as a verbal blessing when the family gathers so that all members get a chance to hear nice things said about themselves. It can be very gratifying to see children and adults nodding their heads in agreement and saying things like, "Yes, Hannah really does have a very positive outlook on life," or "It is so true that Lee is the kindest boy in our neighborhood."

Link Letters

Ask a son or daughter in the military or a relative living in a foreign country to write or tape a newsy letter for you to wrap as a surprise gift for someone you know who would be pleased. Wouldn't Mom love to hear from her sister in Spain, or wouldn't Dad enjoy getting a cassette tape from his first-lieutenant son stationed in Turkey or from an old army buddy? You will need to get started on this idea several months ahead.

GIFTS OF GOOD TASTE

WHAT BETTER GIFTS than festive food fresh from stovetop or oven? Cloth-lined straw baskets overflowing with mouth-watering sweets and snacks from your own kitchen are a sure way to show that you care. A beautiful pint jar of home-canned veggies from last summer's garden or a quart of peaches or cherries picked in July from your backyard tree makes an attractive and distinctive gift. Perhaps you can wrap your very own gourmet specialty like apple butter, root beer, corn relish, dill pickles, hot pepper or muscadine jelly, or a salad dressing made from an old family recipe. Or give a pint of shelled nut meats. Be sure to label all goodies.

• *Bonus idea.* Slice and dry apples and peaches from yard trees, or dry popcorn, beans, peas, or other garden produce for an authentic old-time gift that will start plenty of good conversation, especially if you enclose a note telling how you did it. Dried foods show off beautifully in glass jars. Be sure to include instructions for storage and cooking. For easy drying instructions, phone your county extension service.

Here are other simple-to-make food gifts to please any palate:

Special Recipes

Bake up the other person's favorite recipe. If sister Ruth's weakness is whipped cream chocolate cake or pineapple upside-down cake or blueberry muffins or fruitcake from Grandma's ancient recipe, surprise her with your own homemade version.

Cover pies, sheet cakes, and cupcakes with clear plastic, and give them in the pans in which they were baked for a double gift. Or place baked goods like sticky buns or a fruitcake on a wooden chopboard, then swirl on plastic wrap. The receiver will think of you every time she chops veggies.

Cookies

A plastic-wrapped stack of delicious cookies tied with a bright ribbon will especially please women who always bake for everyone else. Or fill an apothecary jar with cookies and top it with a bright-colored plastic cookie cutter for your child's hardworking teacher, your secretary or boss.

You can wrap cookies to look like a glowing Christmas candle. Cut three cardboard circles to cookie size. Place cookies in a stack with one cardboard piece at the top, one in the middle, one at the bottom, and roll the stack firmly in silver or red foil. Or stack cookies inside a potato-chip cylinder and wrap with foil or pretty holiday paper folded over and taped at the ends. Cut a flame shape from heavy red or orange cardboard and attach it to the top.

Homemade Breads

Regardless of its reputation, bread is really easy to make. It doesn't cost much either! The variety is endless—white, whole wheat, rye, banana nut, pumpkin, salt rising, cranberry, dilly bread, and dozens of others. Most can be baked weeks in advance, wrapped in plastic or foil, frozen, and thawed to taste oven-fresh just before giving. Add a note with your yeast-bread gift that says something like "Everybody kneads someone like you. Thanks for being there when I needed you."

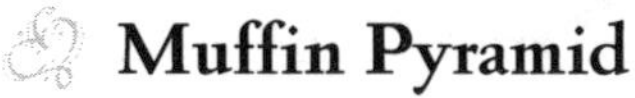

Muffin Pyramid

Pile a dozen muffins or homemade dinner rolls into a triangle tower on an extra-large Christmas plate or platter. Add a couple of sprigs of holly, and wrap this delicious pyramid with plastic so it holds its shape until delivered. Include a jar of jam or a stick of butter if delivery is just down the street or around the corner.

Candy

Fill an oversize recipe card box with a delicious batch of homemade fudge, peanut brittle, or nougats, then tuck in the handwritten recipe.

Coconut Cake Wreath

You can quickly create this delightful kitchen gift from a box of white cake mix baked in a tube pan and topped with a white or green frosting sprinkled with coconut. Decked with a big red bow, this wreath is a surefire winner for someone having a holiday tea, or it makes a terrific centerpiece.

Meals

For people who hate to cook, meals are a good idea. Double or triple each night's main dishes for a month. Cook and freeze the extras in well-sealed aluminum pie plates. (Use plastic for microwave.) Add a note saying "Next time you don't feel like cooking, defrost this meal and enjoy my gift." These meals in a plate are a super supper for someone living alone or for a busy working couple. Maybe you can give frozen meals as gifts to Dad for use when Mom goes out of town or to Nellie while her elderly mother is in the hospital. Be sure to label the contents of each packet and include defrosting and reheating directions. For an extra surprise, include a gift certificate from a nearby bakery to be redeemed for dessert.

• *Bonus idea.* Cook up appropriate foods for someone on a low-calorie, diabetic, low-cholesterol, or meatless diet. Tape the recipe to the dish of prepared food so the recipient can make it to enjoy again. Or deliver a pretty, empty casserole dish and a half dozen recipes. Let the recipient choose one and you arrange to fill the casserole with it in the next month or so. Most libraries carry plenty of books with recipes for prescribed eating plans.

HEIRLOOM GIFTS

THERE IS A special joy in passing along to someone else keepsake gifts from a jewelry box, closet, dresser, or cedar chest. Such gifts often create a warm bond between giver and recipient. After all, only kinfolk and best friends have a common interest in these treasures. And there is great satisfaction in seeing valued articles put back into use by someone who will appreciate them.

A birthday or Christmas may be just the right time to pass on your wedding dress and veil, a blue garter, or the white lace ribbon saved from your wedding bouquet to an engaged daughter. A hand-sewn baby bonnet or christening dress fashioned by your mother makes a wonderful keepsake for a niece with a brand-new baby about to be baptized or dedicated. You may be the only one who can give an old diary that contains invaluable insight from a witty and talented uncle, now deceased, or a baby book holding long-forgotten and fascinating facts about your grown child.

Maybe you have a romantic poem stashed away that was written by an aunt to her fiancé, a cross-stitched baby sampler, or a leather-covered book of John Wesley's sermons printed one hundred years ago in

England. Interesting mementos like Grandfather's pocket watch on a chain, Mama's doll that she carried everywhere with her as a child, her ruby ring or jade necklace, Aunt Anna's cut-glass bowl that was always filled with mints on her piano, or Great-grandfather's magna-cum-laude gold medal received in college—these all make wonderfully sentimental love gifts. I saved my bridal flowers and mixed them with other sweet-smelling potpourri in a beautiful covered glass cylinder jar.

If you choose to give these treasures, package them with wit and imagination, and be sure to spend time helping the other person understand their significance by writing the history of each item in longhand.

Old Photos

Got an old, old album of family photographs stashed away in a drawer? Give it away on a gift occasion. Or remove and frame a single old lithograph of a great-grandmother wearing high-button shoes, long skirt, and plumed hat or a great-uncle in high-button collar and monocle. Label the photos for easy future reference with the approximate date each was taken, the location, and individuals, telling your relationship to each. You may be able to have an old photo copied to give as a gift to several people who would appreciate it.

• *Bonus idea:* Select photos of a now-grown son or daughter as a baby or toddler being hugged or rocked or held by loving family members. Most folks find it hard to believe old photographs of themselves. My daughter Vicki reacted with astonishment, especially to the antique automobiles and familiar hometown places shown. I was the only one who could give this gift. Vicki's children love to look at the old photos over and over, and the photos have led to some good conversations.

Granddad's Old Bible

A well-used Bible, handled over and over by a beloved relative or friend, can bless the lives of many upcoming generations. Some personal Bibles have valued handwritten margin notes, which reveal deep insights into thoughts and attitudes about God, death, family, and other matters.

• *Bonus idea.* Purposely prepare your own Bible (or the big family Bible) to give to someone in years ahead. If the paper permits, use a yellow marking pen and highlight favorite Scriptures that have encouraged and strengthened you during daily devotions. Neatly write your comments and personal thoughts in the margins, and initial them. Include your application comments like "This passage helped me most when Jim died," or "My wife reminds me of the treasured and faithful wife mentioned here in Proverbs 31." The Bible will be passed on to children and grandchildren in years ahead. Each new owner can add initialed comments at inspirational places with a different colored marking pen.

What a joy it was for me to hand my personal Bible to my ten-year-old daughter who had not owned one before, and to observe her newfound interest in this important book because I had marked some of the wonderfully uplifting sections. She read them over and over and after a while began to read whole chapters at one sitting. Somehow, the highlighting sparked her interest in Scripture.

Mementos

• *Memory box.* Fill a cigar box or shoe box with small keepsakes, school awards, newspaper clippings, baptism or school certificates, postcards, war medals, organization pins, and blue ribbons that show activities and achievements of one person in days gone by. Cover and decorate the box, and label and/or mount each item for easy identification and long life.

• *Letters.* Packets of old handwritten family letters make fascinating gifts. Maybe you have letters from college kids relating dorm escapades or containing heartrending pleas for money, old love letters sent by Uncle Marvin to Auntie Jan from Europe during World War II, or a collection of notes sent from a missionary sister relating harrowing experiences in a foreign country. Tie them with a ribbon, or enclose them in clear plastic covers to be punched and placed in an album. Or choose one particularly sentimental item to frame as a gift, maybe Dad's letter of proposal to Mom.

Heirloom Collections

Do you have accumulations of Indian head nickels, arrowheads, spoons, cups and saucers, or other collectibles that you are ready to give away? Wrap them individually in tissue, or make or buy a simple wooden rack for spoons or a small printer's or curio cabinet to show off such things as miniature ceramic bells, turtles, or elephants. Coins look pretty in old glass canning jars, and both will likely become more valuable as years go by.

• *Ornaments and knickknacks.* An assortment of Christmas tree ornaments or tabletop knickknack treasures from the family home will be appreciated. Old items labeled with date and origin can help young people continue fond traditions.

- *Household and personal items.* Antique dish or silverware sets or even something like Grandfather's mustache cup or his razor and leather strop can mean much to younger people who have heard about their use in earlier days. Old lockets, brooches, and cuff links need not have intrinsic value to be welcomed by those who recall much-loved relatives wearing them.
- *Textiles.* Old hand-knit, crocheted, or embroidered dresser scarves, tablecloths, bedspreads, or afghans made by family members are sure to be wanted by someone who loved these folks. Wash them or have them dry-cleaned, and include a note about where the item was used. On Aunt Tillie's bed? On Mom's nursing home chair? On the back of Dad's recliner? Even though somewhat worn, these nostalgic gifts warm the heart. You can frame several hand-crocheted chairback covers and doilies to make a wonderfully unique wall grouping. Lacy doilies, starched and framed in brass or wood hoops to be hung in windows, resemble gigantic snowflakes.

RECYCLED HANDMADE ITEMS

Patchwork Pieces

Before you throw away Grandma's tattered patchwork quilts, consider making treasured gifts from these scraps of sumptuous fabric like velvet and satin. Recycled items like these are beyond value and can bring back wonderful memories. Use undamaged parts to make up a pair of sentimental antique couch pillows. Some old heirlooms were fashioned as community quilts, exquisitely hand-sewn with seldom-seen decorative stitches and personalized with the names of various hometown handicrafters embroidered on the blocks.

You can also use these worn-out quilts to add a colorful handcrafted touch to your Christmas tree by stitching up a dozen plush mini-pillow ornaments to hang with lavish red velvet ribbons. Pretty them up with beads and a lace edging.

Children's Art Pillow

Locate a piece of artwork done in earlier years by a now-grown-up child. Cut a piece of linen, unbleached muslin, or some other light-colored fabric an inch larger than a pillow-sized piece of soft foam, and trace the child's drawing on the fabric with carbon paper. Using a chain stitch, embroider the design in the same colors used in the original, or use liquid embroidery. Cut another piece of fabric the same size, and sew the two pieces together inside out on three sides. Turn, stuff in the foam piece, and stitch up the fourth side for a made-of-memories pillow to be genuinely appreciated by the artist for years to come.

You could also frame this heirloom piece or make a wall hanging by fraying the two side edges and sewing fringe on the bottom edge. Hem the top and insert a wood or brass rod for hanging.

Hands-of-Love Quilt

Here's how a family can create a beautiful heirloom to wrap the "gifted one" in warmth. Ask each family member to trace around one hand and give you the pattern. Then cut each hand pattern from fabric and appliqué it onto a square of cloth. Decorate the hands by sewing on cuffs, embroidering rings and fingernails in place, and adding lace. Appliqué or embroider names and favorite hobby symbols like a baseball or a tennis racket.

FAMILY ROOTS ON TAPE

THERE COMES A time when people yearn to know their origins. You can make a keepsake oral history to give your family by interviewing the elderly on tape or video. Or you can write down their memories in a journal. Chances are, you will be spellbound listening to an older relative reminisce about life in the past. Begin the interview by recording the time, date, place, and full name of the one speaking. Ask the person to tell about place of birth, childhood experiences, events from the lives of parents and grandparents, and idiosyncracies of deceased aunts and uncles. Get the older person to talk about how early immigrants made the trip and survived in a new country and about any relatives still living overseas.

Ask about schools, houses, hobbies, values and concerns, military service, how parents met and courted, and family sayings. Maybe the person would be willing to sing a favorite ethnic song, recite an original poem, or speak in a native language. Older folks will be so pleased that you care about the past, and future generations will treasure this nostalgic record that adds priceless continuity to the family. State and local history societies often have low-cost or no-cost pamphlets to help with such projects, and their staff people can give more ideas. A good book for this project: *Reaching Back,* an album with spaces to fill in five hundred questions by Alice Chapin (Betterway Books).

• *Bonus idea.* Write your own simple biography about personal memories of past times titled *I Remember.* Just let the ideas spill out; no great writing ability is needed. Tell future generations about your childhood, courtship, wedding, the day each child was born or married, your frightened or sad feelings during their illnesses or during times of bereavement, your dreams and hopes in times of struggle and during pleasant years bringing up the family. A good book to help you write your personal memories: *Good Times with Old Times* by Katie Funk Wiebe (Herald Press).

Or write up a history of the house where your family lived. Tell who built it and when, the cost, who else lived there, and how it was reconstructed after a fire or an earthquake.

GOODWILL TOWARD ALL: THE BEST OF GIFTS

THE NEXT FEW gifts cost much more than money. They involve difficult acts like deciding to change habits or attitudes, to make a wrong right, or to invest yourself in someone else's life. Some may even prove risky because they involve revealing deep feelings never before expressed. But the satisfaction to be gained outweighs the personal effort and risk, and each idea is based on the philosophy of giving away love. These goodwill gifts may be given secretly behind the scenes, or you may choose to let the recipient know your loving intentions.

The Gift of a Better Attitude

(From an Atlanta wife): For a long time, my husband told me that my outlook seemed very negative and that I was often too demanding. But I argued that I was just telling him how I felt or that I required his special help. One day I decided to listen to my thoughts from sunup to sunset. I was astounded to see how many complaining thoughts there were! I saw clearly that developing a better attitude would be a profound way to show love for Allen. So I secretly tried a small experiment. I didn't criticize, complain, or make demands for a whole week. I deliberately expressed more hopefulness, more positiveness, more understanding, and tried to be less demanding. My husband sensed the change immediately, and during that short week I quietly watched our relationship bloom more than it had in years. Allen stopped ranting over small things, and we both smiled and joked more. I may not have a perfectly positive outlook yet, and I still get too bossy now and then, but I know that I am doing better. Concentrating on my own behavior has been enough to inspire Allen's willingness to change too. Last week he told me that he loves me more than ever and asked what he could do to please me more.

The Gift of Openly Showing Love

Someone wise once said, "Four hugs a day are necessary for survival. Eight for maintenance. Twelve for growth." Some families never get around to saying "I love you" to each other even though they experience strong ties. Many folks go through an entire lifetime never hearing those longed-for words from certain folks they adore. Most of us blithely go our own way, showing only about as much love as was shown to us when we were growing up and in the same ways. Old habits are hard to change! Dr. David Mace, who counsels troubled families, says, "In successful families, the members keep on letting each other know that they like each other."

A discreet embrace with no demands attached to it can lift another's spirits or quiet anxiety because it says "I care, I understand, I am a friend of yours." Why not deliberately place a hand of love over some distressed person's clenched fist or stroke a sad one's head? Being hugged generously or touched lightly on the back of the neck or stroked between the shoulder blades or having someone gently take your hand feels so good. Yet few of us remember to give this gift of affirmation. If you are not used to showing love, it may not be easy the first or second time and may not be received as cordially as you like (or you may happily reap much greater returns than you bargained for). However, the risk involved makes the gift worth all the more. Just go ahead and show love anyway, expecting nothing. You can do it as a secret agreement between you and God.

Making Time for Others

Perhaps you have become a workaholic with too few hours and a dearth of energy to expend on others when you get home each day. Or maybe you have simply let your partner do most of the nurturing of your children or caring for elderly parents. Your decision to give more time to loved ones is a gift that you may or may not want to mention, but it *can* be given, and it will probably be received with as much gratefulness as any tangible purchase made at a department store.

Purposely planning more hours together may be the only way. Parents can decide to accept fewer responsibilities at church for a year in order to be at home with their children more. A husband can give up Scouts or community fund-raising for a while to spend two more evenings at home every week. Grandparents can purposely invite grandchildren over individually to share activities like playing ball or picking peaches in the backyard or to teach them how to knit or drive.

Pledges of Personal Change for Another's Sake

You may know you need to make some kind of change in your daily life, and your loved ones want you to change as well. Your greatest gift could be one of the following pledges:

"I know that I spend too much money. My gift to you is a personal plan to do better on budgeting. I have made an appointment to visit a financial counselor at the bank in January. I will try harder to stick to whatever budget he recommends. HAPPY BIRTHDAY! I love you."

"I know that it hurts you and the children to see me smoke. As my gift to all of you, I plan to attend the stop-smoking clinic. Your wanting the best for me has helped me make this decision."

"I know you have wanted me to go to church and Sunday school with the family for a long time. I appreciate that you have not harped at me on Sunday mornings and just quietly taken the responsibility for our family's spiritual growth by yourself. You deserve help in this task. As my gift to you, I will set the alarm at 7:30 A.M., and will go along with all of you for a six-week trial period. Who knows? I may like it!"

An alcoholic can promise to seek help from Alcoholics Anonymous, or a person who abuses drugs can enroll at a drug treatment center as a gift to the family. Caring adults and children worry about loved ones whose habits seem out of control. One popular television commercial shows a small child saying to Santa, "I just want my daddy sober this Christmas."

Mercy Mild: The Gift of Forgiveness

Maybe you have had an argument with a good friend and have not spoken to each other since. Perhaps a sister or brother or parent or child has offended you. Or maybe your church has split, with one group opposed to the other. Why not use Christmas, Thanksgiving, a birthday, or some other gift-giving occasion as an opportunity to make up? A phone call, a personal visit, or a card with a message of reconciliation can be your best gift. The most difficult part may be overcoming the pride and self-righteousness that allowed the rift to continue. There are, after all, only imperfect people in the world, and the other person may be reacting to circumstances the best way he knows. So, just jump over the uneasy feelings and get down to the business of mending differences. Christ never said "In your particular set of circumstances or because of what was said or done to you, you have my permission to hold a grudge." His words were "Love your enemies. Do good to those who hate you. Pray for the happiness of those who curse you; implore God's blessing on those who hurt you" (Luke 6:27–28).

Holidays make reconciliation a little less awkward, and even if the recipient does not respond positively, you will have the great satisfaction of having done all you could. James Kenny, a psychologist, and Mary Kenny, an author, suggest eleven steps to end family cold wars:

1. Take the initiative. Someone has to make the first step, and it might as well be you.
2. Seek a wise counselor. A third party can often see danger signs and divert you to other routes of success.
3. Use ordinary means. Often, a routine birthday card is a method by which a person can reestablish communication.
4. Use some preplanned event. Drop by, make a phone call, be easy.
5. Be brief. Rifts that have lasted years cannot be overcome instantly. Have patience.
6. Be personal. Don't place blame or try to figure out what hap-

pened to separate you. Say you're sorry about the split, and say why you want to end it.

7. Accept negative feelings. Don't be defensive; don't try to re-create what occurred in order to sort out blame. You've taken the initiative; so be ready to listen to the other person who might still have to get something off his or her chest.

8. Stay positive. Find ways to establish new links—like grandchildren or updates on mutual friends.

9. Focus on the present. Realize that the problem is the lack of communication, not the original dispute. That's long gone; so let it stay buried.

10. Keep trying. Don't push, but don't give up. It may take time to overcome a period of silence.

11. Include God. Maybe he's the third party from number 2 above, but he should be part of the solution. Prayer for wisdom in how to approach the other person, for a spirit of reconciliation on all sides, and for strength to persevere can help a lot and may be the ingredient that will carry the day.

THE SILENT GIFT: PRAYER

A CHURCH GROUP like a Sunday school class or choir can promise to pray for one another instead of exchanging gifts. Members can each write their names and several specific prayer requests on a slip of paper to be drawn by one of the others. The prayers are begun, and a few months later, secret prayer partners revealed, maybe at a retreat or group gathering. One small prayer group that I belong to has chosen one day a week to pray privately for one another for two years. It has been fascinating to share and compare prayer requests and answers. So many of our petitions have amazingly been granted!

An added bonus came when we all realized how much closer we had become to one another as prayer partners. Prayer is perhaps the best gift of all, comforting and benefiting everybody long after other presents are forgotten.

CHAPTER 2

GREAT GIFTS *for* Grown-ups to Give Youngsters

MAYBE YOU THINK the children on your gift list will feel cheated if you don't spend a lot of money on presents. The following experience in my own family helped bring the "less is more" gift philosophy into perspective.

For many days before Christmas, our own four children and several of the neighborhood youngsters had been having a wonderful time sliding down the big snowy hill behind our house. For sleds they had used big pieces of cardboard cut from cartons and boxes we had collected. Their shouts and laughter made it obvious they were enjoying themselves immensely. So my husband and I decided to make things even better for the little ones. There were hoots and hoorays when the kids saw a brand-new Flexible Flyer and a saucer sled as well as a toboggan under the Christmas tree.

We were astonished a few days later when we peeked out the kitchen window. The children and their friends were gleefully waving the cardboard pieces as they clambered back up the hill. The brand-new sleds? They leaned against the back porch most of the winter, unused.

Here are ideas for great gifts, not available in stores, that will be dear to the hearts of children you care about, and most cost next to nothing.

COLLECTIONS THAT MAKE GREAT KIDS' GIFTS

KIDS LOVE COLLECTIONS of almost any kind. I asked nine-year-old Mark what he would like to do while visiting my house. "Get out Grandpa's old coins and look at them," he said excitedly. How he loved checking the value of buffalo nickels, Indian head pennies, and silver dollars in our coin collector's handbook! Next visit, Mark spent three hours laying out and inspecting scores of seashells and a few insect specimens that my husband had collected over the years. Mark spread the shells all over the living room floor, sorting them by color. He has since been able to identify many species of insects, including a fat tick taken from our English bulldog.

What can you collect for a child that will challenge the imagination and ingenuity? Try a few of these ideas:

Coins

Toss small change into a kiddie bank or a pretty jar all year long for a splendid Valentine's Day or birthday collection that a child will have lots of fun counting and rolling in the coin wrappers you include. Give instructions for opening a bank account, or say, "Spend as you wish!" One grandmother reports, "Sometimes my grandsons play store with the money before taking it to the bank to be exchanged for bills. They have learned how to count money very well even though they are only six and eight years old. The fun Jack and John get out of this small-change collection is way out of proportion to the value of the coins."

Inspirational Packet

Ask your church's Sunday school superintendent or children's teacher to save back issues of Sunday school papers and worksheets containing puzzles, stories, and other activities. Most churches purchase a few extra. Bundle these interesting booklets and flyers into a packet of reading material that will provide many hours of profitable pleasure. Include the most outlandish pencil or pen that you can find and perhaps a brand-new box of watercolor paints or crayons.

Buttons

A see-through plastic jar chock-full of buttons is just right for most kids ages four to six years. They love to separate the buttons by size, shape, and color. Provide an egg carton or some other small compartmentalized boxes for sorting. Be sure the buttons are colorful, not too small, and all mixed up in the jar.

Paper Dolls Galore

Collect colorful monthly Simplicity, McCall's, and Butterick flyers, and ask for outdated pattern catalogs for a little girl to cut out paper dolls to her heart's content. Cut out a few characters and several outfits with tabs extending from the shoulders and underarms to show her how. Include blunt scissors.

Geological Specimens

Here's a grandfather's idea for the child who loves digging around for rocks. "All year, I pick up pretty pebbles and stones to give to my grandson Danny. Some sparkle with mica. Others are bright blue or green or bright white, and some show signs of iron or have shell patterns embedded. I separate the specimens for safekeeping in a leftover candy box with partitions and include tags so that later we can share time identifying and comparing them to photos in a paperback book that I gave him."

Postage Stamps and Matchbooks

One mother in Georgia says, "Last year, I cut stamps from all our home mail, and my husband brought home used envelopes from his office, some from foreign countries. We tossed these in a box along with matchbooks picked up at restaurants, banks, and special events. At Christmas we sorted and placed them in small glass fishbowls and then wrapped the bowls as gifts for our delighted daughter. The stamps we saved were a much better assortment than kits purchased in stores, and our daughter's accumulation of matchbooks, mostly from grown-up places, is the envy of her friends."

The United Nations has the only international post office in the world and will send kids information about its special programs and stamps from various countries. For a free booklet, call 212-963-7684.

Celebrity Autographs

Watch newspapers for ads about a sports, theater, or music celebrity coming to town. A notepad or football autographed by a famous player or the signature of a favorite star like Alan Jackson can become a child's proudest possession. Maybe you already own an autographed baseball, record album cover, or book that you would be willing to pass on to a young person as a gift.

If the youngster is an autograph hound, perhaps he would enjoy reading one of these how-to books with you: *How to Write to World Leaders* by Rick Lawler (Avon Books) or *Autograph Collecting Made Easy* by Allan Kaufman (Carlton Press).

ACTIVITY KITS

Very, Very Busy Box

A young child's mind will open in all sorts of creative directions with the gift of small treasures and trinkets and a few instructions in a box. The simplest, most ordinary item can become charming and captivating when painted, covered with fabric, or combined with something else that is colorful or whimsical. Cover a big brown cardboard carton or hatbox with pretty fabric, and fill it full of crafty items for a super-duper make-it kit that can provide many hours of fun. Include glue, blunt scissors, a big needle and thread, and diagrams or pictures of things to make.

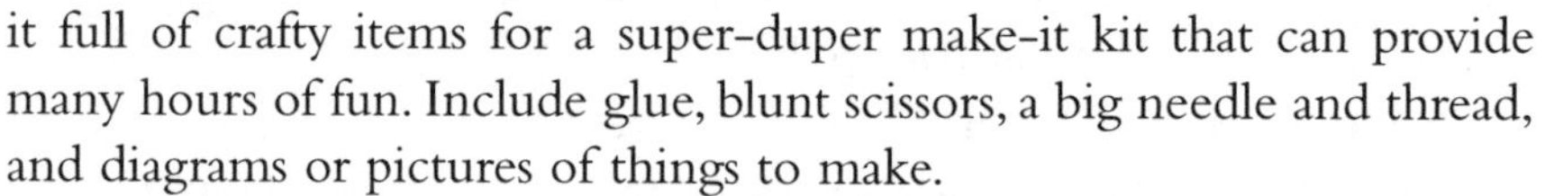

Other items for the busy box:

- Pipe cleaners
- Drawing pads and pencils
- Felt squares, fabric scraps, patterns for doll clothes
- Glitter, sequins, beads
- Bits of yarn, ribbon, lace, string, cord
- Bits of burlap, fake fur, velvet
- Buttons, buckles, spools of all sizes
- Velcro
- Embroidery thread, hoops
- Foam packing pieces
- Pillow stuffing
- Plastic foam meat trays, washed
- Wallpaper leftovers and borders

- Old gloves for puppets
- Plastic foam and paper cups
- Plastic lids for coffee and juice cans, plastic squeeze bottles
- Cardboard tubes
- Round ice cream or butter tubs
- Cigar boxes
- Carpet samples
- Old jewelry
- Balloons
- Magnets
- Magnifying glass
- Pinecones, pebbles, acorns, other natural items
- Macaroni
- Old Christmas tree ornaments (nonglass)
- Watercolors
- Straws
- Shirt cardboards
- Corrugated cardboard pieces
- Crepe paper, Con-Tact paper, graph paper, construction paper, tissue
- Aluminum foil
- Newsprint
- Baby food jars
- Aerosol can lids, bottle caps
- Clothespins of all kinds and colors
- Seashells
- Rubber bands and paper clips
- Brass paper fasteners
- Corks
- Small pieces of pegboard
- Cookie cutters
- Dried beans or seeds

- Cartons from L'eggs nylons
- Small sponges
- Cotton balls, tongue depressors, Popsicle sticks
- Balsam wood scraps
- Old hinges, locks, screws
- Toothpicks
- Artificial fruit
- Paintbrushes
- Party favors
- Decals
- Markers
- Sticky wall hangers
- Feathers and plumes
- Magazine pictures of animals, insects, trucks and cars, sports, or any other subject of interest to the child

Bathtub Kit for Preschoolers

Collect empty squeeze bottles, rubber syringes, and liquid soap and shampoo bottles of all sizes and colors, especially those with spouts, to be placed in a small plastic washbasin or sieve and tied with a bow. Include a few kitchen castoffs like plastic cups, a bar of soap that floats, a packet of bubble bath, and a dishcloth just in case the child wants to wash dishes like Mommy does.

Nurse's Kit

Start with a discarded nurse's hat (or make one from paper) and a small tote bag or old suitcase. Other items: Band-Aids, candy pills, bottles of colored sugar liquid for medicine, prescription pads and pencil, roll of gauze wrap or pull-on stretch bandage, old white smock or vest, and a paper-cup stethoscope.

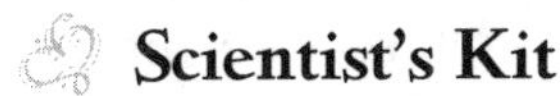

Scientist's Kit

Collect a magnifying glass, magnet and paper clips, test tubes and bacteria trays, bird feathers and nests, wildflower and leaf specimens, and whatever else you think your would-be scientist would enjoy.

Dress-up Kit

A few years ago I created a fun-without-limits kit. For months I saved clothing items in an old trunk to make a dazzling dress-up kit for the children to become models, actors, and actresses, to disguise themselves as detectives, or to become mommies and daddies. Into the trunk went old scarves, shirts, dresses, suit coats and vests, belts, bangle bracelets and earrings, aprons, ribbons, sequined party sweaters, gloves, high heels, hats, nylons, eyeglasses, wigs, half-used lipstick and rouge, purses, an old velvet evening cape, a Japanese paper fan, and a few Halloween items like a fake mustache, rubber masks, big noses with eyeglasses attached, and wax buck teeth. I stuck a fairy story book inside the trunk before giving it to the children as their combined Christmas gift. What a gift it was! They spent hours dressing up and acting out dozens of different roles. One of the girls even became Mary, mother of Jesus. I was amazed at my tomboy girls' delight in dressing up like real ladies and at my nine-year-old son's creativity in writing little playlets to match the costumes in the trunk.

Do-It-Yourself Baking Kit

Wrap up a box of cake mix, a couple of your shaped cake pans (hearts, bunnies, or Santas) for some holiday. Raid your pantry shelf and include a box of confectioner's sugar, your pastry tube, and red food coloring. (Or you can buy a tube of red frosting.) Include instructions on how to decorate. P.S.: Remind the youngster to return your tins and pastry tube afterward.

Bonus idea. Type up a no-cook or super-simple recipe for fudge, peanut brittle, brownies, pralines, or penuche. Tuck it into a pretty box with most of the necessary ingredients conveniently premeasured into appropriate cup measures and covered with plastic wrap. Rubber-band them for no-spill security. Include a can of evaporated milk (best for homemade candy) and a package of nuts.

Fabric Design Kit

Cut out about one hundred felt circles, squares, rectangles, and triangles of various sizes and colors for a make-your-own-designs kit. Include a background piece of black felt or suede about twelve inches by eighteen inches for the cut figures to cling to and an envelope or box to store the pieces when not in use. Imaginations can run wild here!

Manicure Kit

Include Mom's leftover nail care items like nail polish and remover, cuticle tools, emery boards and files, small squares of cloth for dabbers, cotton balls, and Q-tips. Add makeup samples for extra fun.

Soap Carving Kit

This should include several different-sized bars of Ivory soap and a booklet of ideas. For patterns and tips on soap carving, send to Procter & Gamble Company, P.O. Box 599, Cincinnati, OH 45201. P & G will also send directions to whip up a batch of artificial snow for making holiday window wonderlands.

Grab Bag Basket

Pack a basket of tiny brown paper bags filled with things like homemade candy and cookies, nuts, dried fruit, or dime-store goodies. Tie a note to the basket saying that the child can draw out and open one each day until all are gone. This intriguing grab bag will extend the child's excitement for many days after the gift occasion.

Hobby Library

If you are a garage-sale hound or if you love flea markets, buy a collection of five- and ten-cent books that relate to the youngster's special interest—weather, archaeology, scuba diving, flying saucers, photography, stamp collecting, or whatever. Give a basketful of these books as your gift.

Wallets

A used wallet in good shape can be stuffed with play money to make a small child feel grown-up. Include a see-through ID section for carrying photos. Perhaps you can tuck a bit of real money away in one compartment.

FASCINATING FREEBIES IN THE MAIL

CAPITALIZE ON THE child's latest hobby or interest by sending for free or nearly free booklets and bulletins. A book loaded with freebie ideas is *Free Stuff for Kids* by Penny Warner (Meadowbrook Press).

ONE BIG THING

WITH SOME NEIGHBORHOOD scouting, you can give a child one big item for hours of fun. Announce the gift with a brightly wrapped note tied with a ribbon. The message should describe the item, tell its possibilities for use, and say where it can be found.

• A huge cardboard tube from a carpet store to be used for a play army's hiding place, for foot rolling, or whatever.

• An inner tube to blow up and use as a swim float or raft (under parent's supervision).

• A carton from a refrigerator, washing machine, or dishwasher to make a castle, clubhouse, train station, mansion, or terrific teddy bear dwelling. Save cardboard tubes from paper products, tongue depressors, and wood and fabric scraps to make furniture and curtains. Or glue a picture of a television set or other items on tiny boxes. Provide safe markers and crayons for drawing on small doors, roof shingles, flower boxes, and shutters.

Two or three smaller boxes with ends pushed out and set one behind the other make wonderful tunnels to climb through.

• *Cartons-a-go-go.* Paint a twelve-by-eighteen-inch box in a bright color and draw on headlights, bumpers, gas cap, and radiator with markers. Some children will know how to draw wheels on boxes. Cut the sides down to about twelve inches, and cut two holes to stick legs through the bottom so the youngster can get inside and hang on under the armpits to walk the go-go machine along with his feet.

LITTLE FOLKS EMERGENCY PHONE DIRECTORY

DELIGHT A VERY young child who cannot yet read with a personalized picture phone directory to hang on the wall, using snapshots to identify important people. In an emergency or maybe just to help out a busy mom, a youngster needs to know how to use the telephone without help. A four- or five-year-old can learn to call Grandma, a neighbor, the fire department, or police, even though he can recognize only numbers and ABCs.

PERSONALIZED ADDRESS BOOK

CAN YOU IMAGINE how grown-up nine- or ten-year-olds will feel to have their very own custom-made address/phone book? Cut and decorate a pretty felt cover for an inexpensive address book. Include names of relatives and good friends in school, church, and clubs, as well as emergency numbers and those for doctor, minister, dentist, and parents at work. A child will love seeing what a wide circle of friends he has. This is an especially good gift for a youngster who has a bedroom phone. If not, suggest that the private phone book be kept in the same drawer as yours.

COOKIE MESSAGES

BAKE! BAKE! BAKE! . . . a cookie message for all the kids on your gift list. One plastic-wrapped super-cookie with the child's name or a fun message frosted on will make almost any youngster merry. If it suits your fancy, color the dough with food coloring, and tie up the treat with a big bow. Add to the message with shapes. Cut hearts for Valentine's Day, bunnies for Easter, Santas for Christmas.

Spell out your message with more than one cookie. You can purchase an inexpensive plastic alphabet set of twenty-six cookie-cutter letters plus comma, question mark, and ampersand at cooking specialty stores or hobby shops to custom-cut your best cookie wishes:

GRANDMA LOVES JIMMY
WORLD'S BEST KID
HAPPY NEW YEAR
WE ARE GETTING A KITTEN
LET'S TAKE A HIKE
FUTURE SPACEMAN

Punch holes in the top of each cookie letter with an ice or nut pick before baking so that yarn can be woven through to hang your message. Or attach the cookie letters to lovely lace paper doilies or foil-covered cardboard.

You can wrap up lots and lots of assorted loose cookie letters (make more vowels) in plastic wrap to play spelling games with young children. For an older youngster, why not give the cookie-cutter set along with this recipe and make an appointment for the two of you to bake together?

Alphabet Cookies

1 stick (1/2 cup) butter or margarine, softened
1 1/4 cups granulated sugar
1 egg
1 tablespoon evaporated milk or cream
1 teaspoon vanilla
2 cups all-purpose flour
1 teaspoon baking powder
1/4 teaspoon salt

In a large bowl, beat together butter and sugar. Add egg, milk, and vanilla and beat until well mixed. In a small bowl, stir together flour, baking powder, and salt. Gradually add flour mixture to butter mixture and beat until dough is well blended and smooth. Dough can be placed in refrigerator overnight or in freezer for 20 minutes to stiffen some, if necessary. Roll about half the dough to one-eighth-inch thickness and cut out alphabet letters. Place on ungreased Teflon cookie sheet about an inch apart. Roll out remaining dough and cut. Bake one cookie sheet at a time in 350° preheated oven for 7 minutes or until slightly brown. Cool on wire rack. Makes about 5 1/2 dozen cookie letters.

HEIRLOOM TOYS

CHECK THE ATTIC for Dad's Flexible Flyer sled or old handmade wooden toys, or maybe Mom's favorite doll and dollhouse to pass on to your children at gift-giving time. Kids enjoy trying to imagine what Dad and Mom must have looked like when they were seven or eight years old playing with these things, so include parents' childhood photos.

INSECT HOUSES

A VARIETY OF bugs and other interesting live nature specimens can be collected and observed in easy-to-make houses. Cut side openings in rinsed-out milk cartons or plastic detergent bottles, and cover by taping on nylon hose scraps. To make these "bug houses" more realistic, place a twig and leaves inside. Include a magnifying glass if you have one—and maybe one outrageous-looking bug to spy on.

STICKERS

PUTTING THINGS AWAY in the same place every time is more fun if a child has made his own labels. A box of self-stick labels of many colors, sizes, and designs can match-code toys with shelves. Stick a label on the front of each shelf and matching labels on toys that belong there. Even youngsters who cannot read will know where toys belong when asked to pick up. They will enjoy working with you to apply stickers to get this neatness-counts project started.

SEW WHAT?

IF YOU ARE handy with a sewing machine or thread and needle, you can create kids' items that are absolutely "cute beyond dispute."

Designer Socks

No store will have socks like the ones you create by sewing on teddy bear appliqués and buttons. Embroiderers can add initials or interesting messages like "These socks are made for walking." Perhaps you could run ribbon along the top edges of socks.

Bean Bags

These bags for tossing are easy to make. Cut various shapes like rectangles, circles, or smiley faces from felt, sew three sides, turn, and stuff them half full with navy beans. Stitch up the fourth side.

Pillowcases

Sew these for every occasion. Use fabric remnants, or purchase material at giveaway prices after each season is over. Kids will adore sleeping on valentine hearts in February, merry Santas in December, rambunctious bunnies at Easter, or smiling jack-o'-lantern faces at Halloween.

Hand Puppets

Hand puppets are just right for preschoolers who love to act out their fantasies. You could choose a favorite storybook and make puppet people to match the characters. Then stitch up a drawstring bag to store these fun figures.

Stuffed Creatures

Use patterns available in sewing departments and fabric stores to stitch up and stuff cuddly teddy bears, smiling dinosaurs, terrifying tigers, or dangly-legged Raggedy Anns for adorable special gifts for children. Most stuffed toys can be made from fabric leftovers and stuffed with old nylon hosiery or foam scraps for easy washing. Your child's imagination will make these lovable creatures come alive.

Doll Wardrobe

Even an inexperienced seamstress can sew tiny designer clothes to give children for their "in-house" doll residents. Patterns are available for nearly any doll that lives with your youngster. For extra fun, pin the little garments on a small Christmas tree with clothespins of many colors or hang them on a ribbon clothesline strung between two chairs. Post a big sign with the recipient's name: FOR MARY LOU'S DOLL.

Quilts

Piece together half a dozen doll-sized quilts in vivid colors to comfort any small child's doll on cold winter days. Tie with a blue or pink ribbon, or pile high in a mini-basket that resembles a bassinet. You can use well-loved traditional designs or make up a few simple block patterns of your own.

If you really enjoy quilting, make a lovely single-bed-sized coverlet each year for one of the children on your gift list. Personalize each quilt by using the child's favorite colors and fabrics. The youngsters will all wonder who is getting a special quilt this year. Eventually, every child will have one, and you will have created an heirloom for years to come.

"Just Like Me" Doll

What child would not love such a doll? Ask the youngster to lie spread-eagle on a sheet of newspaper and trace a body outline. No need to tell why. Now cut two patterns from old white sheets and stitch them together, leaving an opening on one side. Use felt-tipped markers or crayons to sketch in eyes, hair, clothing, and shoes to resemble the child. Stuff with polyfoam scraps and stitch. Strap on a real wristwatch, and add sunglasses, hair ribbon, wig, socks, necktie, necklace, or whatever else you can think of to make the "me" doll true to life. Young children will adore dragging around their twin or showing it off to friends.

I-Can-Do-It Book

Sew an I-Can-Do-It book for small children learning to dress themselves. Use different-colored felt pages, and sew on a zipper to practice zipping, buttons and holes to learn buttoning, snaps for snapping, and buckles for buckling. Then stitch on the cloth front of an old sneaker so the child can practice tying shoelaces. Decorate the cover by pasting on felt geometric designs or an outline of the child's hand or initials. Or tightly sew on bright beads and sequins. A more experienced seamstress can sew these zippers, buttons, and snaps on the front of an oversized clown doll.

ABC Book

You can create an ABC first picture book by pinking edges of a dozen seven-by-seven-inch pieces of heavy material like denim, felt, or duck and stitching them together along one side with extra heavy thread. Draw on simple everyday objects like an apple, baby, car, or house with a permanent marker, and print identifying words underneath in capital letters. Or use colorful ABC pictures from old magazines. Cut the child's name in felt letters and paste them on the cover.

Christmas Ornaments

Make a Christmas tree ornament for each child every year. Stitch tiny tartan teddy bears, sew and stuff mini–candy canes, fashion yarn angels, crochet starched snowflakes, or cut and paint wooden soldiers. Patterns are available at craft and sewing stores. Then paint or embroider each youngster's name and the date onto the ornament. Every year the child's collection will grow, and he will have a sentimental and beautiful accumulation of handcrafted ornaments to put on a first Christmas tree in his room or when he moves away from home.

Banners

Sew a felt banner for the child's room with a motto or saying:

BEST KID IN THE WEST
LOVE ME, LOVE MY DOG

I LOVE BEETLES AND SNAKES

IF YOU SMOKE IN OUR HOUSE,
MY MOM CALLS 911

ALL SNAKES ARE POISON!
TAKE MY WORD FOR IT

Christmas Stockings

A snazzy Christmas stocking makes a fun gift that will be hung with pride from year to year. Cut any whimsical shape you wish—a fancy high-heeled boot for a little lady or a cowboy boot for a would-be cowboy. Use green or red denim, corduroy, or cotton duck material, and trim the creation to your own delight with checked toes and cuffs, appliqués, sequins, and festive stick-ons, or embroider the edges with metallic yarn.

Then stuff with little gifts like a perfect orange or apple, healthful treats like dried fruit or nuts, a popcorn ball, little cans of juice with straws, sugarless bubble gum, dime-store toys like whistles and marbles, toothbrush and toothpaste, pencils and erasers, or liquid bubble-maker and wand. An oversize stocking will hold three narcissus bulbs and a small planter. Include instructions on how to plant and care for them.

More Ideas from Books

Refer to pattern books in fabric shops for instructions on sewing other intriguing items for children like stuffed cloth baby blocks, novelty ice-cream-cone-shaped pillows, cheerleading and ice-skating outfits, nighties, and Halloween costumes. You may be surprised by the myriad of ideas for things you can make for youngsters.

Better Homes and Gardens Books publishes several handicraft paperbacks packed with ideas to make your Christmas gift giving more personal and less commercial.

SHOP PROJECTS

EVEN FOLKS WITH very limited band-saw skills can make nice, sturdy toys that are lots of fun for kids. It is very satisfying to watch a youngster enjoy a plaything you have created.

Sources of Toy Ideas

For free catalogs of books, hardware, materials, and parts for making wood items:

Woodcraft, P.O. Box 1686, Parkersburg, WV 26102-1682

Constantine, 2050 Eastchester Road, Bronx, NY 10461

The Woodworkers' Store, 4365 Willow Drive, Medina, MN 55340

A good book: *The Wooden Toy Book,* Rodale Press, 33 E. Minor Street, Emmaus, PA 18098 ($13.95)

Back issues of *Wood* magazine carry many woodworking projects to make for kids. Write to P.O. Box 9266, Des Moines, IA 50306-9266.

GIFTS FOR THE CHILD WHO LIVES FAR AWAY

IF YOU DON'T live right around the corner from your beloved little people, here are special gift ideas that help you keep in touch. Your creativity can make a gift memorable without much more money than the cost of mailing. Almost any child will appreciate the "extra something" involved in these imaginative ideas.

Balloons

Insert money (a dime, quarter, or rolled-up dollar bill), an IOU, or a gift certificate inside a brightly colored or unusually shaped balloon along with a special "I love you" message. Stick the balloon inside a birthday or Halloween card that you make or buy, and give instructions: ask an adult to help you blow and pop the balloon for the secret inside. You can be sure the child will not receive a duplicate of this gift.

Cassette Tapes or Videos

Send a few good picture books to a young child (could you buy them at a thrift shop?) along with a tape that the child can play to hear (or see) you reading the stories aloud as she follows along in the book. Be sure to make comments about the pictures. Maybe you can use a little clicker or a bell to signal when to turn the page, but be sure to give instructions about this at the beginning of the tape. Not only will children enjoy being read to, they can become accustomed to your voice. Saves busy parents reading to kids too.

Family Tales

Youngsters love the magic of taped tales about their parents' childhood antics, especially about Mom or Dad misbehaving and what happened afterward. True family stories with surprise endings or plans that went awry can be wonderfully intriguing. Surely Mom and Dad never got spanked! Or did they? What about the time Dad fell in the ditch and got covered with mud? Or when Uncle Joe surprised everybody by unexpectedly coming in the front door on Thanksgiving morning from overseas army duty? Or why not tape the story of the birthday when Mom's family was too poor for her to receive anything except a promise note for a new doll next June when the farm crops would be harvested? Older folks can tell about what happened on the day the child was born and why her name was chosen. Was the name handed down for six generations? Did Mom have to hurry to beat the stork to the hospital?

Fantasy Book

Write and illustrate a fantasy book that includes all of the child's favorite things in the story: baseball, chocolate pudding, or a favorite doll, for example. Your drawings can be simple stick figures. This customized book is bound to be a winner because it contains what the child likes best.

Special Mail

A surprise every month by mail can be very exciting for a child. Wrap up a newsy letter in a glitzy envelope (enclose a surprise too), letting the youngster know that this is the first of many to come during the upcoming year. Since a fat packet is more fun to receive because it is bursting with exciting possibilities, each month you can tuck in a dollar bill, a packet of flower seeds (sunflowers grow fast and big), a card of barrettes, a decorated hair comb or pretty ribbon, puzzles or mazes cut from magazines, a few balloons, refrigerator magnets, dinosaur stickers, gum, baseball cards, or a mini-book. Choose items to match the child's age. One letter might contain a surprise message like "Gramp and I will be flying out to visit you June 23 to 26."

Postcards

If you travel a lot, promise year-round postcards to children on your list. Of course, kids don't get very much mail, so a beautiful postcard with a personal note once a month means a lot. Cards are often free in hotels or in chamber of commerce offices. When you're waiting in an airport terminal or riding a bus, scribble out a message to a child, keeping a record to be sure they all get a few during the year. Look for humorous cards with crazy cartoons that just fit one particular child's hobby or interest. If ten-year-old Jimmy loves dogs, send him cards with colorful pictures of cockers, collies, sheepdogs, or his favorite breed. Three-year-old Nancy would love teddy-bear cards that seem easy to locate right now, and teenager Roger will get a kick out of race-car pictures. This continuing effort strengthens the bond between adult and child because the card shows how often you think about them, and it doesn't take a lot of time either.

Film

Send camera film to an older child along with a note telling him to take pictures of everybody in the family and to mail the exposed rolls back to you for developing. Get two-for-one service so you have a set to keep and to send to the child. Not only do you get to see how everybody is growing up, but you have kept in touch.

GIFTS OF TIME AND TALK

ONE RESEARCHER NOTES that fifty years ago, children spent about four hours a day in some kind of personal involvement with one or more members of the family—parents, grandparents, aunts, uncles, cousins, and so on. Adult-child interaction in today's busy family has dropped to fourteen minutes a day, and that includes time spent in discipline and reproofs.

An adult's gift of an uninterrupted block of time to a child can be the most precious gift of all. Kids want to be wanted. They naturally think, *If they love me, they'll want to spend time with me.*

What amount of time can you give your child? Whatever it is, write it on a beautifully decorated card along with a list of proposed activities that you know the youngster will enjoy. Maybe you can pledge an hour every Saturday in January or a choice of any four Tuesday nights to do something the child chooses, or plan a "just-us" weekend to be spent camping. Include two blank calendars with your gift, one for you and one for the child, so that both of you can pencil in tentative dates for two or three activities. Could you take a tour of the fire station? Work crossword puzzles or mazes together? Go roller-skating, hiking, biking, or backpacking? Play catch, hopscotch, croquet, badminton, marbles, or paper dolls? Do coin rubbing with pencils, or collect and press beautiful leaves?

Spending time with a child encourages friendly spontaneous talk and good communication. Best of all, it lays the groundwork for discipline needed at a later time.

Excursions

• *A bus, train, or subway ride* downtown for some big-city shopping. Enjoy the views from the tops of tall buildings, and be sure to take young children on escalators, elevators, and moving sidewalks. At Christmastime, the decorations in large department stores and on downtown streets are also big attractions.

• *A visit to your place of work.* Choose a slow day, and give the child small chores like running errands, sticking on labels, or running off photocopies. Let the youngster stay with you for a morning and talk to your colleagues. What happens when you disappear for work each day will become a lot clearer to your child, and she will better understand why you sometimes seem too tired to play in the evening.

• *Bonus idea.* Take the child along on your next out-of-town business trip. Most hotels charge no more for two persons.

• *A trip to a nearby orchard* to pick nuts or fruit for eating or canning when the season arrives. Most children will also enjoy helping you pit, peel, pack, and can the produce.

• *Fishing or mountain climbing* for a day.

• *Panning for gold* or digging for semiprecious gems in abandoned mining areas that have been reopened to the public.

• *A nature hike* to search for rocks or terrarium moss or to identify birds or wildflowers.

• *A visit to several garage sales* some Saturday to look for good used toys.

• *A day's bike hike and picnic.*

• *A trip to a big flea market.*

• *A visit to a live television show or broadcasting studio.*

• *A factory tour.* Many manufacturers offer free guided tours to watch their product being made from start to finish with fun samples offered at the end.

• *A visit to the local humane society or animal shelter* to adopt a pet.

Mystery Trip

Is there a special place in the community that your child has yearned to visit? The zoo? The museum or art gallery? The new public swimming pool or a nearby park where exciting playground equipment was recently installed? Write an invitation on stationery requesting that your youngster accompany you on a mystery excursion. Give clues, but do not tell the destination. Guessing will be half the fun! Include a list of things to take along. Tell who else will be going, or leave blank spaces to fill in names of friends the youngster chooses.

Here is a sample letter inviting a child for a day's canoe excursion into a nearby wilderness area:

Dear Tommie,

Our gift to you this year is a family mystery trip on Saturday, January 25, weather permitting. We will tell you that day exactly where we are going, but here are some clues. Try guessing! We'll have lots of fun.

1. *It is a place you said you wanted to go.*
2. *Your best friend has been there twice.*
3. *It takes one hour and twenty-five minutes to drive there.*
4. *We will leave early in the morning and plan to stay all day.*
5. *You will need to take a warm sweater, camera, sandwiches, good walking shoes, a little money, maybe popcorn or some other snack.*

Love,
Mom

PROMISE GIFTS THAT KIDS WILL LOVE

PROMISES KEPT ARE labors of love. Make yours fit a child's particular need or desire. One creative mother wrapped her promises individually inside small pieces of foil and tucked them into the batter of cupcakes before baking. The children loved breaking open the cakes to find that each contained a splendid surprise of a gift to come.

Important: Be sure to let everybody know ahead what to expect so they will not bite the foil.

Here are IOUs for your special youngster that are sure to mean much more than spending a lot of money.

I promise to:

- *repair a bike or other toy.* You can cut a picture of the item from a catalog or magazine to paste on the promise card.
- *be in the audience every time you play clarinet with the school band this year.*
- *celebrate your eighth-and-a-half birthday with a "half-birthday" party.* Plan a "half-birthday" cake, "half-birthday" ice cream, two overnight "half-birthday" friends, a half pizza at midnight, and a gift divided and hidden somewhere in the house.

A regular birthday party for a beloved doll, teddy bear, or some other stuffed animal pal is fun for a small child.

- *build the world's biggest sand castle with you next summer at the beach.* Include small, appropriate items with the promise card, like pail and shovel, sieve, cookie cutters, and molds.
- *allow you to stay up as late as you like any two nights in the upcoming year. Your part is to make your request known at least twenty-four hours in advance.* (One dad says he found his ten-year-old daughter happily sitting cross-legged on her bed reading *Little Women* and eating popcorn at 2:00 A.M.)
- *Bonus idea:* Give the privilege of one more hour per week of television viewing or give up your own favorite program for an upcoming one you know the child wants to watch. For extra fun, promise taking the youngster's turn at cleaning up the kitchen after supper for a week or give a nonpenalty coupon for a day when the child just does not feel like picking up his room or doing chores.
- *plant a garden with you* (or crocus bulbs or strawberry plants along the sidewalk, or pumpkin or sunflower seeds, or popcorn, tomatoes, or

zinnia and marigold seeds). Radishes, carrots, and beets grow easily and make a pretty vegetable garden. Allow young would-be farmers to grow their own "eggs" by putting in Easter eggplant. The fruit is round, white, and edible.

There will be plenty of good times checking the garden together or picking produce or flowers. A child keeping track of new life is a delight!

• *teach you how to write secret invisible messages.* Use a pen (not ball-point) or a toothpick dipped in lemon or orange juice or milk and heavy writing paper with lines. Since the message will disappear as it dries, place a finger where each word ends to avoid writing over it. The message will reappear in brown for a friend who holds the paper over heat like a warm light bulb or toaster (never use a match or open flame!).

• *Bonus idea:* Write your promise in a secret code by giving each letter a number: A = 1, B = 2, C = 3, etc. Example: 13-5-18-18-25 3-8-18-9-19-20-13-1-19 is MERRY CHRISTMAS.

• *tell ghost stories.* Let your imagination run wild as your kids are tucked in safely beside you under the afghan on the couch and lights are turned low. Begin with an original sentence, then let the kids take turns making up the remainder of the tale, one line at a time. Just watch eyes widen when you begin with something like "Once upon a time in the middle of the night, the lights went on in the Smith house on Summer Street. It was two o'clock and everybody was sound asleep. . . ."

• *take you to the library every week during January and February.* Include a list of good books you enjoyed reading as a child or that you and the youngster can locate together to be read aloud.

• *become a leader for your Brownie troop.*

• *drive you to school the next four times it rains.* A child who walks every day will especially appreciate this promise.

• *hang a rope swing in the backyard.*

• *plant a tree so we can watch it grow together.* Try digging up a small tree in the woods that has been alive and growing about as many years as the youngster. Let the boy or girl help locate the tree, dig a hole, then fertilize and plant it in a sunny spot near the house. For good survival, include a jar of fertilizer spikes and explicit instructions for using them. Provide a journal to write down changes that occur in the tree as the seasons change and maybe even a yardstick to measure growth. Most kids will thoroughly enjoy watching new buds, first leaves, fall colors, birds that nest there, and small trees that sprout from the parent. This idea is a memory maker as various family members stand beside it every now and then to compare their heights to the tree's.

• *teach you to play chess* (or shoot a bow and arrow, crochet, weave or knit, whittle, bake pies, or some other skill the child wants to learn). Maybe you can teach the secret of some magic trick your child has been wanting to know so the two of you can work private tricks on the rest of the family.

• *fly kites together.*

PROMISE GIFTS FOR TEENS

MANY OF THE previous promise gifts to children will also be appreciated by preteens and teens. But this group has more particular needs. They understand better the high value of sentimental presents and those that give extended freedom. Such affirmative gifts offer an unspoken message that says "It's wonderful that you are growing up."

I promise to:

• *teach you to drive.* Set a definite time to begin and a regular series of follow-up lessons.

• *give you sewing lessons* (or instruction about use of power tools like band saw and lathe). Include simple patterns and lesson books.

• *tutor you in algebra* (or chemistry or any other subject needed). Set definite times to get together over the next weeks.

• *let you use my video camera* (or one of your most cherished, "untouchable" possessions for a day or a week, maybe your computer, camera, or sewing machine).

• *lend you my car for the prom.*

• *extend your weekend curfew* (or omit room checks for a month).

• *take you to the local department store's cosmetic department for a free makeover.* Watch newspaper ads for the next time a company-sponsored makeup expert visits with complimentary services. Any charge can usually be applied toward cosmetic purchases.

• *stitch up a felt or denim or canvas caddy* for your locker door. The pockets on this handy hanger will hold anything from hair spray to *Hamlet* to ham sandwiches.

• *prepare a month of diet meals for us to share.* An overweight youngster who wants to lose weight will appreciate this teamwork in dropping a few pounds. At the top of your promise note, print in big letters WE'LL SHOW 'EM! WE CAN DO IT! GIRTH CONTROL IS IN! REFRIGERAIDING IS OUT! Perhaps you can borrow a good diet book from the library to discuss together or from friends who have been successful in losing weight. A month of sensible dieting (ask your doctor first) usually means a four-to-eight-pound weight loss.

• *stick with you no matter what happens.* This can be a very important gift for a troubled or discouraged or very ill child. Perhaps you can paste a photo of the two of you together on special stationery or use a picture from a magazine showing parent and child hugging and touching to help the youngster realize that you really mean it.

Other ideas for promises that improve relationships with teens:

OUACHITA TECHNICAL COLLEGE

1. Give at least one sincere compliment per day.

2. No criticism or grumbling allowed unless accompanied by a positive statement.

3. Whenever necessary, say "I'm sorry" or "I was wrong."

4. Ask questions that lead to open discussion like "What are your thoughts about this?" or "How do you want to handle this situation?" or "What do you expect to get out of this if we go with your idea?"

5. Ask the young person's opinion in making family decisions and then act on it when possible. Ask the teen to help you plan a monthly family council format so that everybody can meet to discuss things important to them. It will add a positive tone for your family to open in prayer and sometimes end with each person telling one thing they like about every other person at the table. Doing these things keeps the family united in spirit even when ideas differ.

6. Be more casual in reacting to the youngster's mistakes and failures. Say "I know you are not perfect, and I love you."

7. Listen! Listen! Listen! Try to see things from behind the other's eyeballs. Begin by reading one of the good books on parent-teen relations like *Givers, Takers and Other Kinds of Lovers* by Josh McDowell and Paul Lewis (Tyndale). Maybe your teen would enjoy *Preparing for Adolescence* by Dr. James Dobson (Tyndale).

CHAPTER 3

NIFTY NO-COST GIFTS *for* Children to Give Grown-ups

WHO CAN RESIST a child's charming hand-fashioned gift, especially when long hours of planning, cutting, pasting, sanding, or polishing were involved? Children love to give what they have made from start to finish and to see their gifts displayed openly or used daily.

One of my most cherished possessions, a crazily off-center red clay pin dish dotted with red and blue circles, was lovingly sculpted by my seven-year-old daughter. For twenty-five years it has given me pleasure every time I mend or sew. I recall vividly the proud sparkle in Mary Jo's eyes when she handed me that little birthday treasure. Last week I was astonished when she casually asked, "Mom, why don't you throw away that funny little dish now that I'm grown up?" I was indignant. "Not me!" I exclaimed. "Every time I use it I remember how much we love each other. I plan to pass it on to your own little Mark." After a long pause, she replied with a pleased look on her face, "I would like that a lot."

Here is an extravaganza of ideas for home-fashioned gifts that kids can make for grown-ups "in a twinkling." All are simple, costing little or no money. Perhaps the most cherished are the promised gifts of special kindnesses or chores to be completed. Whatever gift your child makes, let him or her do the work. The instructions are written to you only so that you can guide and direct the child's efforts to the extent needed. Since you know your child best, be sure to offer safe and age-appropriate work tools and materials, and be there when they are used. Painting, cutting, ironing, or use of the stove may take especially close adult guidance.

BOOKS, BOOKS, BOOKS

HAS YOUR CHILD always wanted to be an author? Then why not have him write an original short book to give as a gift? Let the child choose what kind of book to write—a mystery with a surprise ending, a book of poems or riddles, or a rebus story that substitutes little drawings for some of the words. A homemade book can be stapled together, or you or some other willing adult can sew the pages with a zigzag sewing machine stitch. Or punch the pages and tie with shoelaces, yarn, or leather thongs, or poke metal or plastic notebook rings through the holes. The pages of a looseleaf book handle more easily. See page 88 for terrific ideas on decorating book covers.

Ask your child: "Could you write one of these?"

• *A humorous story about some family event,* like "The Day Our Family Got Snowed In" or "How We Rescued the Cat from the Pine Tree."

• *An illustrated ABC book on a special theme.* Draw your own sketches, or cut illustrations from magazines:

Cooking with Mama ABC Book
A Birthday ABC Book
A Christmas ABC Book
Life with My Four Brothers: An ABC Book

• *A scrapbook with pictures and captions of the family's summer vacation.* One youngster made stick figure drawings of the funny things that happened to her family on the tour bus and in the hotel room in Washington, D.C. She included photos Mom and Dad took of the family standing in front of the Smithsonian Institution and the Washington Monument. She gave full credit to the author (herself!) inside the back cover, where she pasted her photograph. Then she autographed it before giving it to her aunt.

• *A sing-a-ling-along book of favorite songs or carols.* Have your child carefully copy words from a songbook or church hymnal onto separate sheets of paper and staple them together inside a pretty cover. If the family enjoys singing together around the piano or going caroling, photocopy a book for each person. Decorate the pages with pictures clipped from magazines or old greeting cards. Perhaps your child's Sunday school or Scout group would appreciate several copies.

• *A book of famous family quotations.* Ask your child to listen for things family members "always say." Is Uncle Bill always saying, "Just bring an honest face"? Is Aunt Lorna's favorite expression "Mercy me!"? Your child can have a lot of fun finding these familiar phrases used by folks in your family—and each one of them would probably like a book of them.

88 COVERS, COVERS, COVERS

DOES YOUR CHILD need to put his newly created book in a cover? Extra heavy cardboard is ideal since the cover must be durable. After all, this may be the one and only copy of the precious manuscript in existence! Help your child cut the cardboard three-fourths inch larger than the pages on each of the three unpunched sides. Make it more attractive by covering with self-stick Con-Tact paper, or by gluing on wallpaper, velvet, or a cotton print fabric—whatever seems best for the type of book. Decorating with stickers or letters cut from contrasting colored material is an especially fun activity.

Other ideas for eye-catching covers: Ask the child to clip tiny pictures from old magazines that fit the theme of the book like food, babies, boats, grandmothers, etc., and glue them on the cardboard or a thin piece of plywood. Clip edges even with scissors and place the pictures so they overlap each other. They should cover every square inch. Help the child varnish the cover with several coats for a shiny look and longer wear. Or paste on a copy of the recipient's favorite saying and outline the edges of the cover with gold braid.

Phone Book Covers

Is the family phone book cover icky and sticky? Maybe your child can create a looks-like-new directory. Have her cut out a felt cover to fit over it or any other much-used book like a dictionary, a Bible, or an atlas.

Necessary supplies include felt or some other heavy fabric remnants from your sewing box. Help the child lay the book open on the material, and cut all around with pinking shears, allowing about one and a half inches on all edges so the cover can adjust in size when the book is closed. Cut two separate flaps about four inches wide and sew them onto both ends to form pockets. These pockets will hold the book firmly in place when its front and back covers are inserted inside. If you have felt of another pretty color, cut and glue on appropriate letters like PHONE DIRECTORY, or let your child decorate the cover in her own creative way, maybe by adding a pocket on the front to contain a pad and pencil.

BOOKMARKS FOR BOOKWORMS

HANDSOME BOOKMARKS CAN be made from 1½-by-5-inch pieces of cardboard or cut shapes like a snowman or Christmas tree or heart. Cardboard can be decorated with marking pens and crayons. You may want to add a personal message like "I love Grandma" or a Bible verse. Although bookmarks do not have to have a plastic coating, it will make them shiny and durable. Stationery stores carry inexpensive laminating kits.

A piece of stiff fabric also makes a good bookmark. Let your child fray the ends of the cloth by pulling threads for fringe. No decoration will be needed if cloth already has a flowered or plaid pattern.

TAPED INTERVIEW

YOUR CHILD CAN use the tape recorder or VCR camcorder to record a newsy personal message for grandparents or old friends living in a distant town. Encourage the child to tell what's happening at school—good and bad, clubs he has joined, hobbies, awards, sports, grades, best pals, vacation plans.

Let the child tape everybody in your house doing a favorite thing—playing a musical instrument, reading a poem. Even baby's gurgles and goos and the cat's meowing can be fun. Young children can recite a Sunday school memory verse or read a beginner's book or sing kindergarten songs like "Itsy Bitsy Spider."

Love on Tape

Older children can come up with some "just right" interview questions to ask brothers and sisters and produce a treasured cassette. It will delight Mom and Dad so much, they will request a follow-up next Christmas. Here are some of the questions siblings can ask each other:

What do you like about our family?

What is the best thing about Mom? About Dad? Others who live here? The second best thing about each? Third best?

Why is our home a nice place to live?

What is the most important thing that Mom (Dad) taught you?

What is the funniest thing that ever happened to our family?

Are you most like Mom or Dad? Why?

Suggest time for free talk at the end of the interview. For more fun, let your child ask neighbors, friends, or teachers what they like best about the person they're taping for. Or what about interviewing Fido and Kitty and catching on video their tails wagging or their begging for handouts?

PARENTS' POSITIVE REPORT CARD

A CHILD CAN let parents or other important adults in her life know that she's glad they belong to her. Encourage the child to grade as high as she can on character, skills, and personality traits that she especially admires. Suggest making a report card that resembles the child's in format. For example:

Name: Mom
Address: 21 Summer Street
Age: None of your business

Sense of humor	A
Cooking	A+
Sharing	A (Except for fudge, chocolates)
Listening skills	A (I love our long bedtime talks)
Keeps secrets	B+ (Remember last Christmas!)
Creativeness	A (You always have great ideas for English composition topics)
Generosity	A+ (Thanks for loan of the car keys)

Mom's other traits:
Honest
Dependable

Home when needed (I'm glad you
are there for me after school)
Hospitable

Mom needs work on:
Raising allowances
Sticking to 1,200 calories a day
Baking bread as good as Grandma's
(but you're getting there!)

• *An acrostic of compliments.* Show the child how to arrange the letters of a favorite person's name one below the other. Think of acrostic words to show positive qualities, hobbies, and fun facts about the individual. Example (for Gramp):

Great at making campfires and caramel corn.
Rates "A" for good attitude on losing at checkers when playing against the Checker King (me!).
Always smiling; adventurous too. I loved backpacking in the mountains with you in January.
Makes the best cherry pies in the world!
Plays baseball better than my Little League coach—pitches better too!

• *A wall collage of compliments.* Ask the child to draw the person's name in extra-large letters in the center of a big piece of plain shelf paper and then to illustrate the person's favorite activities, hobbies, foods, etc. When the drawing is completed, he can roll it up and tie it with a ribbon, or even frame it.

• *A "great person" wall plaque.* Let your child sand and smooth a good-looking piece of wood and attach the letters any way he chooses. Have him write a letter to accompany the plaque, letting the recipients know what they mean to him and why he thinks they are great. Did they delay buying a much-needed new living room couch so he could have a bicycle at Christmas? Did an adult friend stand by him when he was in trouble last year? Is he proud of some couple's solid, long-term marriage and commitment to their family? This is a creative way for him to tell them so.

- *A brass-nail plaque.* Have the child start by drawing a simple design like a leaf or a heart on plain paper. Sand, then stain, paint, or varnish a piece of wood that measures about eight by ten inches and is three-fourths of an inch thick. Allow plenty of time for it to dry. Then secure the paper pattern on the wood with easy-to-remove Scotch Magic Plus Tape, and lightly hammer decorative brass-head upholstery tacks at even intervals along the lines. After going all the way around the design, carefully tear the paper pattern off. A lovely nail-art masterpiece to fit almost anyone's decor is the result.

HAPPY FAMILY CALENDARS

YOUR CHILD CAN help favorite adults keep track of special occasions for a whole year. Ask for a free calendar from the local drug or hardware store around New Year's, or mark off a big piece of posterboard into a calendar showing the upcoming twelve months. Write in birthdays, anniversaries, and other special days. Highlight birthdays in yellow, anniversaries in pink, other occasions in green. Make a calendar for each person so the family can plan ahead for celebrations.

Children who have begun to study history will enjoy making a family history time-line mural. On a piece of plain shelf paper, use a yardstick and a dark-colored marking pen to draw a long solid line. Starting at the left side, make a small X on the line and write the date below it for 1950, 1955, 1960, 1965, and so on—one for every five years—to the present. Leave space between them to fill in other dates. Then indicate birth dates of grandparents, parents, brothers, and sisters; include important events like when Grandma and Grandpa married or when ancestors came to the United States; record the date when their house burned down, when the family moved, when Aunt Harriet sold the farm. The child will need to ask questions from older folks for information. Illustrate the time-line chart by using marking pens or by pasting on photos of familiar places and people. Future generations will be most grateful for this unique gift.

GIVING IT BACK

A MUCH-APPRECIATED GIFT from children is memorizing and reciting an adult's favorite poem. This can be especially meaningful if tied in with special events—Christmas Eve, Mother's or Father's Day, birthdays, etc. Adults will be delighted that something dear to their childhood has become a permanent part of the child's memory. Other things to memorize include musical pieces on instruments, Scripture verses, parts of a play, and songs.

GIFTS FROM DOUGH

Clay Cookie People

With gingerbread men and angel cookie cutters and the salt-flour dough recipe on the next page, your child can cut a cookie figure representing every person in your family. Make hair by pushing a small wad of dough through a piece of new window screen or a squash press and then pressing it on each cookie person. Push a hole through the top of each figure with a drinking straw so the clay people can later be strung with yarn or ribbon and hung as ornaments. Bake and cool as directed. Paste a real face cut from a snapshot on each. Draw on buttons, necktie, collar, sleeves, cuffs, and shoes with a felt-tipped pen. A set of these would be a perfect gift for Mom, Dad, or grandparents.

• *Bonus idea.* A small child's handprint dried into a round of salt-flour dough will make a great paperweight. Roll dough to a one-fourth-inch thickness. Cut a circle with a large jar lid and leave the clay inside the lid. Firmly press the child's hand into the center. After removing the lid, bake the circle and cool it as directed in the recipe. Paint it with poster paints and leave it to dry thoroughly. A coat of shellac will give a more permanent finish.

Salt-Flour Dough (not to be eaten)

4 cups white flour
1 cup salt
1 1/2 cups water

Mix flour and salt together in a large bowl. Add water gradually and mix. Using a little flour on hands, roll with a floured rolling pin to about a one-fourth-inch thickness. Cut and shape with a knife, cookie cutters, or jar lids. Bake at 200° in oven until hard (about two to three hours).

More Dough Projects

For other salt-craft dough recipes and projects, send $1 for *Dough-It-Yourself Handbook,* Morton Salt Company, Dept. 1137, 100 North Riverside Plaza, Chicago, IL 60606.

Young artists can also create jewelry, candlesticks, and many other gift items from a mixture of cornstarch, baking soda, and cold water. For recipe and craft suggestions, send a stamped, self-addressed envelope to: Arm & Hammer, P.O. Box 826, Springhouse, PA 19477.

SILHOUETTE PROFILE

PARENTS AND GRANDPARENTS will love having an exact likeness of their child or grandchild, and youngsters will enjoy looking back at their own silhouettes in years ahead to recall how they looked "way back when."

The materials needed include a piece of dark blue or black posterboard or tagboard about twenty-four by twenty-six inches, an extra-large sheet of lighter colored construction paper, scissors, paste, and a stick-on picture hanger.

Have the child sit very still against a blank wall with construction paper tacked up. Use a bright lamp with the shade removed or a slide projector to cast the youngster's shadow onto the construction paper. Trace the outline carefully. Next, cut around the silhouette with great care, and paste it on the posterboard or tagboard. On the back, apply a picture hanger, and write the child's name, age, and date. The gift is ready!

DECK THE WALLS

GOT A SCHOOL photograph of your child? Mount it on a piece of tagboard or colored cardboard that measures about two inches larger all around so the picture looks framed. Or cover cardboard with patterned fabric, wallpaper, or Con-Tact paper before pasting on the photo. Add a picture hanger.

Other Things to Frame as Gifts:

- *Family portrait.* Sketch a family portrait, including parents, grandparents, aunts, uncles, brothers, and sisters. Identify everybody by name.
- *Treasured words.* Frame a favorite Scripture, recipe, or sentimen-

tal message. Or copy a best-loved saying on parchment or other plain paper to mount on cardboard. Words can be typed, neatly handwritten, done in calligraphy, or cut from a magazine.

• *Greeting card.* Glue an artistic or unusual greeting card on colored cardboard that picks up one of the shades of the card.

• *Yarn picture.* Children will enjoy making a yarn picture by first outlining a design or scene on a piece of heavy cardboard. From a pile of yarn scraps, select colors to glue on the lines drawn. Use a glue bottle with a pointed spout or a glue gun to spread glue along the lines before applying the yarn. For a more elaborate picture, fill in between the lines of larger objects like houses, clouds, and trees. Fill in the frame itself with yarn, or decorate it with tiny dried flowers glued on in patches.

• *Plastic foam art.* Have your child draw an outline of her hand or foot, a flower, an animal, or some other figure on white plastic foam; the meat trays home from the market are perfect for this. Cut out the design, glue it on a colorful cardboard backing, and attach a stick-on picture hanger.

• *Melted wax artwork.* Shave worn-down crayons or mostly used candles with a vegetable peeler or pencil sharpener. Keep various colors separated in small paper cups. Your child can draw the outline of an animal, a flower, or something representing a hobby or special interest of the recipient on a big piece of cardboard. Protect an ironing board with an old sheet before placing the drawing on it. Sprinkle wax shavings inside the lines and carefully cover with waxed paper. Iron over waxed paper with *low* heat until shavings melt. Allow artwork to cool.

• *Photo collections.* Show off a terrific photo collection by displaying it inside a theme frame. Example: Spell out THE JOHNSONS if you have several family photos or THE ATHLETE if you want to feature photos of your sister's gymnastic abilities. Cut the letter slots three inches high in an eight-by-twenty-inch piece of cardboard. Let your child personalize the frame by decorating the cardboard with his thumbprints dipped in poster paint. Or he may prefer to paint it a solid color. On the back, lightly spread glue around each cutout letter and press on a photo so it shows through the slot. Finish by gluing the whole project onto a larger cardboard or have it dry-mounted. Add a stick-on picture hanger.

THINGS CHILDREN CAN COLLECT FOR GIFTS

• *Nuts and seeds.* If there are nut trees in your backyard or big sunflowers that have produced lots of seeds, have your child fill a little paper basket or brightly covered box with the best of the harvest; then add an "I love you" note, and wrap it up for a delicious treat.

• *Coupons.* Children can clip and collect cents-off coupons from newspapers and magazines for a month to give as a gift to the person who does the shopping at your house. Coupons should be sorted into groups like dairy, drugs, frozen foods, canned goods, medical, meat, and deli. Be sure the child checks expiration dates.

• *Kindling.* Remember how much trouble Dad had starting a fire last winter? Have your child gather up small bundles of dry twigs from the yard for kindling in the fireplace or wood stove. She can even tie them together with a bright ribbon. Bundles like this cost as much as four dollars in some stores.

• *Greenery.* For midwinter gift-giving, your child could collect an armload of greenery from bushes and trees like holly and magnolia to tie together in beautiful bundles for decorating. The best time to deliver this gift is a few days before the holiday. Or she can make bouquets or corsages by using wire twists from bread wrappers to tie together a few smaller stems of greenery that contain bright red berries. Mini-bouquets make great decorations for topping off gift packages too.

• *Prizes from the beach.* Have your children collect seashells, sand dollars, pebbles, coral, and driftwood on your next trip to the beach. Large ocean-washed stones and conch shells make pretty and practical paperweight gifts. Glue on items like small shells, tiny pebbles, little pinecones, dried flowers, acorns, or half nutshells to large, smooth stones for coffee-table display pieces. Depending on its size, driftwood can become a mantel piece or decorate a bookshelf. Children can stick on a label that says "This gift courtesy of [your child's name here]'s Olde Time Gift Shoppe."

• *Bonus idea for sea treasures.* Your child can ask Dad to help her drill holes into the thickest part of small shells. Then string them together on nylon dental floss for wonderful shell necklaces (very popular but very expensive in stores). Or string a velvet ribbon through a hole in a single extraordinarily beautiful shell to make an unusual pendant.

• *Bottle caps.* Your child can use bottle caps to make a doormat for wiping shoes or scraping snow or mud off boots. For a base, she will need a 20-by-24-inch piece of five-eighths-inch-thick plywood. The caps should be turned upside down, in rows touching each other on the plywood. Pound a small nail in the center of each one. Leave as it is, or spray-paint the doormat.

• *Shopping bags.* Any child can save grocery and other shopping bags to decorate with crayons, finger paints, or stickers as gifts for Mom and Grandma. An outline of the child's hand or a favorite slogan or Bible verse done with water-based paints will add a personal touch. Or have the child draw a picture of her house, pet, or school. Does a family member like to write? Show her or him at the typewriter. Does Grandma swim in the neighborhood pool? Draw her diving off the board. See page 119 for a finger-paint recipe.

• *Cartons.* Have your child save pint, quart, or half-gallon cardboard milk or juice cartons to make a shadowbox showcase for hobby collections. Cut off tops and wash out eight to ten cartons thoroughly with lots of hot, soapy water with a little chlorine bleach added. Dry thoroughly. Staple containers together to look like a beehive. Your child will enjoy painting the outside of the showcase box with poster paints, or covering it with colorful wallpaper or Con-Tact paper.

• *Colorful cards.* Your child can collect unusual greeting cards to make a dozen party coasters for entertaining. Cut 3½-by-4-inch rectangles from one-eighth-inch-thick plywood or extra-thick cardboard. (If you choose to use plywood, smooth the corners with sandpaper.) Paint both sides and allow to dry. Let your child glue on the greeting-card art to decorate one side. A coat of clear polyurethane will protect these good-looking coasters, and they can be wiped off with a damp sponge or cloth.

GIFTS OF LIFE

GIFTS THAT GROW are appropriate for any occasion—birthday, Christmas, or Easter—or for no special reason, just to say "I'm thinking of you." Maybe these plants would appeal to someone you know.

Sprouts

For healthy giving, let your child make a sprout-growing kit. Supplies needed are: a large glass mason jar (institution-sized is best), a piece of mesh screen, cheesecloth or some other loosely woven cotton fabric to cover the top of the jar, and a rubber band to hold the covering tight. Sprouting seeds like alfalfa, wheat, and others can be purchased inexpensively from health food stores, or have your child ask a gardener you know for a half cupful. Pack all these items into a box, and include these instructions:

Soak seeds in warm water overnight in the mesh-covered jar. Drain off the water by leaving the jar turned upside down in the sink for several hours. Place the jar on its side, with seeds lying along the length, in a dark place like a pantry or cupboard. Rinse seeds, drain, and re-cover the jar daily for five days. On the sixth day, place the jar of sprouted seeds in the sun to green. Sprouts will keep well for about two weeks in the refrigerator. They are rich in protein and delicious in salads, casseroles, and sandwiches. For creative ideas to use sprouts, see *The Jar Garden—Making Delicious Sprouts: A How-to Book for Boys and Girls* by Dorothy Weeks and Don Berggren (Woodbridge Press) and *The Sprouting Book* by Ann Wigmore (Avery).

Forced Flower Blooms

Help your child cut off several healthy branches from a dormant flowering tree like cherry, crab apple, plum, dogwood, forsythia, redbud, or azalea. Place them in a large container of warm water inside the house for about an hour. Then put them in cold water and set where it is cool and rather dimly lighted. When buds begin to swell, move to a brightly lighted spot. In about six weeks the delicate pink, white, red, or yellow blossoms can be forced into spectacular bloom. Who wouldn't love an armful of these fragrant flowers as a gift to enjoy in the house, no matter what the weather is outdoors? This is a great group project too.

Dyed Blooms

Your child can snip off the stem of a white daisy or carnation at an angle and set the flower in a vase of water tinted with a few drops of food color. Watch the delicate edges take on a beautiful hue! Why not have your child color a pair, one red and one green, to brighten someone's Christmas, or use orange or brown for Thanksgiving?

Avocados

For this gift, you'll need to start several weeks ahead of the gift-giving occasion. Exotic avocados have golf-ball-sized seeds that grow into showy plants. Have your child follow these instructions: Remove the outside meat and insert four or five toothpicks in a line around the middle of the soft pit. Suspend the pit over a full glass of water with toothpicks holding the top half of the big seed above the water and the base submerged. Place it on a windowsill for four to six weeks. When three- to four-inch shoots emerge, the pit can be planted in potting soil in a ten-inch pot. Be sure to leave the top half above the soil line. With plenty of sun and occasional pruning (after the plant is eight inches tall), the avocado will make wonderful greenery.

Other Plants

Citrus fruit seeds like orange, grapefruit, lemon, and lime, soaked a few days in water and then pushed down about one-half inch into fertile soil, will usually grow well in a sunny place and make pretty plants if kept watered. Your child should plant eight or ten soaked seeds in a ten-inch pot to make sure that at least one sprouts. Some grow into very large plants that have been known to produce tasty fruit right in the family living room.

• *Bonus idea.* As a continuing reminder of your child's good wishes, have him cover the message inside a used greeting card by gluing on a packet of seeds of pleasantly scented herbs like mint or sweet basil that will grow nicely in a window box.

HANDY GARDENING ACCESSORIES

THE PLANT LOVERS on your gift list will be reminded of your thoughtfulness every time they give their plants a shower.

• *Spray mister.* An empty spray bottle like the kind containing window cleaner can be washed out with baking soda and water, decorated with stickers, and given as a gift to spray-mist every blooming thing. Be sure your child includes a note telling how to use this gift.

• *Vases and flowerpots.* To make a flower vase, cut off the top of a plastic shampoo or detergent bottle, then let your child paint it and sprinkle on glitter while it's still wet. If you plan to include cut flowers with the vase, have your child place sand or pebbles in the bottom before adding water to keep the container from toppling over. Painted coffee or shortening cans, butter tubs, milk carton bottoms, plastic foam cups, or yogurt cartons also make good plant and flowerpots. They can be covered with aluminum foil or flowered Con-Tact paper, and tied with a bow. Plastic foam meat trays or plastic lids from coffee and juice cans make excellent saucers to protect furniture or windowsills from plant spillovers.

• *Bonus ideas.* Your child can make lovely fake flowers for her vase by following these simple steps. Mount cupcake papers of assorted colors on tops of stiff plastic or paper straws with glue or staples. Gather up small seashells of various shapes and colors. Squeeze a large dab of silicone rubber sealant into each shell, and stick a piece of florist wire into it. Use wire of varying lengths. Allow a couple of days for drying. Stems will easily bend back at the bottom if they were cut too long.

• *Watering can.* To make a handy watering can for porch boxes, large houseplants, or new shrubs and seedlings, clean out, paint, and decorate a plastic gallon milk or bleach jug. If the family's old watering can is a bit rusty, Con-Tact paper makes a great cover-up.

UNDERCOVER IDEAS

CONTAINERS FOR STORING things from cookies to scissors, paper clips, rubber bands, and safety pins are welcome gifts your child can make at a very low cost. Round oatmeal cartons, coffee cans or orange juice cans, small matchboxes, shoe or cigar boxes, and small metal files can be covered with felt, wallpaper, or Con-Tact paper, or they can be painted. Depending on their intended use, they can be trimmed with lace paper doilies, ribbon, sequins, beads, or metallic tape. He could also personalize the containers by adding initials or the individual's name.

- *Carryalls.* Cardboard boxes with handles or kids' lunch containers from fast-food restaurants are especially easy to cover and will hold craft and sewing gear or small repair supplies.
- *Pencil holder.* Your child can clean out and cover a frozen orange juice can to provide full-time help for the home office. Choose a favorite color or a color that matches the office.
- *Ice-cream-carton wastebasket.* Have your child paint the outside of a large round container a dark color. When it's dry, glue on macaroni of all sorts, sizes, and shapes. After the glue dries, she can paint some macaroni pieces lighter colors, and finish by gilding a few of the edges with silver and gold paint. Or she can simply cover the ice cream carton with fabulous fabric and glue rickrack around the top and bottom edges. She may want to make it elaborate for Grandma or very simple in design for Grandpa.

• *Cassette tape holder.* Cover a shoe box with wood-grained Con-Tact paper.

• *Canister set.* Covering a three-pound shortening can and a three-pound, two-pound, and one-pound coffee can with flowered Con-Tact paper makes a long-lasting kitchen canister set. Save the plastic tops to seal canisters of sugar, flour, tea, and coffee.

FANCY STATIONERY AND NOTEPAPER

EVERY ADULT WRITES personal notes from time to time. Your child's favorite adult will always want a package of this good-looking stationery with one-of-a-kind designs.

• *Snapshot stationery.* Have your child gather duplicate family snapshots to cut up. Snip tiny circles around individual faces or groups of people and paste one in a lower corner on sheets of a five-by-eight-inch tablet. A dozen pages of this personalized stationery will be appreciated by almost any family member, and photographs will likely be pulled off and cherished by those receiving letters.

• *Etch-on-a-sketch stationery.* Your child will enjoy painting or drawing a tiny outline sketch or stick figure in the upper right corner of each tablet sheet for a pad of distinctive writing paper. Encourage the child to match the theme to the other person's hobby or special interest like tennis, fishing, cross stitch, or a special breed of dog. Or he can use stencils to repeat the same pattern. Stickers will work well too. Make matching envelopes.

• *Thumbprint stationery.* Dip a thumb into safe, waterbase paint, then make a print or two or three, or more, on tops, bottoms, or in corners of several sheets of paper. Add details to thumbprints to make animals, people, and motifs for invitations, greeting cards, or gift wrap. This is a great idea for children who think they cannot draw very well.

• *Needlepunch stationery.* Your child will need a twelve-inch square of one-fourth-inch Styrofoam, blank sheets of five-by-eight-inch plain paper to be folded in half, a piece of lightweight cardboard to fit the front of his stationery, and a big T-pin or any pin with an extra large head. On the cardboard your child can sketch a small basket, heart, or your own clever design. Place the blank paper on the Styrofoam, then center the design over the cover of the notepaper. Prick pinholes at even intervals along the lines. Let your child glue on ribbons or lace for a lavish touch.

• *Wallpaper stationery.* Have your child cover the entire front of a piece of folded five-by-eight-inch plain paper by gluing on a cutting from wallpaper remnants or sticking on cutouts of bold designs. If your child wants, she can glue a piece of narrow matching border across the lower portion of the notepaper, and use a distinctive coordinating pattern to line the inside of the envelope.

• *Outdoor stationery.* Have your child cut small snippets of tiny flowers or leaves and press them between sheets of waxed paper inside a heavy book or magazine with a heavy object placed on top. When they are dry in about two weeks, have him glue items on the front of a folded piece of note paper. Cover with clear Con-Tact paper if you desire.

HOLIDAY SHELF EDGING

DECORATE YOUR CUPBOARDS and shelves by creating colorful shelf edgings. With these fun creations, you'll find green Christmas trees or cherry-red Valentine hearts peeking out every time someone opens a cupboard door!

You will need the following materials: wrapping paper, both in white and in a color appropriate to the holiday (for example, white and green for Christmas, or white and red for Valentine's Day), masking tape, and scissors. Have your child measure the width of each cupboard shelf. Cut strips of paper—one white and one colored—four inches wide and a few inches longer than the width of the shelf. Fold the colored strip evenly along the edge of the shelf, leaving about a three-inch overhang, creasing the paper at the shelf edge. Tape down the one-inch section of the strip that is lying flat on the shelf.

Next, fold the white strip into three-inch accordion folds (similar to the way people used to make a string of paper dolls). Leaving one inch at the top, draw one-half of your holiday design (one-half of a Christmas tree, or one-half of a heart) on the front panel at the fold. Cut through all layers on the fold, then scallop the bottom edges of the white strip. Finally, unfold and lay it over the colored strip you have on the shelf, creasing it in the same place, so that it forms a kind of "stencil" that the colored paper will peek through. Tape in place.

TABLE ACCESSORIES

THESE PLACE MATS, napkins, and rings are glorious little gifts that are so easy to make, your child can give a dozen. Just think how pleased a favorite person will be to set a table with your child's unique creations.

Place Mats

Old window shades can be cut into twelve-by-eighteen-inch rectangles and decorated for long-lasting and distinctive table mats. Other, less sturdy material like construction paper or cardboard can be used but will last only a few meals. Designs can be made with thumbprints, marking pens, crayons, stickers, or glued-on figures cut from magazines, wallpaper, or old greeting cards. Covering each with clear plastic will make the paper and cardboard mats more durable and easier to clean up.

Your child can weave fancy ribbon place mats in a flash. Materials needed: four yards each of one-and-one-half-inch wide grosgrain ribbon in color A and color B (use red and green for Christmas, red and white for Valentine's Day, orange and brown for Thanksgiving), T-pins, plastic foam board or cardboard about sixteen by twenty inches, scissors, and instant basting adhesive. Have your child follow these instructions. Cut color A ribbon into eight pieces seventeen and one-half inches long; pin one end of each to the top of the plastic foam board in vertical rows with sides just touching. Cut color B ribbon into eleven pieces thirteen inches long, and pin in a similar manner in horizontal rows, with a pin in each ribbon end along one side only. Weave color B over and under color A to make a checkerboard pattern, leaving one inch excess all around. Use basting adhesive to glue the ribbons together at the ends of the rows to hold the weave in place. Take out the pins and remove the place mat from the board. Press the ribbon ends under on the wrong side; glue them in place with basting adhesive.

Your child can wrap cardboard with fancy paper to create a place mat resembling a beautiful gift. Then she can swirl ribbon around, as she would in wrapping a package, and create a big bow in the very top corner.

Napkins

Let your child draw her own turkey or other holiday design on twelve-by-twelve-inch muslin squares with heat-set fabric crayons. Let your child fray the edges of a bright plaid or flowered or patterned fabric that coordinates with the dinnerware. Used material is just fine for this project.

Napkin Rings

With some supervision in cutting, your child can use cardboard tubes from paper towels or toilet tissue to fashion elegant rings that will make any meal a special occasion. Have him cut tubes two and one-fourth inches long, and glue on colorful strips of construction paper or wallpaper. Decorate with pictures and words cut from magazines or old greeting cards. Or have him cut designs like circles, rectangles, turkeys, holly leaves, hearts, animals, or anything else your child can think of from felt or other fabric scraps, and paste them on with a glue gun.

PLANT A FAMILY TREE

HERE'S YOUR CHILD'S chance to present facts about the family in gift form. Have him cut a flowerpot shape from construction paper, then print the family name on the upper rim. Glue two sides and the bottom edge of the pot to the lower center of a large piece of posterboard; leave the top edge open. Using pipe cleaners or flattened paper drinking straws as stems, paste on a cupcake paper flower for each family member, planting stems into the open edge of the pot. Add names, birthdates, birthplaces, and whatever else your child wishes. Encourage the child to be as creative as he likes by gluing on a photo or adding a stick figure sketch of each person or by drawing in background with crayons. Birthdays will be easy to remember with this creative piece hung on the wall.

• *Bonus idea.* Help your child make a goodwill table tree to honor a special family member, maybe a grandparent, aunt, or cousin who has just been through an illness or won a blue ribbon. Use a sturdy little green plant that resembles a tree, or anchor a small branch in clay or plaster of paris inside a colorful flowerpot. Have your child ask everybody to write three notes on rectangular slips of paper beginning with "You are very special because . . ." or "I love you because . . ." or "I am proud of you because . . ." Roll these up in scrolls, tie with brightly colored yarn or ribbon, and attach to branches of the tree. Be sure each is signed. The messages will show the family's love and admiration for the honored person.

OTHER IDEAS FOR NO-COST ADULT GIFTS

• *Pot holder.* Have your child weave a pot holder to delight the cook every time she or he uses it.

• *Name board.* Your older child can use a wood-burning set to make a name board for the mailbox or yard. Be sure she makes it large enough to be seen from the street.

• *Key ring.* Let your child decorate a wooden clothespin, insert a screw eye tightly at the top, and hang on a lightweight metal ring to hold keys. Let best-loved teachers know how wonderful they are by having your child make several key rings using a felt-tipped marker to inscribe ABCs or SUPER-TEACHER or TEACHERS HAVE CLASS.

• *Doorstop.* Have your child paint a brick white and decorate it with stencils to match the holiday season. Or let her cover it with fabric to match drapes or upholstery.

• *Bookends.* For heavy bookends, a child can cover a pair of bricks with wood-grained or patterned Con-Tact paper, and paste a picture postcard on one side of each. Or cut pictures from magazines that reflect the recipient's hobby or special taste.

IOU COUPONS

IOU COUPONS REQUIRE more of your child's time and energy than most other gifts, but he will be blessed in greater measure too. Here are great ideas that will warm adult hearts. Have your child print them on decorated notepaper, or wrap up a book of IOU coupons. They will likely be the best gift the grown-up receives.

This coupon good for:

One week of picking up and dusting the living room after school
One month of keeping Dad's shoes shined (four Saturday shines)
One car wash
One breakfast in bed for two
One trip to the store
One hour of window washing
Potatoes peeled once for dinner
One vacuum cleaning job downstairs
One night of getting supper for the family
Three hours of baby care so you can work on a project

Let your child come up with her own promises. Some possibilities include wash and fold laundry, polish silverware, clean the garage, wax the kitchen floor, be a partner for a favorite game like chess, or make caramel corn for the family watching a football or baseball game on television.

Be sure your child is aware of the recipients' needs and makes his coupon fit. If a nearby relative or friend is planning a trip, have him offer plant or pet care for several days. If Grandma works outside the home, your child could let her know he is available for *her* choice of work sharing. Your child can provide several blank coupons for her to fill in. Brothers or sisters can give coupon suggestions too.

CHAPTER 4

NIFTY NO-COST GIFTS *for* Children to Give Other Children

One of the best presents I received as a child was a minibox of cinnamon red hots from my older sister, who had saved them for me from her school Valentine's Day party. She knew they were my favorite candy, but I was well aware that they were also her favorites, which made the little gift a real sacrifice. On another occasion she stitched up a colorful apron in her sixth-grade home economics class—just what I needed to complete my costume for a party. Warm memories of both of these gifts have remained over the years when others have been long forgotten.

Kids don't have to be great artists to fashion nice presents that will gladden the hearts of their friends. Here are gifts with a different spirit that show your child cares. They are simple to make, do not take a lot of time, and cost nearly nothing. Be sure to look in other sections of this book, especially Chapter 3, for other things that might appeal to your child's best pal or cousin.

FOR PET LOVERS

YOUR OLDER CHILD can easily make a fashionable sweater for a small dog from an old ski mask. Instructions: Lay the mask face down, and carefully use small scissors to clip open enough seam at the crown so the pet's head will go through. The youngster may need your help if scissors are sharp. Hold the ski mask up, and your child will see that the eyeholes can now be used for the pet's front legs and the mouth slit for the rear ones. Puppy's tail will go through the neck opening. Since most head coverings for skiers are very colorful and made of heavy knit materials, Fido will be snug and warm, and maybe even fluorescent, wearing this bright new sweater in cold weather.

An old sweatshirt may fit a larger dog—have your child cut off the arms with a pair of pinking shears. Your child can make designs or write the dog's name on it with markers. Slip the dog's front legs in the armholes and then pull over its head.

Nobody likes looking at a litter box. For your favorite kitty owner or kitty, make a stand-up screen to keep it hidden from view. Fold a twenty-by-thirty-six-inch piece of heavy cardboard in three equal parts and cut an arched top. Your child can paint and decorate this folding screen to provide privacy for Kitty.

Most any pet lover would enjoy browsing through instruction booklets or a catalog of unique and hard-to-locate items that make life with Spot or Kitty much nicer. Ideas:

Pedigrees Pet Catalog, 1989 Transit Way, Brockport, NY 14420, offers a free catalog featuring feeders, waterers, grooming supplies, name tags, and dozens of other items for special and not-so-special breeds.

Almost any veterinarian's office has racks loaded with free pet care booklets, usually supplied by nutrition companies. Or send for a few to give to a dog or cat owner:

Puppy Care Guide, Pedigree, P.O. Box 58853, Vernon, CA 90058
My First Puppy, Cycle Pet Care Center, P.O. Box 9001, Chicago IL 60604-9001
Caring for Your Kitten, Hill's Pet Nutrition Inc., P.O. Box 148, Topeka, KS 66601-0148

Bonus idea: Wrap up a pet book borrowed from the local library as a gift along with a promise to read it through with your child in the two weeks before due date. Time spent together may be as important as learning from the book.

PASS-THEM-ON GIFTS

YOUR CHILD CAN have fun and accomplish something important all at the same time. Have him select good toys that he has outgrown like bikes, sleds, skates, games, books, and building sets to give to a younger child who will appreciate them. Your child can clean them up, or paint those that need it. Be sure games and sets are complete. Other hand-me-down ideas: flash cards, jump ropes, dolls, trucks, table and chair sets, football and baseball cards. One sixth grader said that once she told her sister how much she admired the sister's ring, and the next Christmas, the ring appeared wrapped as a gift to her! Big Sis loved jewelry, but said she would rather her little sister enjoy it.

- *Magazines.* A child can bundle and tie together with a ribbon the last twelve issues of a magazine that she has been receiving over the past year. Some other child will enjoy the stories and articles as much as your child has.
- *Puzzles, stories, and comics.* Your child could save kids' puzzle and story pages from family or children's magazines and special comics

from Sunday newspapers. These can then be mounted on construction paper or cardboard sheets, punched, and put together with yarn or paper fasteners for a fun book. Or attach them to a clipboard for easy removal one by one as they are completed. Be sure puzzle answers are glued to the back of each. For something extra, have your child stick blank labels over the words in comic strips, and add his own captions. Be sure your child leaves a few spaces blank so the other child can write some too. Have your child begin these projects with plenty of time before the gift-giving occasion so he can collect materials from many sources.

JIGSAWS

KIDS WILL ENJOY creating a homemade jigsaw puzzle by pasting on cardboard a favorite photograph or snapshot or a beautiful scene cut from a magazine; then cutting it into pieces. Older children can work with smaller pieces than younger children can, so keep that in mind as they cut the pieces. Adult help may be needed when smaller youngsters use scissors. You cannot buy this personalized gift in any store.

MOBILES

A CHILD CAN make a hanging mobile to match almost any friend's special interest. Colorful tissue paper scraps or other paper remnants can be cut and glued into flowers or butterflies or birds and combined with plastic coffee can covers, used greeting card pictures, and handles from large detergent boxes to make bright hangings just right for the youngster's room. Or cut cars or geometric shapes from construction paper. Use invisible nylon sewing thread to tie pieces together so they hang from a wire coat hanger or a small tree branch to swing at the slightest breeze. Babies love mobiles too, but be careful to hang them high for safe no-touch viewing.

SPOOL PEOPLE

WHEN FACES ARE painted on the sides of large thread spools, they become spool people to illustrate stories for young children or to ride on tiny toy vehicles. Why not have your child paint a spool family with Mom, Dad, and all the kids?

CONE GIFTS

COLORFUL PAPER CONES filled with edible goodies make a sweet surprise from your child at any time of year. Help the child cut 2½ inches from the bottom of an 8½-by-11-inch sheet of construction paper to form a square, or use brightly colored shelf paper or wallpaper. Save the extra. Roll the square to form a cone. Glue the edges, and attach a handle made from the paper you saved. A cone can also be made from a half circle. Let your child trim the cones with lace glued around the top edge or use his own imagination. Fill with peppermints, tiny wrapped candies, or any small items you think the other child would enjoy. At Christmas, make cone gifts to hang on the tree. For extra fun, fill a larger cone with popcorn for the whole family to enjoy.

TOY BOX

ASK A PRINT shop owner to save a sturdy ten-ream copy-paper box with its top. Have your child cover the box inside and out with colorful wallpaper, fabric, or foil. Tuck in several empty mesh bags saved from fresh fruit or stitch up cloth drawstring bags to hold toy sets with lots of parts like Construx, building blocks, Legos, small cars, and puzzles.

PAINTER'S PARTY

Easy Easel

Children love "constructing." Help your child mark and cut out a triangle from a cardboard carton to make a no-tip table easel for another child's painting or drawing projects. Colored clothespins will hold papers in place. To add to this gift, your child can make finger paints from the recipe below. For a flannel board, simply attach felt to the easel. A shoe box prettily covered with wrapping paper or wallpaper will handily hold supplies and flannelboard figures.

Painter's Caddy

For a handy carryall to hold paints and art supplies, have your child cover a six-pack drink carton with brightly colored paper. Round food canisters can be used for articles like brushes, chalk, yarn scraps, or crayons. Wash out small glass jars to store finger paints.

Finger Paint

2/3 cup cornstarch
1 cup cold water

1 envelope unflavored gelatin
$2\frac{1}{4}$ cups hot water
$\frac{2}{3}$ cup soap flakes (don't use detergent)
4 tablespoons food coloring

Mix cornstarch and $\frac{2}{3}$ cup cold water in a medium-sized pan. In a cup, mix together $\frac{1}{3}$ cup cold water and the gelatin. Pour the hot water over the starch mixture and bring it to a boil, stirring constantly. When the mixture is clear, remove from the stove.

Stir in the gelatin mixture. Add the soap flakes and stir briskly until they are dissolved. Mixture should be thick. Stir in the coloring and mix well.

Note: Play dough and finger paint recipes will definitely require adult guidance since they involve use of the stove.

HOMEMADE PLAY DOUGH

A BATCH OF play dough will give many hours of fun to a young child. With a little adult help, your child can make it from this no-fail, no-mess recipe that will keep for months in a covered plastic margarine or butter tub. If your child wishes, she can pack items like birthday candles, drinking straws, and cookie cutters with her gift.

Play Dough

$2\frac{1}{2}$ cups plain flour
$1\frac{1}{2}$ cups salt
1 tablespoon alum (look in the spice section of grocery stores)
2 tablespoons cooking oil
2 cups boiling water colored with food dye

Mix together flour, salt, and alum in a large bowl. In a small bowl, add cooking oil to colored boiling water. When it is cool enough, add to the flour mixture gradually. Knead. If play dough is too soft, add a bit more flour.

FOOD FOR THE BIRDS

Peanut Butter Cone

Your child can make a bird feeder that will draw a flock by spreading peanut butter or bacon fat on a large pinecone. Press on cornmeal, and then push in sunflower seeds, birdseed, cranberries, and raisins. Use a pipe cleaner, piece of wire, long yarn string, or an ornament hook for a hanger. Wrap the feeder lightly with colored cellophane, and tie it with a bow. Be sure your child includes instructions so the recipient will know to hang this treat for feathered diners on an upper branch to discourage cats. Squirrels will likely steal spillovers on the ground. Your child may want to suggest counting the birds who come for their peanut butter snack.

Feeder for Small Birds

Help your child remove the label from a twenty-eight-ounce plastic detergent or shampoo container, and cut a rectangle about two inches high by three inches wide in the lower front of it. Tie a string around the neck of the bottle to hang. Fill a plastic bag with birdseed, and include that as part of the gift.

Coconut Shell Feeder (a shop-wise adult needed to help with this project)

Help your child drill a hole in a coconut, and empty out the milk. Saw off the top third, and scoop out the meat. Drill holes at three evenly spaced places around the edge. Loop pipe cleaners through the holes, and twist them into a hook at the top. Include birdseed with the feeder.

OTHER EASY THINGS CHILDREN CAN GIVE

• *Flash cards.* Your child can make up a set from plain index cards for a younger child who is struggling with reading words or who is having trouble with math.

• *Line viewer.* Make a line viewer for a new reader to keep the place. Help your child cut a wide slot from a piece of cardboard that measures about four by six inches. The viewer can be moved down the page as the story progresses. Be sure your child includes instructions.

• *Magic garden.* Send for directions on how to make a magic salt garden to grow mysterious crystal flowers from common household ingredients. Send a stamped, self-addressed envelope to: Luther Ford Company, P.O. Box 201405, Bloomington, MN 55420. Have your child wrap up the recipe plus jars containing the necessary ingredients (salt and laundry bluing). The recipient will only need to add water to make a unique growing gift.

• *Knitted items.* Can your child do simple knitting and purling? Eight six-inch squares of knit-one-row, purl-one-row worked in different colors, then sewed together in a strip, make a cozy scarf. Or have your child knit four seven-inch squares to be sewed together for both front and back of a pillow. Old nylon stockings will stuff it nicely. Knit larger squares to make a gigantic floor cushion.

MY TIME IS YOUR TIME

YOUNGER CHILDREN ARE almost always delighted when an older child chooses to spend a block of time with them. Your child can make a "Time Coupon" promising an hour to play the other's favorite game (even if your child doesn't particularly like tiddlywinks!) or to show the younger child how to play solitaire or dominoes. Your child can promise a half hour of reading favorite stories or books aloud or listening to an excited new reader read. If your child knows another child has not learned to ride a bike, she can set a time to help. Or she can promise to take the child along next time she goes roller-skating or for a walk to the store. She could make a coupon pledging the use of her bike, wagon, or some other highly valued possession for a week.

Have your child slip a promise coupon in a pretty box, and wrap it exactly like any other gift. Encourage her to say yes with a smile when she is asked to carry out the pledge later.

Your child could take a sibling's turn making beds or doing dishes, or promise to take out the garbage for a couple of weeks or feed the cat for someone who will be away at camp. If you have a teenager, perhaps he could commit to driving a younger child to a friend's house or any other place he knows the younger child would like to go.

CHAPTER 5

GREAT GIFTS *for* Grandparents

GIFTS FOR OLDER people are perhaps the most difficult to select. Their material needs are often less, so choices are fewer. Their inner desires are very different and sometimes not understood by younger friends and family who have not yet walked in more mature paths. Most of the gifts described here cost nothing more than loving time and effort, but I have included some store-bought ideas just in case you want to give something more tangible to Grandmother or Uncle Willis.

Time spent with the aging can be the most satisfying gift of all. Older men and women often yearn for a casual conversation with another human being or even a telephone call or letter. Their need for being with others is expressed graphically in these stanzas from a poem entitled "Waiting" by Theresa V. Meyer.

Waiting

I watch from my window day after day,
For someone may come to my door and say,
"I was just passing by on my way to the store,
I really meant to have called before."
"Oh, do come in and sit a while!"
"Yes," she answers with a friendly smile.
"Perhaps a warm drink and a little chat?
Won't you sit down? I'll take your hat."

PROMISES OF TIME

Your time spent with an older person can put strong wings on a weary heart. God gave himself. Can we do otherwise? Here is how others have given promises of their time to someone older who needed it. Maybe you can think of a friend who would like to receive one of these notes or something similar:

- "The first Tuesday of every month is reserved on my calendar for you and me to spend together with your choice of things to do. I will call you each time to make plans, so think about some things we could enjoy. If you just want to talk or watch television or sip tea, that will be fine. I look forward to time spent with you."
- "Here are twelve certificates, good for dinner at our house the second Tuesday of each month for the coming year. Tom or I will pick you up and take you home afterward."
- "Would you allow us to adopt you this year, please? Our children need a grandparent stand-in who lives nearby to help them understand how the wisdom and love of a wonderful older person can enrich their lives. We want you to visit when we have special birthday or holiday celebrations this coming year, and we would like to bring the children to visit you as often as we can. We also want to keep in touch by letter and phone to check on how things are going with you. It would please us greatly and we would feel honored to have you join our family in this way. We enclose a stamped envelope for your reply."

The promise of long-term commitment takes time and energy, but the rewards can be great. Perhaps everyone in the family can list ways to make the elderly person feel a part of the family and pledge together to carry out the ideas.

- *Bonus idea.* A ladies' church group can compile names of lonely older folks for year-round gifting. Members draw names monthly to pay a visit, send a card, telephone, or take a small present.

A BOOK OF HAPPY COUPONS

CHOOSE A FEW of these ideas to make up a book of things to do for your favorite older person. On the first page, you can write something like "Here is a book of happy coupons that you can cash in by calling me ahead. HAPPY EASTER!"

• This coupon good for one day of shopping together for clothes. (Maybe you can scout the stores ahead to see what is available in preferred clothing, lingerie, dresses, shirts, or coats to save time and effort for the fragile elderly person.)

• This coupon good for a chauffeured ride in the country to see the springtime flowers or fall leaves. (Other ideas: a trip to the zoo or museum, a ride past the old homestead, a visit to the grave of a loved one, lunch for the two of you at a nice restaurant, a trip to the nursery to select plants for the yard or window box or cemetery urn.)

• This coupon good for a secretary for a day (me!) any time you need one. I will come and pay bills, make phone calls, run bank errands, sort papers, balance your checkbook, take dictation and type letters, write thank-you notes, organize your calendar, or take you to the lawyer's office. Let me know which day you need help.

One thoughtful couple gave this commitment to their elderly neighbor in the next apartment: This coupon good for five hours of help from your neighbors throughout the coming year. You can call us to help your arthritic hands open jars, grate cabbage, carry a heavy package upstairs, or hang pictures. We enclose a checkoff chart to keep track of a few minutes here and there as the year progresses. No cheating! This is our Valentine's Day love gift to you. It will give us great joy to keep on "gifting" all year. Just give a ring!

This couple says the gift prompts a lot of laughter as they tease the neighbor about keeping track of the time. Of course, the full five hours are never entirely used up.

You can promise to:

- Wallpaper a room, or paint a porch, front door, or kitchen woodwork.
- Chop and split firewood and bring it in from outdoors.
- Wash windows, pull weeds, mow the lawn, or shovel snow as needed.
- Repot plants or stick flower bulbs in the ground for someone who has trouble kneeling.
- Leave the morning newspaper on an elderly neighbor's porch or behind her storm door as soon as you have finished with it each day.
- Pick up the older person for church each Sunday.
- Send or deliver church bulletins or club newsletters to someone who cannot attend regularly.
- Do grocery shopping once a week or once a month, or shop for Christmas or birthday cards and gifts for the elderly person to send.
- Help the other move when the time comes.
- Bring books from the library once a month and return them.
- Allow the other to stay at your house for two weeks after he is dismissed from the hospital following surgery.
- Sew a dress or shirt, mend, or put in a hem during January.
- Knit a requested item like a shawl or slippers.
- Glue a squeaky rocker.
- Take a pet for grooming services or to the vet for annual shots.
- Install a smoke detector, door bar, chain, or peephole.
- Send for a medical data necklace or bracelet engraved with personal health facts such as blood type, allergies, or special health conditions: Medic Alert, Turlock, CA 95380. Such readily available health information saves precious time in case of an emergency.

HELPS FOR OLDER EYES AND EARS

MANY OLDER PEOPLE are in fairly good health but have some loss of sight or hearing. Try some of these terrific ideas that others have used and recommended to make special days a little merrier for some wonderful elderly person you know.

Large Print Hints

For the person who loves to cook but has trouble reading small print, copy off favorite recipes in big bold letters onto notebook pages and place them inside plastic sheets in a three-ring binder. Give it a special title like "Mary Jo's Cookbook."

Or make an alphabetical list of the addresses and phone numbers of best friends, the bank, gas and electric companies, department stores, doctor, fire department, hospital, police, and others needed in emergencies, and write them in a personalized large print address book.

The National Association for Visually Handicapped (22 West Twenty-first Street, New York, NY 10010) will send large-type instructions for knitting, crocheting, and gardening as well as other guides for the partially sighted. You can also obtain a free newsletter, *Seeing Clearly.*

Many-Colored Threads

Many older people can do their own mending and sewing on of buttons, but threading needles often is difficult because of failing eyesight. Last Christmas, we threaded about seventy-five needles of different sizes from spools of various colors of thread and poked them side by side through eight color-matched felt squares for easy identification. Gram selects the color and takes the needle she needs. The others are left in place for future sewing tasks.

Self-Esteem Builders

For a man or woman in a nursing home, frame pictures of him or her as a younger person and hang them on a bulletin board for all to see. It will boost the person's self-esteem and remind visitors, younger relatives, nursing staff, and doctors that this resident was once stronger and good-looking.

Type up a brief biography telling facts of the person's early life, jobs held, special awards received, or any other interesting things. The older person will feel new dignity when visitors ask about past experiences, and the photos will remind care givers that folks who are old, wrinkled, and sometimes confused deserve respect for their past accomplishments.

News from Friends

Mail is a vital link to the outside world for the older person living alone. Elderly folks will sparkle when even a postcard is delivered, letting them know that someone is thinking about them. In early December, you can phone or write to everyone you can think of requesting that each send a newsy note, Christmas card, or some other holiday remembrance to the oldster. Get in touch with old friends, members of a garden club the older person once belonged to, or a Sunday school class attended regularly in younger days. Your favorite senior citizen will have a mailbox full of holiday goodies as a result. Do it again on a birthday, for a special event, or when the person is ill. Maybe coworkers at your office would enjoy helping in this project even though they have never met your mom or dad or great-aunt Julia.

Good Grooming

Write an elderly friend a note like this on a birthday or Mother's or Father's Day: "As my gift to you, I want to be your wheels to the hairdresser [or barbershop] whenever you need to go. All it takes is a phone call, and I'll be at your door."

Daily Calls

Do you know a person advanced in years who prefers to live alone but often feels uneasy? Perhaps he or she would be very relieved and grateful to receive a note like this on a special gift-giving occasion:

> *Dear Dad,*
>
> *From now on, I will call every morning and evening at seven to see that all is well with you. I know you may not need this every day, but I want to keep in close touch. I'll feel better knowing someone I care about is OK.*
>
> *Love,*
> *Estelle*

Special Occasion Calls

A telephone call from a beloved family member that comes at just the right time can pick up sagging spirits and make an isolated older person feel connected to others. After checking with children and grandchildren or nieces and nephews, send a letter to Aunt Em or Uncle Bart explaining that your gift for all occasions in the upcoming year will be a series of phone calls from loved ones. Enclose six postcards, one to be returned to you just before each occasion (birthday, Valentine's Day, Easter, Mother's Day, Thanksgiving, and Christmas). Paste on hearts or bunnies or other appropriate stickers or use gold seals to make them look "official." Each can say:

> THIS CERTIFICATE good for one phone call from the_________________ family. I would like to redeem it by having you call me on _________________(date) about ______ o'clock ______ A.M. _______ P.M.

Then you alert the callers to the time and occasion and wait for the happy response.

Search-a-Puzzle

Aging people often say they feel worthless or no longer needed. At Christmas, turn the tables on an avid reader of newspapers and magazines and ask her to "gift" your puzzle-loving family by cutting out all the crosswords and mazes she can find in the upcoming year. She will feel useful with this ongoing work that gives pleasure and may even enjoy enlisting friends and neighbors to help! Folks in your family will think of the elderly one every time someone gets out a puzzle during long winter evenings.

Safety Mirror

One woman says she knew that her aged mother, who lived alone in a second-floor apartment, often felt uneasy about answering the doorbell. The elderly lady felt threatened by the possibility of a stranger at the door because she could not see who was there on the ground floor. Getting downstairs was difficult because of severe leg problems. Occasionally, fun-loving children rang the bell. For her birthday, the daughter's husband mounted an oversize mirror rescued from a junkyard truck to the outside frame of the window beside Mom's favorite rocking chair and slanted it to show the door below. No more painful and unnecessary steps down steep stairs. The older woman said she felt much, much safer.

IDEAS FOR SHARING CHRISTMAS ACTIVITIES

HOLIDAYS CAN BE especially trying for older folks who recall rich memories of Christmases past and often find themselves anticipating less fulfilling celebrations this year. Many cannot join in the festivities with full vigor even if invited. Personal needs for friendship and intimacy become even more compelling for the elderly as they watch loving family groups get together and enjoy each other on television. These creative gift ideas can help older persons you know get involved during this joyful season.

- Offer a wheelchair ride through the mall to see the elaborate Christmas decorations.
- Go Christmas shopping with an elderly person, and help select gifts for loved ones.
- Take children to visit. Have youngsters read the Christmas story aloud or recite a holiday poem. Maybe holding hands and praying together before leaving would mean much. Or perhaps you could take along a well-behaved pet for someone who loves animals. Would the person enjoy holding your baby or talking to your two-year-old? Be alert for signs of overtiring.
- Make sure your church or club caroling group sings Christmas songs outside your elderly person's apartment or window. Or if possi-

ble, be responsible for pushing a wheelchair-bound person so that he or she can accompany the group of carolers around the neighborhood.

- Volunteer to take the person to Christmas Eve services or to midnight mass.
- Invite the older person to join your family on Christmas Day for dinner.
- Ask an older friend to your house to share in preparing old-time recipes for cakes or cookies. Maybe the other person can't help mix but can be involved in simpler tasks like picking out nutmeats or cutting and frosting cookies.
- Spend an afternoon helping wrap and label gifts for someone who finds the task tiring. Turn on the radio for festive background music. Take along a teapot, tea, some pretty cups and saucers, and homemade cookies for a little party afterward.
- Help an older person buy and trim a Christmas tree or assemble and decorate an artificial tree.

GREAT LOW-COST GIFTS TO BUY OR PUT TOGETHER

BECAUSE FOLKS WHO are getting on in years do not have the opportunity to get to stores frequently and because gift choices are limited, you may want to wrap something you purchased at a store to give your favorite elderly person. Inexpensive gift ideas like these require your taking time to select "just right" items to give or assemble into meaningful and worthwhile gifts. Maybe your much-loved older person would appreciate:

- *A live plant.* It can be nurtured and appreciated as a companion. Growing things beautify a room by adding color and life, and plant slips can be passed on to others with joy.

• *A windowsill garden.* A wood or metal box filled with potting soil and planted with seedlings makes a fun-to-watch windowsill garden. Sow sage, rosemary, thyme, and parsley for an herb garden, or put in tomatoes or flower plants that do not grow too tall. Promise to mount the box on a window if needed. For extra fun, type out recipes that make good use of herbs and veggies.

• *A small Christmas or Easter tree.* Decorate it with tiny framed snapshots of beloved people. Or clip around snapshot figures, and paste them on brightly painted wooden squares or ornaments. If you have no photos, paint a name on each square. Lighting up the family photograph tree each evening will be a reminder of how many people care.

• *An eyeglass care kit.* Include small wipes, a mini-screwdriver for making adjustments, and a new case to carry glasses. Look on racks in an optician's office for other practical items like nose pads and eyeglass chains.

• *A lap writing kit.* Inside a foldover clipboard, place stationery and envelopes, return address labels, plain and picture postcards, stamps, several kinds of pens and pencils, a tablet, and an address book with as many names, addresses, and phone numbers of the other's friends and relatives as you can think of. Wrap up a small decorative box to contain paper clips, tape, a paste stick, rubber bands, mini-stapler, ruler, and marking pens to keep handily in a desk or bedside drawer.

• *A package of preaddressed cards.* Christmas, New Year's, and birthday cards to send to family and friends will be much appreciated. Attach stamps and return-address labels to envelopes, and include a felt-tipped pen so a message can be written just before the card is mailed. Many older folks love to keep in touch on special days but lack writing skills or energy to go out and select just the right cards or to address and stamp them. The mailing date for each addressed card can be written in pencil on the envelope, and the envelopes kept together and in order with a rubber band for easy remembering when the mailing date arrives. Include a packet of stickers that reflect a special interest like birds or flowers so that the elderly one can add a personal touch. If kids are on the mailing list, enclose a few children's cards.

- *Puzzles.* They can be new or used, as long as all pieces are intact.
- *A Membership in AARP ($8).* Write to the American Association of Retired Persons, 601 E Street NW, Washington, DC 20049. A membership in CAP ($13), Christian Association of Primetimers, P.O. Box 777, St. Charles, IL 60174. Both offer pharmacy and medical discounts, health and homeowner's insurance, book and travel bargains, and a subscription to a magazine for senior citizens.
- *A catalog and gift certificate.* Look on page 14 for catalog ideas. For those with special handicapping conditions, give a certificate from a catalog with things designed to make day-to-day living easier. A wealth of health care products is available to reduce or eliminate frustration and struggle in daily tasks: convenient one-handed cutters, a sock aid to put on hosiery without bending over, medi-crush for those unable to swallow medication in tablet form, and even utensil handclips for those who have difficulty grasping. A good book on this subject is *The Gadget Book: Ingenious Devices for Easier Living,* American Society on Aging ($10.95).
- *A special telephone.* One with oversize numbered buttons is convenient for a person with poor sight. Someone with limited mobility will love getting a cordless phone.
- *Other books of interest:*

The Quiet Moment: Devotions for the Golden Years by Jeanette Lockerbie (Standard Publications)

AARP publishes a variety of special-interest books for folks in their later years and for caregivers of the elderly. For a catalog, send to: AARP Books, Scott, Foresman & Company, 1865 Miner Street, Des Plaines, IL 60016.

Struck Down But Not Destroyed: A Christian Response to Chronic Ill-

ness and Pain by Doug Wiegand and Stan Scott, Rainbow's End ($9.95)

Gardening in the Shade (choosing, growing, and caring for plants in shady environments), a Better Homes and Garden Book

Accessible Gardening: Tips and Techniques for Seniors and the Disabled by Joann Woy, Stackpole Books ($15.95)

Seniors Acting Up: Humorous New One-Act Plays and Skits for Older Adults, edited by Ted Fuller, Pleasant Hill Press ($17.95)

• *A catalog of large-print books and a gift certificate.*
Big print publishers:

G. K. Hall
70 Lincoln Street
Boston, MA 02111

Walker & Company
435 Hudson Street
New York, NY 10014

Wheeler Publishing
PO Box 531
Accord, MA 02018-0531

• *A subscription to a large-print magazine or newspaper.* Prices vary, but any additional cost will be worth it. Contact:

Reader's Digest
Pleasantville, NY 10570

Guideposts
Carmel, NY 10512-9970

New York Times
229 West Forty-third Street
New York, NY 10036

• *Taped books and devotionals.* Books on Tape (P.O. Box 7900, Newport Beach, CA 92658) and Recorded Books (P.O. Box 409, Charlotte Hall, MD 20622) offer many listening choices for folks with failing eyesight who love good books or those who tire easily holding heavy objects. The Bible on tape is available at most religious bookstores, but be sure to choose a version preferred by the older person. The Upper Room offers a subscription to a daily devotional guide on cassette tape ($35 yearly) or in large print ($8.95). Write to P.O. Box 37153, Boone, IA 50037-0153 or call 1-800-925-6847.

• *A small cassette player and tapes.* Favorite music or speakers on tape will provide hours of delight. Perhaps you can include a promise to tape Sunday church sermons for a shut-in.

• Tartan Books (1-800-233-8467, ext. 507) offers a catalog of books discounted for senior citizens who are members of the American Association of Retired Persons.

• American Printing House for the Blind, P.O. Box 6085, Louisville, KY 40206 and Low Vision Aids Clinic, 301 E. Mohammed Boulevard, Louisville, KY 40202 offer various helps for the visually handicapped.

GIFTS FOR THE ELDERLY IN A NURSING HOME OR HOSPITAL

THESE PRACTICAL GIFTS will lift the spirits of older persons you care about:

• *Warm clothing items that do not button or do not zip up the back.* Be sure that everything is permanently labeled for easy identification after laundering. Favorite items include sweaters, underwear, pajamas, socks or stockings, nightgowns, shirts, slacks, and dresses.

• *An inexpensive piece of jewelry.* It can make a real difference in a woman's appearance and boost her self-esteem.

• *A bedjacket for a woman;* a nightcap for a man.

• *Soft slippers with leather soles* that will not slip or slide.

• *Sneakers with Velcro closings* instead of laces.

• *An extra warm blanket or blanket bag* that zips shut for cozy warmth while napping or while watching television in a chair on cold evenings.

• *A machine-washable pillow and flannel sheets and pillowcases.*

• *A pillow backrest with arms.*

• *A tote bag to carry books, crafts, and personal items.* Use cord or binding to sew ties onto the bag's corners so it can be attached to the arm of a wheelchair or secured to a walker.

• *A denim caddy with deep pockets that hangs at bedside* to contain personal items. These caddies are usually designed so one part slips under the mattress for a firm hold.

• *A small battery-operated radio with built-in earphones* for easy handling—no cords to tangle and no earplug attachment needed. A care giver can set the dial to an older person's favorite station, and the handy little earphone set can be hung over a bedpost for convenient later use. Those who are hard of hearing often find this kind of radio better than a conventional table model.

• *A gift certificate for beauty or barber care.*

• *A sunshine basket with small wrapped gifts for opening one per day until all are gone.* Include skin cream, talcum, disposable razors, aftershave lotion or cologne, soap, comb, and brush. Ask the nursing home director for a list of other sundries that older people appreciate.

• *Favorite homemade food,* always a welcome change from institutional meals. Be sure it fits the recipient's diet, however. Or fix a box of snack food. Include mini-packets of crackers, cookies, potato and corn chips, small cakes, and packaged dried fruit.

- A *wrapped box of candy* for the elderly person to give to a favorite nurse or aide.
- A *bouquet of fresh flowers* or a more lasting basket of silk flowers.
- A *bulletin board* on which to hang greeting cards and photos.
- A *magnifying glass* for easier reading, sewing, or handiwork.
- A *label-maker* to mark personal possessions.

CHAPTER 6

GIFTS FROM STORES *and* Catalogs for Just About Anybody

MAYBE YOU WANT to spend only a small amount of money to buy gifts for folks you care about. These sure-to-please presents won't break your budget, because we have tried to keep them at a low-cost level. The emphasis here is on buying and giving the gift that fits best what the recipient wants or needs. Of course, choices (especially for kids) must match abilities.

One Christmas, I watched my excited little preschooler rip open her biggest and prettiest package, only to burst into tears. What a surprise! We had shopped so carefully, and everybody thought she would love her bright blue robe and matching slippers to wear on Saturday mornings, munching cereal and watching cartoons. But five-year-olds often have their hearts set on receiving certain items long before gift days arrive. Why didn't someone ask?

The solution: Post a "What's Your Wish?" list on the side of the refrigerator. Leave a space after each family member's name so they can list their desired gifts there. Set a limit on the cost at that point and make it clear. If you hear parents or married sons and daughters or grandchildren express a yearning, jot it down. Children and teenagers love to let you know the desires of their heart long before birthdays. Before shopping for gifts at any time of year, study the list. It's nice to know your money is spent for presents that fulfill the recipient's desire or need. The "What's Your Wish?" list helps you buy more intelligently and there are fewer disappointments.

BABIES AND TODDLERS UNDER THREE YEARS

CURIOUS BABIES ENJOY brightly colored playthings to handle and inspect. Busy little toddlers love to push and pull things and to experiment with their hands. Parents will appreciate some of these too.

Baby Maybes

- Clothing items
- Clutch ball
- Crib gym
- Crib mobile
- Baby shoes or booties
- Teething ring, pacifier
- Baby mirror
- Blanket for crib or carriage
- Diaper bag
- Cloth book
- Squeaky rubber toy
- Soft fabric doll
- Musical chime toy
- Plastic oversize beads and rings
- Electronic nursery monitor
- Playpen pad

Toddler Pleasers

- Pull toy
- Stacking toy

- Small stuffed animals or dolls
- Shape sorter
- Plastic or ceramic cup, tumbler, plate, small eating utensils
- Big ball
- Child-sized rocking chair
- Doll carriage
- Jigsaw puzzles with oversize pieces
- Books
- Toy musical instruments like drums, horn, xylophone, tambourine

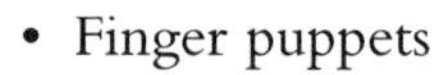

Preschoolers

Three- to six-year-olds are at the make-believe age, and they love to say, "Let's pretend!" These low-cost gifts will help little people imitate the world around them in a thousand and one situations and become almost anybody or anything they want.

- Finger puppets
- Toy cash register
- Toy telephone
- Blocks
- Sandbox toys, pail, shovel, plastic cups, spoons, funnels
- Cooking appliances and utensils that look like Mom's
- Play store or gas station
- Toy villages, farms, forts
- Small cars and trucks
- Construction toys and tractors
- Finger paints
- Crayons, watercolors, coloring books

- Cuddly toys and dolls
- Inflatable animals
- Nesting boxes
- Balloons
- Balls
- Dollhouse and furniture
- Slinky
- Plastic backyard pool and swim float
- Picture books
- Records, cassette tapes

SIX- TO TWELVE-YEAR-OLDS

THESE KIDS ARE beginning to learn social strategies. They enjoy competitive games and physical play. Some of these gifts challenge their minds and arouse their curiosity; others encourage outdoor activities. You're bound to find some exciting ideas for your favorite children.

- Sports equipment
- Table tennis set
- Ice or roller skates
- Sled
- Kite and string
- Card and board games
- Action figures or fashion dolls
- Bicycle
- Bicycle basket, lock, pump
- Backpack
- Overnight drawstring survival bag con-

taining towel, washcloth, soap, brush, toothbrush, toothpaste, magazines, snacks

- Supply of clay, molds, cookie cutters
- Rubber stamp with child's name and address, ink pad
- Personalized pencils
- Big tablets and oversize pencils
- Felt-tipped children's marker set
- Art supplies
- Swim float
- Nose plug, swim fins, or snorkle mask
- Stationery kit

Include personalized paper, envelopes, self-stick return address labels, stamps, pens, address book, tracing paper, clips, pencils, small stapler and staples, paper punch, and thank-you notes.

- Magnifying glass
- Extra-strong magnets
- Prism
- World globe
- Beginner's stamp packet and collector's album
- Coin collector's album and a book to identify value of coins
- Model kits
- Science and craft kits
- First makeup kit
- Rocks or shells to add to a collection
- Money in a wallet or purse
- Roll of new nickels, dimes, or pennies
- Wind-up alarm clock
- Top or yo-yo
- Ant farm
- Building sets
- Baseball or football cards
- Headbands, hair barrettes, brush
- Carpenter tool set (appropriate to age)

Include hammer, screwdriver, pliers, a couple of wrenches, nails, bolts and nuts, sandpaper, and precut wood.

- Glass globe that "snows" when shaken
- Lunch box
- Mug with hot chocolate packets
- Volumes of an encyclopedia purchased weekly at grocery store
- Bookplates to personalize new books
- Initialed teaspoon
- One Christmas tree ornament
- Kids' calendar
- Fishbowl and fish, food, and instructions for care
- ID tag for a pet

Send to Walter Drake, 66 Drake Building, Colorado Springs, CO 80940 for a tag that hooks to the collar; include pet's name, owner's name, address, and phone number.

- Cozy comforter or juvenile sheet set with colorful design
- Comic books and puzzle books with crosswords and mazes
- Autographed book by a favorite author

Write a letter to the author in care of the publisher and enclose a check for an autographed copy. If you already have the book, send it in a padded envelope along with return postage and a note asking for the signature. Most children's writers enjoy helping out in this way.

- Illustrated instruction books for craft projects and materials for completing one project
- Stamped, preaddressed Christmas, birthday, or New Year's cards to mail to friends and relatives
- A bank account in the child's name
- A gift subscription to a magazine:

Clubhouse
Focus on the Family
Pomona, CA 91799

Pockets
The Upper Room
P.O. Box 37146
Boone, IA 50037-0146

Faith 'n Stuff (from *Guideposts*)
P.O. Box 1400
Carmel, NY 10512-9909

World
National Geographic World
P.O. Box 63001
Tampa, FL 33663

Ranger Rick
National Wildlife Federation
P.O. Box 777
Mt. Morris, IL 61054-8276

MUSE (Smithsonian for ages 6–14)
Box 7468
Red Oak, IA 51591-2468

TEENS

AFTER ABOUT AGE twelve, children's interests become more sophisticated. Whether the teen is younger or older, these gifts will likely be enjoyed:

- Sports fitness kit with headband, athletic socks, knit leg warmers, sweatshirt, or soothing body lotion

• Make-your-own sundae basket

Include ice-cream scoop, assortment of toppings and nuts, maraschino cherries, a bunch of bananas, cones or plastic sundae dishes, and maybe a few crisp dollar bills to help pay for ice cream.

• Popcorn party basket

In a pretty ribbon-tied basket, place microwave popcorn packets, paper napkins, plastic bowls, and maybe a few cans of soft drinks. If you have one, include a recipe for popcorn balls.

• New driver's kit with car keys on a jazzy chain, flashlight, flares, car polishing items, chamois cloth.

• Bath soak kit with fragrant soap, bubble bath, shampoo and conditioner, oversize towel, washcloth, a paperback mystery novel

• Home manicure kit with polish, remover, emory boards, hand lotion, cotton swabs, nail clippers, scissors

• Album, photo mounting corners, glue, self-stick labels, marking pen

• Subscription to a contemporary inspirational teen magazine:

Campus Life
465 Gunderson Drive
Wheaton, IL 60188

Devo'zine (Upper Room)
P.O. Box 37140
Boone, IA 50037-0140

• Denim- or plaid-covered modern language version of the Bible

• Diary that locks with a key, or a blank journal

• Box that locks to store very private items

• Zany socks, shirts, caps, shoelaces

• Appliqués to sew on jackets

• Current fad items like polka-dot suspenders

• The biggest of anything: a foot-long pencil, extra wide pens, outsize paper clips in fluorescent colors, huge Mexican siesta hat, five-foot teddy bear, maxi-sunglasses, jumbo-sized oranges or apples, colossal ten-quart pail filled with ready-to-eat buttered popcorn, or the world's largest bright red Christmas bow to tie on a pet's collar.

• The smallest of anything: Bible, set of playing cards, or flashlight

• Colorful magnets to hang in home or car; choose from an assortment of things like rainbows, ladybugs, mottoes, butterflies, flowers, or animals

• Wall posters

• Tickets for the amusement park, movies, circus

• Plastic fashion watch

• T-shirt or button with slogan

• Bus tokens

• Personalized initial seal with colored wax to close envelopes

• Whittling and rock-hunting tools with information flyers about these hobbies

• A share of stock and a pamphlet about how the stock market works

• Gift certificate for local music or department store

• Record or cassette of a favorite music group

• Record or cassette storage rack

• An easy-to-learn musical instrument like a recorder or harmonica and an instruction book. *Easiest Harmonica Book* by William Bay, Mel Bay Publications ($4.95).

ADULTS

HERE ARE IDEAS for practical or pretty gifts that grown-ups of any age will welcome. All can be easily located in hardware, department, or discount stores or in mail-order catalogs. Perhaps you can discover the perfect store-bought gift from this smorgasbord of ideas, which includes traditional oldies as well as some newer ones.

- Music or audiocassette or CD
- Big box of candy, dried fruit, select coffee or tea, or assorted cheeses
- Small glass jar filled with cracked nuts like macadamias, cashews, Brazils, black walnuts
- Basketful of grooming products in mini-bottles—shampoo, hair conditioner, soaps, hand lotion, cologne, sunscreen, loofah sponge
- Basket of fragrant soaps
- Set of combs or hairbrush
- Makeup brushes
- Hand mirror
- Fix-it set of basic tools
- Book on a subject of special interest
- Sunglasses
- Specialized magazine

Bird Watchers' Digest, Box 110, Marietta, OH 45750, and *Astronomy,* P.O. Box 1612, Waukesha, WI 53187, are two possibilities.

- Subscription to a daily devotional guide magazine

Write *Walk Through the Bible,* P.O. Box 80587, Atlanta, GA 30366, or *Day by Day,* Forward Movement Publications, 412 Sycamore Street, Cincinnati, OH 45273-9204

- Current issues of several different magazines that the other person would like but probably not buy, rolled up together and tied with a gigantic bow

- Spiral copy of the church hymnal. The recipient's name can be imprinted to personalize the gift.
- Book donated to the local public or church library in the other person's name
- A well-worn Bible or other favorite book, rebound good as new
- For someone thinking of buying a new car, a collection of brochures from many automobile dealers
- Instructional do-it-yourself videotapes
- Travel videotapes of special interest to the person
- Travel diary or foreign language dictionary for the traveler
- Calendars

Museum gift shops almost always have gorgeous wall calendars showing local scenes or famous collector prints. Your gift money will do double duty for a preservation project if you order from Friends of Earth, 1025 Vermont Avenue NW, Suite 300, Washington, DC 20005, or American Horticultural Society, 7931 E. Boulevard Dr., Alexandria, VA 22308

- Telephone gift certificate
- Gift certificate and a copy of any interesting catalog
- Gift certificate for services from a beauty shop or barbershop, clothing alterations or appliance repair shops, food specialty or ice-cream store, dry cleaners, lawn care experts, plumber, maid service, video store
- Restaurant matchbook with gift certificate for one or dinner invitation attached
- An overseas call to a missionary, young soldier, or relative in a faraway place.
- Extra-long phone cord
- Monogrammed notepad
- Compartmentalized desktop organizer for small items
- Desk calendar
- Appointment book

- Checkbook holder
- Accordion file envelopes for organizing papers
- Blank computer discs, printer or keyboard dust covers, or other computer supplies
- Fireproof or metal document box
- Playing cards
- Photograph or print of a favorite place like the Grand Canyon, Monticello, Epcot
- Packet of picture postcards of the old hometown
- Pocket calculator
- Flashlight and batteries
- Emergency flares to carry in the car trunk
- Extra set of car or house keys
- Tire gauge
- Rain gauge
- Barometer
- Thermometer
- Umbrella
- Belt
- Folding outdoor chair
- Wall hanging or picture
- Bedroom slippers
- Sweater stone to remove yarn pills
- Lint brush
- Big Christmas stocking filled with personal items
- Coffee mug decorated to reflect the other's hobby or interest
- Good grooming kit for the office with small mirror, cologne, needle and thread, toothbrush and small tube of toothpaste
- Mailbox
- Small jewelry items, liquid jewelry cleaner and brush
- Kitchen or garage gadget
- Wallet or purse

- Set of mugs and a jug of cider
- Money

Order an uncut sheet of dollar bills, available from the Bureau of Engraving and Printing, Mail Order Sales, Room 602-11A, Fourteenth and C Streets SW, Washington, DC 20228.

- Paid-up membership dues in an organization of special interest
- Season pass to anything
- One time paid-up fee for an ardent golfer or tennis enthusiast
- Tickets for a local tour of homes
- Dish garden
- Decorative wood or brass pot for plants
- Flower press
- Gift certificate from a nursery for a flowering tree or bush
- "Secret indulgence" gifts

These show intimate knowledge of the other's little quirks: a whole chocolate pie for a chocoholic; a box of Northern Spy apples for your sister, who complains of mushy apples since moving to Florida.

- Tongue-in-cheek collections of small items

My sister never can find toenail clippers, so I gave her a pair for each room in the house. How about a case of toilet tissue for a close friend who had none in the house the last time you visited, or twenty-five lightbulbs for someone who cannot remember to turn off the lights? For extra fun, if Uncle Joe is crazy about dill pickles, arrange for everyone in the family to give him a jar.

PEOPLE WITH SPECIAL INTERESTS

DOES RETIRED COUSIN Henry seem to spend all day in his workshop? Does Mom sneak away to her sewing machine every chance she gets? What about your friend who loves to bake cakes? Take advantage of special interests and needs to make gift shopping a breeze.

Seamstresses

- Pair of precision dressmaker scissors
- Several yards of special fabric with pattern and necessary notions rolled up inside, all tied with a measuring tape bow
- Whimsy basket

Line it with print fabric and load it with sewing notions, fabric remnants, beads and sequins, fancy trim and binding, thread of many colors, snaps, unique buttons, a pincushion, Velcro, and cord. Sometimes sewing odds and ends can be purchased at sell-out sales for as little as a dime.

- Wood sewing basket with handles
- Ceramic or silver thimble
- Thread organizer

Other Needlework Enthusiasts

- Pattern, yarn, crochet hook or knitting needles for a sweater
- Supply of small frames
- Gift certificate from a local frame or needlework shop
- Subscription to a handiwork magazine:

Quilter's Newsletter
Box 394
Wheatridge, CO 80033

Sew News
PJS Publications
News Plaza, Box 1790
Peoria, IL 61656

Threads (sewing, knitting, quilting, etc.)
63 S. Main Street
Newtown, CT 06470

Women's Circle
P.O. Box 299
Lynnfield, MA 01940-0299

The Workbasket
KC Publishing
1700 W. 47th Street
Suite 310
Kansas City, MO 64112

Serious Cooks

- Recipe box
- Cookbooks

Local Junior League or church group publications are usually outstanding.

- Membership in Better Homes and Gardens Cook Book Club, 1-800-678-2701
- Crockpot
- Mixing bowls
- Coffee mill

- Whatever is brand-new (or antique) in kitchen gadgets
- Basket of unusual herbs, spices, and sauces and corresponding recipes
- Contemporary cookware
- Plastic salad spinner
- Matching kitchen towels, potholders, trivets
- Antique glass canning jars
- Microwave turntable
- Spice rack
- Decorative kitchen timer
- Cookie press, cutters
- Marble rolling pin
- Extra-deep pie plates

Mostly for Men

- Pocketknife
- Small hand tools
- Portable tool carrier
- Pattern books or plans for building or carving projects
- Plastic workshop organizer to hold nuts and bolts, odds and ends
- Shoeshine kit
- Sleep mask for a night worker
- Tickets to a boat or an auto show
- Pen-and-pencil set
- Car cleaning and waxing supplies in a bucket with sponge
- Car mirror, emergency flares, litter bag, first aid kit, maps
- Lock for gas tank
- How-to book about car repairs
- Man's shower kit with soap on a rope, talcum, oversize bath towel, aftershave, and body lotion
- Sports calendar

- Hunting accessories
- Fishing tackle and lures

Parents of Young Children

- Subscription to a parenting magazine
- Book on practical parenting or marriage enrichment

Gardeners

- Sprayer
- Leather yard gloves
- Oscillating sprinkler
- Problem-solving books or handbooks on specialized subjects like organic gardening, rock gardens, insect control, azaleas
- Wildflower identification book
- Framed prints of flowers or plants
- Straw hat or watering can filled with things like canvas gloves, kneepads, cleanup bags, hand trowel, liquid fertilizer
- Any new garden gadget or labor-saving device
- Bag of selected spring bulbs
- Flower or vegetable seed packets
- Unusual seeds like muskmelon, herbs, midget vegetables
- Paperback copy of *Growing Midget Vegetables at Home* (Lancer Books)
- Paid membership in a local garden club
- Subscription to a gardener's magazine:

Organic Gardening
33 East Minor Street
Emmaus, PA 18049

Flower and Garden
4251 Pennsylvania Avenue
Kansas City, MO 64111

American Horticulturist
7931 E. Boulevard Drive
Alexandria, VA 22308-1300

- Books for gardeners:

The Weekend Garden Guide by Susan A. Roth, Rodale Press

Illustrated Guide to Gardening and 1,001 Hints and Tips for Your Garden; both Better Homes and Gardens books

Clergy

- Book on best-selling religious books list
- Magazine subscription:

Catholic Digest
P.O. Box 64090
St. Paul, MN 55164

Discipleship Journal
NavPress
P.O. Box 35004
Colorado Springs, CO 80935-0004

Moody Magazine
820 N. LaSalle Blvd.
Chicago, IL 60610

Decision
Billy Graham Association
1300 Harmon Place
Minneapolis, MN 55403-1988

• Coupon a month for your services (see sample coupons on p. 178)

Maybe you can visit shut-ins, volunteer to answer the church office phone, or type letters the next time the church secretary is ill.

• Dinner-out and baby-sitting coupons for pastor and spouse

• Coupons for once-a-week housekeeping help at the parsonage for a month

• A small good deed done each day for someone else in the pastor's name

Afterward, write the deeds on a piece of paper and enclose it in a birthday or Christmas card if you wish.

162 THE WHOLE FAMILY

YOU AND YOUR relatives can simplify gift giving by exchanging gifts from one family to another rather than between individuals. Everybody can enjoy trying out the gift sent to the whole family.

Here are gifts that cost from twenty dollars to about sixty dollars, which is fifteen dollars each or less for a family of four. One or two cost a bit more but may be worth it.

• Magazine subscription that fits a family hobby

Do they raise dogs, own horses, or ski? Tie a ribbon around the current issue, and attach a card that says "subscription on its way."

- Family membership for a local natural history museum, planetarium, botanical gardens, or science center.
- Tickets to community drama or concert events
- Pedometer to measure miles walked or hiked
- Oversize coffee table book
- Board or group games
- Sports equipment like a croquet set, basketball and hoop
- An aerial photograph of the recipient's home area, which you can enlarge and frame
- Bluebird or martin house and instructions for hanging it
- Bird feeder and year's supply of bird food
- Family pet gifts like a homemade doghouse or a dog or cat goody kit
- Oversize picnic basket with plastic dishes, silverware, salt and pepper set, napkins, foam cups, hand wipes, tablecloth
- Large thermos with handle
- Camping equipment: lantern, small stove, mess kits, air mattress, or freeze-dried trail foods
- Camera that is easy to use

Include cut-rate newspaper coupons for developing or for double prints.

- Disposable cameras with preloaded film
- Five-foot stick of salami, crackers, loaves of French bread
- Gift certificate for videotape rentals
- Oversize floor pillow set
- Vacation trip guidebooks, car activity books for young children, gift certificates for fast-food restaurants
- Paper table settings, cups, tablecloths, napkins, and enough candles to celebrate family birthdays for an entire year
- Hammock or porch swing
- Front-door mat imprinted with family name
- Small kitchen appliance like a toaster or popcorn popper

• Kitchen gadget kit

Include items like a manual can opener, jar opener, tongs, measuring cups, strainer, spatulas, cooking spoons, a candy thermometer, and a colorful plastic sieve, along with a couple of terry cloth dishtowels.

• Outdoor thermometer

• Electric pencil sharpener

• Wicker bathroom hamper

• Reading lamp

• Dental kit with two toothbrushes for every person, toothpaste, dental floss, mouthwash

• A money plant

Tie envelopes with small sums of money, each marked with someone's name, on the branches of a big poinsettia plant. It can be tagged "For everybody at 203 Jackson Street" and delivered on December 24. When the tissue is removed, the bright branches will fly out for everyone to grab his or her own money envelope.

• Adopt a child for a family

Let them know with a letter such as this:

> *Dear Jim, Mary, and Children,*
>
> *This year, we would like to do our Christmas giving a little differently, so we think we have a wiser way to spend money and better honor Jesus on his birthday.*
>
> *In your family's name, we have adopted José Rezito, a nine-year-old boy from a very poor home in Bolivia. Each month for the next year, we will be sending twenty dollars to the Christian Children's Fund, 2821 Emorywood Parkway, Richmond, VA 23294, to provide some of the necessities of life for José. Our kids have pledged monthly money from their allowances too. These few dollars will go a long way to put a smile*

back on José's face. We enclose his photograph and biography received last week from CCF. You will be getting letters from José from time to time. We will send in the pledge on the first day of each month. We love you lots.

Reflecting Jesus' love,
Alec, Jane, and the kids

CHAPTER 7

WRAP IT UP *with* Imagination and Economy

I'll make it the most gorgeous-looking gift ever given," I promised myself on my husband's birthday last September. Our budget was curtailed when our old washer broke down and we were forced to purchase a new one, so the monetary value of his gift was necessarily limited. Somehow, after buying his small gift, I was able to set aside ten dollars to wrap it in an exquisite box with gold foil, a wide blue velvet ribbon with a huge bow, and a suede tag. He loved the elegant box and thought my gift was nice, too, but later I lamented privately that the wrapping had cost nearly as much as the present inside.

Sure, you can buy gorgeous gift paper and ribbon made from fabric, silver, or even gold lamé. But do you really want to spend five or ten dollars for wrappings that someone will likely rip off and toss aside in a few seconds?

You may be surprised at how many different and beautiful ways there are to wrap up special gifts on a budget. And you will be rewarded as others appreciate your creativity in combining twice-used paper, ribbon, and other leftovers in new, dazzling ways. When all eyes are on an intriguingly wrapped box, folks will not think about how much or how little you spent for what is inside.

FOCUS ON THE BOX

YOU CAN TURN plain cardboard boxes into happy packages that will elicit smiles even before the contents are revealed. If you sewed a flowered blouse for Sis, wrap the box in remnants of the same fabric, and glue on a collar and buttons to resemble what is inside. If you are giving a man's shirt, tickle his fancy by dressing up the box to look like a stuffed shirt. Draw or paste on a collar, cuff links, pocket (leave the top open for a gift card and handkerchief), and bow tie. Or cut a slot in the box top and loop through one of hubby's old ties. Add a loud plaid vest if you like. Where do you get boxes for gifts? Ask for them when you make department store purchases throughout the year. Or ask clerks to save stocking and lingerie containers for you. Be sure to pick them up when asked.

• *Bonus idea.* Create a nest of boxes. Wrap each separately and beautifully, then place inside the next largest until finally the biggest contains them all. You can label the various boxes with a different person's name so the present gets passed around until the smallest box, the one containing *the* gift, is discovered, labeled with the right person's name. To keep folks confused and wondering, put pebbles or beans in some of the containers to add weight and rattles. For more fun, add crazy gifts inside.

DESIGNER PAPER

YOU WILL FALL absolutely in love with these custom-made paper designs and so will the recipients.

• *Professional papers.* For an engineer or a math teacher, use graph paper for gift wrap. Sheets from yellow legal pads work well on a lawyer's present. For a cleric, cut pages from a devotional magazine or pictures and messages from outdated church bulletins. For a telephone operator or lineman, make an enlarged photocopy of a page from the local phone book or yellow pages.

• *Sheet music.* Strike just the right note by using sheet music to wrap up a tape, CD, concert tickets, or almost anything else that fits a music lover's taste. Black-and-white sheet music topped with a red, blue, or green bow makes a dramatic package.

• *Maps.* Raid the car's glove compartment for outdated road maps, almost always a generous size, or cut maps from ancient almanacs for brightly colored wrap to delight a salesman or someone who loves to travel. A jogger might enjoy a map of the city, rolled up and tied with a pair of laces to match his shoes. Use an intriguing poster discarded by a travel agency or a magazine article about some exotic foreign country for a world traveler.

• *Wallpaper.* A leftover roll of wallpaper or pages from an outdated wallpaper sample book make wonderfully appealing wrapping paper. Choose a rocking horse or snowman design for a child, or let a flotilla of boats sail atop a man's package. Open roadsters or racing cars might be the right pattern for a junior sports enthusiast. Wide or narrow coordinated wallpaper borders can perk up plain packages. Someone on your gift list would probably appreciate abstract art designs.

• *Newspapers.* Impress a businessperson or an entrepreneur by wrapping a gift in the stock market pages or a section of the *Wall Street Journal* topped with a little bag of chocolate gold coins. Use stories of famous personalities from the sports section for an avid baseball or football fan, home classified ads for a realtor, crosswords for a puzzle buff, or colorful comics from the Sunday paper for a child or someone young at heart. If you still live in your hometown but your family does not, a copy of the local newspaper will please the recipient, who will likely pause to read the latest news before opening the gift. A young mother I know saves wedding, engagement and birth announcements, pictures of the family participating in sports and community events, and other special news clips from the local paper to paste in strategic positions on her packages for parents, brothers, and sisters.

• *Bonus idea.* A woman living overseas creates sensational wrap by using newspapers printed in Japanese for gifts sent back home. Everybody has fun trying to figure out the day's news in Tokyo before opening gifts.

• *Fabric wrap-ups.* Tying a cranberry-red velvet package with a white eyelet bow is an elegant touch. Save remnants to cut out gift clothes or fabric sacks in exactly the right shape and size with pinking shears. Clip ribbon-width strips from coordinating color material to become ties. Or use inexpensive unbleached muslin or an old sheet or pillowcase for all-over wrap, then add a clump of silk flowers or glue on colorful designs like umbrellas, cars, or contemporary art. Teens will enjoy a denim-wrapped package.

If you have been quilting lately, sew together some appliquéd blocks to wrap a special package.

To make an extra-nice container that can later be a handy storage box, cover the bottom of a hat or boot box with bold plaid or checked gingham or calico and the top with shiny red or gold paper. Attach a crocheted or knit doily with a few careful stitches, or sprinkle confetti on glue in the shape of a festive wreath.

Use bandanas! Place a small gift diagonally in the middle of a colorful handkerchief, knot the opposite ends together on top, and tuck in the corners. For larger presents, cut your own bandanas from big pieces of country print fabric, and use pinking shears to neaten the edges. Wrap small gifts like perfume or sachet in an embroidered or delicately printed scarf to be used over and over.

• *Rubber band bonanza.* For a gift wrap that will stretch anyone's imagination, pull dozens of different colored rubber bands over small boxes covered with plain tissue paper. Place the bands haphazardly at various angles for a contemporary look.

JUNIOR SMART WRAPS

ALMOST EVERY HOME has resident or visiting artists—kids! Their art can provide some "grand openings" on special gift days. Spread a large roll of butcher paper, green wrapping paper, white shelf paper, or newsprint on the floor so children can design wrap that will turn ordinary presents into irresistible gifts. Supply them with finger paints, felt-tipped pens, stickers, gold and silver stars, glue and glitter, stencils, paper doilies, bits of ribbon, lace, fabric, and old magazines and greeting cards to cut up. Then, just watch them go to work!

Suggest that the youngsters write the family's last name or messages like "I Love You!" or "Happy Birthday!" over and over on the paper. They can draw family activity scenes, their own hand and footprints, or stained-glass windows. Or they can print Scripture verses. At yuletide, maybe the kids will enjoy writing "Merry Christmas" in other languages: Portuguese, "Feliz Natal"; Chinese, "Tin Hoa Nian"; French, "Noël."

• *Gift bags.* Trace and paste silhouettes copied from cards, stencils, or cookie cutters on brown grocery bags. For extra smartness, use sewing machine attachments to zigzag, monogram, or appliqué the shapes to the bags. Tie the bags shut with gold cord. Or cut vertical slits about an inch apart nearly all the way down each side of a large bag. Weave ribbon or leftover strips of starched fabric or heavy construction paper through the slots for a basketlike effect. Wallpaper makes eye-catching designer bags to hold awkward items like round loaves of homemade bread.

• *Printed paper.* To make potato block prints, cut a potato in half and use a marking pen to draw a design like a tree or an initial on the flat side. Whittle around it until the design is raised about an inch. Press the potato printer against a sponge dampened with poster paint and then firmly onto plain paper, repeating the pattern all over. Or cut sponges to various shapes and sizes, dip lightly in paint, and press on the designs.

• *Custom-painted wrap.* Kids will enjoy spattering finger paint on wrapping paper with a laundry sprinkler or using a flat brush to smooth on bold plaid designs. Be sure to let one color dry before the next broad strokes of a coordinating color are applied.

• *One-of-a-kind wrap.* Save kids' coloring book pages, perfect spelling tests, finger paintings, school drawings, and other artwork to use as unique and personal package wrap for adoring grandparents, other close family members, and godparents.

WRAP-UPS FOR PROBLEM PRESENTS

BULKY AND AWKWARD items can be disguised or gussied up with no-cost or low-cost materials to make them into presents that please. Here are ideas:

• *Baseball bat or hockey stick.* Tape the item between two pieces of colored cardboard a few inches longer and wider than it is. Punch holes every few inches along the edges, and lace through ribbon or yarn to secure the cardboard pieces together. Tie on a cluster of candy canes.

• *Umbrella or walking stick.* Make a gigantic peppermint stick package by rolling the gift in white tissue paper and leaving the handle free. Use tape to secure the paper just below the handle. Swirl red ribbon evenly around and around, and tie the ends in a bow to hide the tape. Attach a sprig of mistletoe or other greenery, and add a bag of wrapped peppermints to treat a sweet tooth.

• *Yarn and knitting needles or several tennis balls.* Pack them in a big cardboard tube to be covered with foil and topped with a ribbon. Or turn the container into a smiling snowman by painting it white, adding a foam ball on top for a head as well as a jaunty black construction paper top hat. Stick in whole cloves for eyes, nose, and mouth, and use sticky dots for buttons. Tie on a plaid fabric muffler, and use pom-poms or cotton balls for ear muffs.

• *Bottle.* Cut a fabric circle big enough to wrap up as far as the throat of the bottle. Set it in the center of the circle, then gather and secure the edges with yarn loops around the neck. Or paste zigzags of confetti on the outside of the bottle, and top it with your most extravagant ribbon.

• *Large round items.* For a potted plant or a soccer ball, lay two paper rectangles of contrasting colors at angles to form an X. Gather up the ends around the object into a fluffy ruffle, and tie the gathering with a bow. Junior sports enthusiasts will love you for adding a sweatband pulled around the ball.

• *Soft bulky gifts.* Trash bags (which come in all sizes and colors) will disguise floor cushions, bed pillows, a child's extra large stuffed animal, or a comforter. Wrap each item in tissue paper before placing it in the bag. Pull a wide ribbon tightly around the center of the package, and tie it in a bow. Glue on gorgeous glitter for a touch of glamour. For a child's gift, you can tie on a mini–teddy bear.

• *Food.* Items like fresh-baked muffins, cheese balls, fruit, or fudge will fit inside a wicker basket. Recycle old linens with hand-tatted edgings or handmade dresser scarves or crocheted chair sets to make a charming lining. For a country look, tie fragrant herbs and greens to the handle.

• *Giant gingerbread boys and girls or big cookies.* Keep colored cellophane from a fruit basket to wrap such goodies. Pull paper together at the top, and tie it with yarn. Leave yarn ends long enough so these delicious gifts can be hung on the tree if it is Christmastime.

• *Jumbo coffee mug.* Fill it brimful with an unusual blend of ground coffee from a specialty store, and cover it with clear plastic to make an instant present.

• *Nuts.* Pack them into recycled fruitcake tins.

• *Jams and jellies.* These gifts are colorful showing through glass jars, and you can give them a country look by tying on a fabric circle to cover the top. Get a guaranteed thank-you smile by perching a sprig of mistletoe or bunch of tiny dried flowers on each container.

• *Children's gifts of unmanageable size or shape.* A walking doll will be even more appealing by simply tying on streamers of different colored hair ribbons or barrettes. For an extra flourish, fasten on candy kisses or bubble gum.

• *Rediscovered treasures.* An antique butter or pickle crock that has been stored for years makes a unique container when filled with almost anything.

• *Knitted wear.* Roll up a handmade muffler and mitten set or a matching sweater and cap, and stick knitting needles through them.

• *Linens.* A set of table linens can be wrapped inside the tablecloth and secured with a clump of napkin rings. No need for any other wrap. Or place a matching bedsheet set inside one pillowcase, roll tightly, and attach a sachet pouch. A couple of infant receiving blankets can be rolled up and fixed firmly together with the biggest pastel safety pins you can find. Let everybody see the fantastic afghan you created; tie it around with yarn leftovers (for later mending), then give it away unwrapped.

A FINAL WORD

YOU'VE JUST BEEN through a unique experience discovering the joy of giving gifts from the heart. Although this experience is new for many of us in today's world, it is one that actually has been encouraged for generations.

In the Bible, giving gifts of love and celebrating together were common occurrences. All throughout Exodus, Leviticus, and Numbers, the Israelites are given instructions for celebrating several feasts and special events. In Deuteronomy, the Israelites are told to celebrate the Feast of Tabernacles for seven days. Nehemiah 8:12 tells how the people had a time of "great and joyful celebration." In James 1:17, we are reminded that every "good and perfect gift" is from God. And it is God who gave the most personal and precious heart gift of all: his Son, Jesus Christ, to be our Savior. Truly, when we give gifts of love and celebrate together, we are following God's instructions and example!

In light of this, I want to encourage you to continue giving gifts from the heart. I hope you have felt at least a small sense of joy as you have read through this book and discovered ways to personalize your gift-giving events. I hope this book has helped you discover and implement ways to reclaim your holidays and celebrations. And I hope you have discovered that you no longer need to look to advertisers or commercial retailers to tell you what the perfect gift is for Christmas, birthdays, weddings, and so on. Now you can use the most wonderful and effective resources of all to discover that "perfect gift"—your heart, your imagination, and your knowledge of those to whom you wish to give.

There is, however, another aspect of this new and wonderful kind of gift giving that many do not realize is there. When you give heart gifts, you inspire others to do the same. Perhaps you have already experienced the pleasure of having a friend to whom you have given a gift of love, one that came from your creativity and heart, reciprocating in like form. This can be especially enjoyable—and rewarding—when it is a child who catches the excitement of personal gift giving.

So, now that you have some idea of the different types of gifts you can give—and of how easy and inexpensive they can be—I offer you a challenge: Do not grow weary of giving gifts from the heart! It is a sad fact that you will encounter many temptations to give in to the tyranny of time and "convenience." And it is unavoidable that the siren's song of advertisers will tickle at your ears—but do not surrender your celebrations!

In purchasing and reading through this book, you have taken a step toward giving gifts that will bless the recipients for a long time. Keep going! The joys you encounter in doing so will go far beyond anything advertisers can promise or expensive gifts can deliver. Always remember, there are wonderful blessings waiting for you and for those who will receive your gifts of love. And that is something that truly deserves a "great and joyful" celebration!

COUPON EXAMPLES

To ______________________________

Coming your way
on December 15

One Christmas Wreath

delivered and ready to hang!

From ______________________________

HAPPY FATHER'S
DAY

A gift for you of 10 hours next month
to help you get started
on your new computer.

To ______________________________________

I O U

This coupon can be redeemed for a free ride
to and from work every day
for one month.

From ______________________________________

To ______________________________

I O U

A ride a week

To Ridgecrest Mall

for 2 months.

Just for your birthday

(This gift starts immediately!)

From ______________________________

I O U

A special gift for Mother's Day

(and here it is):

Your garden will be planted and tended

from May 1 to June 1.

To ______________________________

Gifts for a full year are coming your way.
You've just been elected to the Pie-a-Month Club

January—pecan
February—cherry
March—lemon
April—chocolate
May—rhubarb
June—strawberry
July—blackberry
August—peach
September—blueberry
October—raisin
November—pumpkin
December—mincemeat

One of the above will be delivered to your house on the 15th of the month with lots of love.

From ______________________________

For your birthday

I O U

5 lessons in how to knit socks.

Love,

From ______________________________

P.S. Let's make it in the coming month.

To ______________________________

A gift of love and music

on Valentine's Day

I promise to give you 4 lessons

in how to play the guitar.

Then we can make music together!

From ______________________________

To ______________________________

Here's a can of tennis balls

and an I O U for

4 tennis lessons at the city courts.

You'll be a smash!

From ______________________________

To ______________________________

You can do

Calligraphy

and I'll help you learn!

This coupon good for 6 lessons.

From ______________________________

A GRADUATION GIFT FOR

____

I promise
to photograph you in your graduation gown
anytime the day before graduation.

CONGRATULATIONS!

From ______________________________

IOU for Christmas 1997
a birdhouse for martins
to be built and mounted in your yard
before nesting time
and enjoyed every day during the year!

My Special Gift
For My Special Neighbor's Birthday

A Free Haircut

Anytime in the next 2 months

To ____

Now that you're __________ years old,

we can do math together.

I promise to help you for 3 months.

1 + 1 = Great Improvement

HAPPY BIRTHDAY!

From ____

To ____

Birthdays Are for Memories—
and Pictures

I O U

A watercolor sketch of your home,
the place for memories.
P.S. I'll make it in the season you wish.

From ____

To ______________________________

A Gift for You
from one who knows and cares

I O U

A visit each day for a month
to check your blood pressure.
(I will bring the pressure cuff!)

From ______________________________

To ____

An I O U!

For Christmas

A cross-stitch

Of a candle

Burning bright

For you

All the year through!

From ____

About the Author

Alice Chapin has written several books, including the best-selling *400 Creative Ways to Say I Love You, 365 Bible Promises for Busy People* and *365 Bible Promises for Hurting People*. A native of Batavia, New York, she and her husband now live in Georgia.

WINNING STRATEGIES IN SELLING

WINNING STRATEGIES IN SELLING

Jack Kinder, Jr.
Garry D. Kinder
Roger Staubach

PRENTICE HALL
Englewood Cliffs, New Jersey 07632

Library of Congress Cataloging-in-Publication Data

Kinder, Jack.
Winning strategies in selling.
Includes index.
ISBN 0-13-961110-X
1. Selling. I. Kinder, Garry D.
II. Staubach, Roger. III. Title.
HF5438.25.K56 1981 81-10518
658.8′5 CIP

© 1981 by Prentice-Hall, Inc.

All rights reserved. No part of this book may be reproduced in any form or by any means, without permission in writing from the publisher.

Printed in the United States of America

20 19 18 17 16 15

ISBN 0-13-961110-X

ATTENTION: CORPORATIONS AND SCHOOLS

Prentice Hall books are available at quantity discounts with bulk purchase for educational, business, or sales promotional use. For information, please write to: Prentice Hall Career & Personal Development Special Sales, 113 Sylvan Avenue, Englewood Cliffs, NJ 07632. Please supply: title of book, ISBN number, quantity, how the book will be used, date needed.

PRENTICE HALL
Career & Personal Development
Englewood Cliffs, NJ 07632
A Simon & Schuster Company

On the World Wide Web at http://www.phdirect.com

Prentice-Hall International (UK) Limited, *London*
Prentice-Hall of Australia Pty. Limited, *Sydney*
Prentice-Hall Canada Inc., *Toronto*
Prentice-Hall Hispanoamericana, S.A., *Mexico*
Prentice-Hall of India Private Limited, *New Delhi*
Prentice-Hall of Japan, Inc., *Tokyo*
Simon & Schuster Asia Pte. Ltd., *Singapore*
Editora Prentice-Hall do Brasil, Ltda., *Rio de Janeiro*

DEDICATION

Winners make things happen.

Losers let things happen.

This book was written for you and the countless thousands who are committed to being self-motivated, independent winners in selling.

THE BEST BOOK ON SELLING I HAVE EVER READ

FOREWORD BY EARL NIGHTINGALE

I was spending the summer in Carmel, California, when the call came through from Dallas, Texas. At first I thought the secretary was kidding. "Mr. Nightingale? Mr. Roger Staubach calling."

I had been a fan of Mr. Roger Staubach's since the time I saw him quarterbacking the Navy team in a game against Army. He was great then, and he's been great ever since. As you would imagine, he was friendly and easy to talk to. And when he mentioned the Kinder brothers, I remembered. On one of our many get-togethers, the Kinders had mentioned their friendship with Roger Staubach and what a super salesman and businessman he was.

I had known Jack and Garry Kinder since the old days in Chicago, back in the late 50's when they were executives with Equitable, the giant insurance company. Over the years I had come to know them as the best trainers of insurance people throughout all of North America. And that also applies to salesmen and women of all products and services, not just insurance by any means.

I had appeared on the platform with them at sales meetings and rallies many times and the better I got to know them, the more I liked, admired and respected them. They are men of the very highest moral calibre, both devout churchmen who have approached and taught their profession with the care, intelligence and integrity befitting any of the higher professions. To Jack and Garry Kinder, selling is an honorable, lifetime profession in which the rewards are as high as we want to set them and in which the whole man or woman and his or her family are taken into full consideration.

After reading this book, you will realize, as I did, that if you never read another on the selling profession, it will be quite sufficient.

What I had not known about Roger Staubach was that he earned more money selling, during the first three years he was with the Dallas Cowboys, than they were paying him. And that he had remained in sales right up to the present and had every intention of making it his life career.

As we chatted on the telephone we agreed that the quarterback of a winning NFL team certainly had to be the best kind of salesman. His very demeanor, his attitude, the tone of his voice as he called the plays in the huddle and at the line of scrimmage, would determine, to a great extent, the spirit and attitude of the entire team. Roger mentioned that that was true and that working with the pass receivers was particularly important.

We're all selling, every day of our lives, whether we realize it or not. We're selling ourselves, most of all, and our habitual attitude tells the world how well or poorly we're succeeding. It shows in our eyes, the expressions on our faces, the way we walk, our posture, the way in which we enter a room and meet people. Our very *self-image* is a matter of salesmanship, as are the attitudes of our children and our spouses much of the time. We set the standard in our families, and that's selling. And our success, regardless of our line of work, will depend upon our selling skills.

Read this book, by all means. Don't read it in a hurry. Read it all. What you already know will not suffer from reminding and reinforcing or from considering a new approach. But most importantly, what you will find here are systems and strategies that never fail if they are faithfully followed. It is, simply, the best book on selling I have ever read. You will find it an endless source of enjoyment and lifelong profit.

Earl Nightingale

AUTHORS' INTRODUCTION

WE BELIEVE

We believe your main mission in selling is to win. Winning doesn't mean getting ahead of others. Winning means getting ahead of yourself. Winning means breaking your own records. It means outstripping your yesterdays by out-selling yourself today.

• • • • • •

We believe it can actually be *easier* to win than to lose in selling. But to win, you must do something that the "average" salesperson doesn't even consider; you must teach yourself to *think correctly.* You must think correctly about yourself, your selling ability, your prospects or clients, and your future in sales.

• • • • • •

We believe that this book will help you clarify your thinking in sales. Our combined 60 years in selling have taught us many things. Perhaps the most important is that right thinking comes to the individual who is reminded often of the following success factors.

1. You must be self-motivated.
2. You must not only want success, you must *need* it.
3. You must set a series of realistically high goals and establish a timetable for meeting them.
4. You must act as if it is *impossible* for you not to be a consistently high achiever.
5. You must form the habit of doing things the right way the *first time!*

• • • • • •

We believe that this book will make a difference in your selling career. We believe you will discover the "idea count" to be exceptionally high. The concepts and strategies are proven. They *are* transferable. We believe that they'll produce dynamic results for you.

• • • • • •

We believe that you'll want to read, study and digest the information developed on these pages until the thoughts and suggestions become a dominant part of your selling equipment.

• • • • • •

We believe that the tested techniques offered in this book will increase your sales and bring you greater commissions. This book encapsulates successful methods that have been used by some of America's leading salespeople. Chapter 4, for example, reveals the telephone selling tip that Jay Lewis utilized to increase his earnings by $2,000 each month.

As every salesperson is painfully aware, objections are a fact of life. Chapter 7 probes the most common reasons for objections, and then goes on to reveal a six-step strategy for overcoming all objections. Chapter 8 deals with the must crucial element of selling and provides you with the five cardinal rules that will make it much more likely that you will close the sale.

• • • • • •

We believe that this is a book that will prove valuable to you in both your professional and your personal life. We believe that this is a book you will want to refer to again and again.

• • • • • •

We believe this is the sure way for you to become a winner in selling!

Jack Kinder, Jr.
Garry D. Kinder
Roger Staubach

CONTENTS

Foreword by Earl Nightingale **7**

Authors' Introduction **9**

1. The Power of a Made-Up Mind in Selling **17**

Make Up Your Mind That Preparation Pays Off (19)
Make Up Your Mind About the Opportunity (21)
Make Up Your Mind About the Importance of Salesmanship (22)
Make Up Your Mind About Playing the Odds (25)
Make Up Your Mind to Expect Great Things (26)
Make Up Your Mind to Give the Impression of Success and Confidence (27)
Make Up Your Mind to Guard Moral Values (28)
Make Up Your Mind to Be a Sound Financial Manager (29)
Make Up Your Mind You Feel Better When You Feel Fit (30)
Make Up Your Mind That Leaders Are Readers (34)
Make Up Your Mind to Keep Your Family Life in Order (35)
Make Up Your Mind It's the Spiritual That Determines the Material (37)
The Power of the Made-Up Mind Illustrated (38)
The Power of the Made-Up Mind Summed Up (44)
The Power of the Made-Up Mind Reminders (46)

2. Planning and Prospecting: The Cornerstones of Winning Selling 49

Examining the Selling Spectrum (51)
The Way In Is Easy—The Way Out Is Hard (52)
The Planning Function (53)
Plan to Wake Up Employed (54)
Subscribe to the "Box Time" Theory (55)
Plan a Monthly Self-Organization Day (55)
The Best Kept Sales Secret (56)
The Prospecting Function (57)
Examine These Six Prospecting Strategies (61)
Planning and Prospecting Summed Up (65)
Planning and Prospecting Reminders (66)

3. How the Buyer Buys and How the Seller Sells 69

Nothing Happens Until Someone Makes the Decision to Buy Something (71)
How Success Is Earned (72)
The Five Buying Decisions (73)
Steps in the Selling Process (74)
Want-Creator vs. Needs-Satisfier (75)
How the Buyer Buys and How the Seller Sells Summed Up (75)
How the Buyer Buys and How the Seller Sells Reminders (76)

4. Making Contact: Winning Pre-Approach Strategies 79

Where the "Ball Game" Is Won (81)
It's a Series of Decisions (81)
Preparing for the Initial Contact Call (82)
Objectives of Planning the Initial Contact (83)
The Most Important Thing (85)
Don't Tell Your Story for the Practice (87)
Take This Pledge Now (89)
Facing the Important Four-Minute Barrier (89)

Five Ways to Cope with Call Reluctance (91)
Crucial Factors (97)
Making Contact Summed Up (98)
Making Contact Reminders (99)

5. Probing: How to Gain Positive Interest in Your Product 101

The Approach and Its Objectives (103)
Probing—Its Objectives (104)
Probing—Its Advantages (104)
Know Where the Sale Is Made (105)
Learning Is Listening (105)
Finding the Facts (107)
Discover the Dominant Buying Motive (108)
Probing Summed Up (110)
Probing Reminders (112)

6. Presentations That Help the Prospect Buy with Confidence 113

What a Good Presentation Must Do (115)
Four Essentials of a Good Presentation (115)
How to Gain Instant Attention (116)
How to Arouse Interest (118)
How to Create Desire (119)
How to Gain the Buyer's Confidence (120)
How to Motivate to Action (122)
Presentation Pointers (124)
Only the Best Is Good Enough (128)
Presenting Summed Up (130)
Presenting Reminders (132)

7. Strategies for Controlling Objections and Converting Them into Sales 135

How You Stay in Control (137)
Always Assert (138)
Our Attitude Toward Objections (138)

Classifying the Objection (139)
Why Do Prospects Object? (139)
When to Answer (140)
Anticipate Objections (140)
Ignore Objections (141)
Ask Permission to Answer the Objection Later (142)
Answer the Objection Now (142)
Master the Six-Step Strategy (142)
Hearing the Prospect Out (143)
Asking the Prospect to Repeat (144)
Restating (144)
Isolating the Objection (145)
Using an Example or Story (146)
Stimulating Action (147)
You Don't Handle Every Objection (149)
Function As an Assistant Buyer (150)
Handling Objections Summed Up (151)
Handling Objections Reminders (154)

8. Leading the Prospect to the Buying Decision 155

An Effective Salesperson Closes (157)
Five Cardinal Rules of Selling to Remember (158)
Deal with Decision-Makers (159)
The Two Vital Closing Factors (159)
Gauge the Prospect's Pace (163)
A Language You Must Learn (164)
When to Stop Selling (164)
Buying Signs to Watch For (165)
Seven and One-Half Strategies for Closing the Sale (166)
Assist the Buyer with These Questions (171)
Ask Yourself These Questions (171)
Closing Summed Up (173)
Closing Reminders (174)

9. Remembering Service and Follow-Through After the Sale 175

The Importance of Follow-Through (177)
Show Them Your Appreciation (178)

Serve What You Sell (182)
Handle Complaints—Fast! (182)
Five Keys to Serving Better (183)
You Are the Firm (184)
Selling After the Sale Summed Up (185)
Selling After the Sale Reminders (187)

10. How to Profit from Time Management in Selling . 189

A Slight Improvement (191)
You Can Give Yourself a Raise (192)
High-Quality vs. Low-Quality Time (194)
A Meaningful Parable (199)
Managing Your Time Summed Up (200)
Managing Your Time Reminders (201)

11. Staying Up: Keep a Vital Self-Image and Expect to Win 203

Your Need for "Upness" (205)
What Is Self-Image? (206)
Changing Your Self-Image (206)
One Thing Not to Surrender (208)
Building Your Vital Self-Image (209)
Be Aware of Two Mental Diseases (213)
Motivation Comes from Within (214)
Six Steps to Self-Motivation (215)
Staying Up Summed Up (217)
Staying Up Reminders (219)

12. Five Steps to Prosperous Goal Setting and Action Planning 221

Plan Your Future Now (223)
How You Set Goals (225)
The Five Key Steps to Goal Setting and Action Planning (227)
Goal Setting and Action Planning Summed Up (242)
Goal Setting and Action Planning Reminders (244)

13. The Thirteen Winning Traits of Super Salespeople **245**

What I've Got: What It Takes (247)
Thirteen Winning Traits (248)
Improving Your Field Position (252)
The Most Motivational (257)

Index **259**

CHAPTER 1

THE POWER OF A MADE-UP MIND IN SELLING

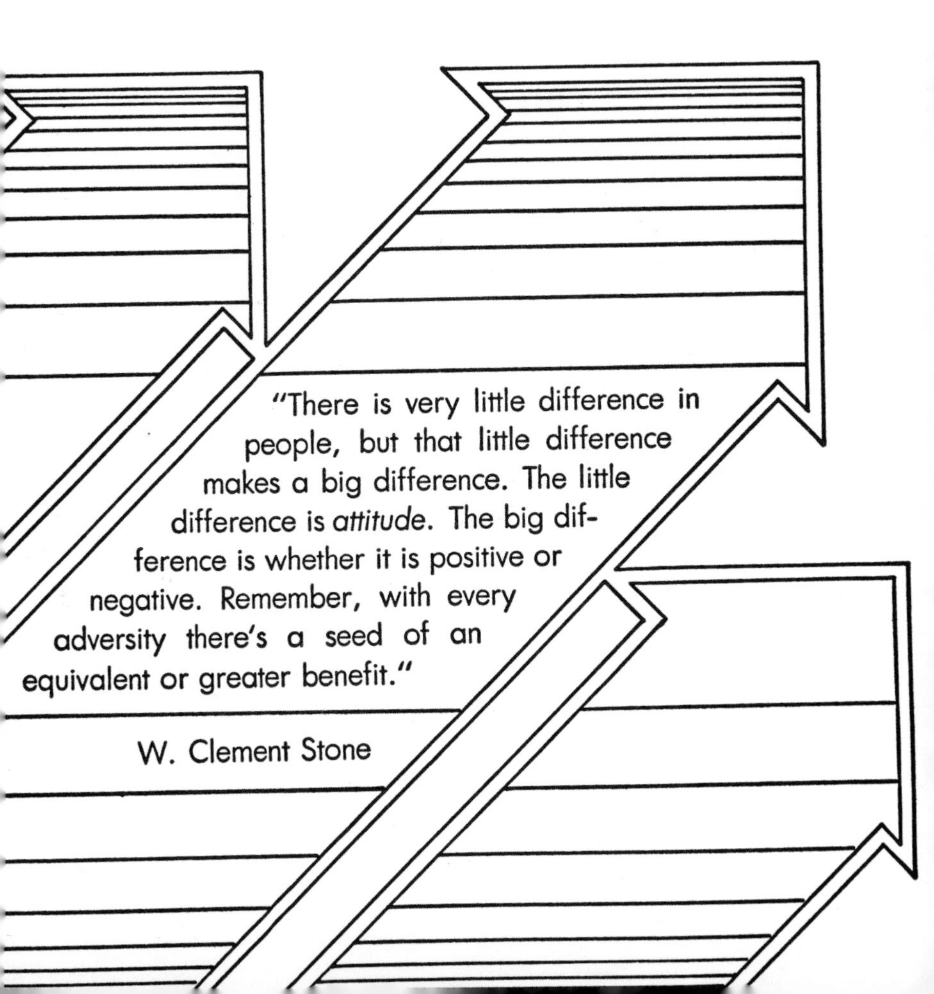

"There is very little difference in people, but that little difference makes a big difference. The little difference is *attitude*. The big difference is whether it is positive or negative. Remember, with every adversity there's a seed of an equivalent or greater benefit."

W. Clement Stone

MAKE UP YOUR MIND THAT PREPARATION PAYS OFF

Metropolitan Stadium in Minneapolis is jam-packed. The NFL Eastern Championship is at stake. The Vikings have played the Cowboys tough. They are leading 14-10. Time is running out.

The Cowboys have moved the ball to midfield. The clock shows time left for one, maybe two, plays.

All-pro Drew Pearson goes deep. Drew and Viking defender Nate Wright are both streaking as hard as they can toward the end zone.

The ball is thrown high and long. A determined Drew Pearson, struggling for position and running at top speed, catches the ball on his hip. Drew holds on. The official signals touchdown. The Cowboys move up in front. The clock shows only 24 seconds left and the Cowboys go on to win 17-14!

Vikings fans thought Drew had interfered with Wright. The only thing known for certain in the stormy aftermath of the Cowboys' title victory was that Drew Pearson had scored the winning points. *Drew had a made-up mind about that catch!*

Spectacular achievements, like Drew's, are always preceded by unspectacular preparation.

The prepared professional captures the winning feeling. Professionals, in any human endeavor, because of preparation, act as if it were impossible to fail.

The scene changes—this time it's Texas Stadium. For nine consecutive times, the Philadelphia Eagles have met defeat at the hands of the Cowboys.

It became apparent, however, that the Eagles were "up" for this one. They established a third quarter lead that the Cowboys couldn't overcome and won the game 31-21.

Along with countless Cowboy fans, that's one game we'd like to forget. However, in the post-game remarks, Eagle Coach Dick Vermeil made a statement that we shouldn't forget: *"Our important victory tonight didn't just happen. This one we played without the fear of losing."* He went on to add, *"It started in the off-season and in training camp. It continued through a lot of tough days and nights. You can't believe the number of hours and the hard work that went into this winning performance!"*

Spectacular achievements are always preceded by unspectacular preparation.

In professional football, it's called "paying the price." In the business world, it's called "self-discipline." In either case, it boils down to *deciding to succeed.* In fact, *not* to decide is *to* decide. If you haven't decided to succeed, you've decided to accept failure.

How do you decide to succeed? First of all, you ask yourself what you want out of your sales career. Once you decide, you plant that seed in your mind. Feed and nourish it as you would any valuable seed. Care for it. Imagine that seed sprouted and grown to maturity. Imagine yourself already harvesting that seed—already having achieved success! Picture yourself doing the things you will be doing when you've achieved your career goals!

Make up your mind that you must live off the fruit of your thoughts. What you think today or tomorrow, next month or next year, will mold your life and determine your future. Dr. Dennis Waitley, a national authority on high-level performance, says, "Be relentless in rehearsing your goal achievements. *Winning is a learned habit.*"

To paraphrase Shakespeare, "All things are ready if our minds are!" That's why it's so vitally important for you to make up your mind to act as though it were impossible to fail.

MAKE UP YOUR MIND ABOUT THE OPPORTUNITY

If you look at your work as a career instead of "just a job," the rewards of selling are substantial. A career in sales has one of the highest profit and satisfaction potentials of any field of endeavor—*if* you have self-discipline, courage and commitment.

The last census of the Department of Commerce showed that there are more people earning above $50,000 a year in sales than in any other profession—and many salespeople earn *twice* that amount or more!

What is the future for salespeople? First, we're on the threshold of the most exciting period of sales growth in history! Marketing, advertising and promotion have worked to make us not only aware of the benefits of technological advances but also of the rewards of financial planning and home comforts. *As never before, prospects are pre-conditioned to want the latest and the best.*

Secondly, the consumer is more affluent. Where once the bulk of our spendable income went for neccessities such as food, clothing, shelter and medical care, more and more consumer dollars are now available to be spent on other items. At the same time, companies and corporations are more willing than ever to look at new or more cost-efficient solutions to traditional problems.

It all adds up to an era of unprecedented opportunity. Make up your mind to be prepared to take full advantage of the opportunities the future will bring!

MAKE UP YOUR MIND ABOUT THE IMPORTANCE OF SALESMANSHIP

Unless you're a modern Robinson Crusoe and this book floated up on your beach in a bottle, you are engaged in sales. You use many of the principles of salesmanship in your daily contact with others. From cradle to grave, we are all salespeople.

To young people faced with the problems of earning a living or of merely getting along well with their associates, no other abilities will be more helpful than those practiced by effective salespeople. *Knowledge of selling principles is a vital element for successful living.*

Can selling be taught? We feel that the answer is

"yes!" Countless companies have either trained their own salespeople or have hired consultants to do the job. By their success, they've demonstrated over and over again that the principles of selling *can* be taught and learned just as surely as can the principles of engineering, law, medicine or athletics. Of course, you can't expect to become a skilled professional in any field without both study and practical experience. It's true that much *can* be learned by "trial and error"—but it's not an efficient use of time—and time in any profession is money.

Modern psychologists tell us that you are molded more by your environment than by your heredity. They insist that it is possible not only to modify your behavior, but even to alter your personality through training. Some go so far as to assert that environment and training can materially raise your I.Q. *Nearly everything essential to your success in selling can be acquired and developed.*

You will hear it said that "salespeople are *born* and not *made.*" While some people do seem to have a "natural" feel for selling, this statement is no more true of salespeople than it is of actors or artists or athletes. In fact, it's *easier* to "make" a salesperson than any other professional—as evidenced by the fact that there are more wealthy salespeople than wealthy quarterbacks!

An individual of only average talents can become an effective salesperson if he or she puts forth the required effort *consistently.* This same person might have no chance of ever becoming a great actor, famous artist or star quarterback for the Dallas Cowboys, *regardless* of effort!

Selling, at its best, is the art of creating in the mind of the prospect the idea that possession of your product or service best satisfies his or her need.

Selling is the art of influencing prospects to buy at a mutual profit that which you are selling.

Selling is the art of understanding human desires and pointing the way to their fulfillment.

Selling is the art of assisting your prospects in buying intelligently. Your aim is not to make each transaction a "win or lose" situation but a "win-win" situation, because selling is the fine art of presenting your product or service in such a way that both seller and buyer feel they've gained something of value.

We've been saying that selling is an art, and it is. However, it is also a science. Science is a systematic knowledge, and art is knowledge made effective by skill.

When you systematically acquire selling knowledge, you're following a scientific approach. When you begin applying these scientific principles to your own products and services, you're practicing art.

There's a growing body of knowledge dealing with selling strategies. Your company provides you with a wealth of updated information about your products and services. Your industry and professional associations provide you with the opportunity to stay current and build your reservoir of knowledge. Selling is part science—because it takes applied research to be successful. It is also an art—because of the unique way that you apply your scientific knowledge to get the desired result.

Art can be poor, fair, good, excellent, or even a masterpiece; it all depends on how much skill the artist has and how he or she applies that skill.

Artists, we mentioned earlier, aren't born, they're made—just like salespeople. If you study the scientific part of selling and practice the art, you will produce good art and good results. You *will* be successful. No one else in the entire world can bring your unique experiences, your unique talent, your unique personality and your unique knowledge to your particular selling situation. With all of that going for you, you will be *successful—if* you have a burning desire for success!

MAKE UP YOUR MIND ABOUT PLAYING THE ODDS

After analyzing the work records of many, many salespeople, we have concluded that the typical salesperson produces little in the way of measurable results in five out of every six working hours! You don't sell to everybody you see, and much of what you do probably won't pay off for some time to come. So you see, very little time is actually spent *selling.*

If you look at your time from this standpoint, it could become discouraging. Furthermore, four out of every five people you call on will have a built-in sales resistance mechanism that can be very ego deflating. When you consider that over 80 percent of your sales time isn't spent selling and that 80 percent of your calls are apt to be negative, you might conclude that you can't beat the odds. But you can, if *you play the odds, and don't let the odds play you!*

Learn to play the odds. A pitcher doesn't strike out every batter he faces. Roger didn't throw a touchdown pass every time he got the ball. Babe Ruth is remembered as the home run king because he hit 714 home runs—but the Babe also struck out 1,330 times! The secret of success is to take each pitch as it comes and do your level best to knock it out of the park. Sure, you'll miss some. You'll even miss more than you hit—but you'll soon be hitting enough to make you a superstar!

To be a winner, you must be an odds player. You must have the self-generated brand of determination that carries you through to victory even though you operate in a negative atmosphere much of the time. Selling in many respects is more demanding than competitive athletics. Many salespeople operate without a coach or a team to support them—they have to build their own egos, recover from their own defeats, manage their own schedules and cheer their own victories. Salesmanship is a one-on-one kind of challenge, and that's what makes selling one of the most rewarding professions in the world!

MAKE UP YOUR MIND TO EXPECT GREAT THINGS

Everything about you—your facial expression, your movements, your dress, your tone of voice, the grip of your hand, the way you walk—tells your prospects what you think of yourself. You cannot disguise the impression you make even if you try. You can guard a few of your actions, but almost everything about you shows your estimate of yourself. There is no common law by which you can achieve selling success without first expecting it. *Great selling results are produced by the perpetual expectation of attaining them.* Despite natural talents, expanded through training and education, selling achievements will never rise higher than the expectation. People can who think they can. People can't who think they can't. It's an inflexible, indisputable law of selling and of life.

As a professional, your self-confidence is the one

thing you can never afford to surrender. Count as your enemy the person who shakes your estimate of your selling ability. Nothing enhances your ability like faith in yourself. In the selling profession, faith can make a one-talent salesperson into a great producer; but without it, a ten-talent sales rep remains mediocre.

The pros in selling are self-reliant, positive, optimistic and assured. They electrically charge the atmosphere they work in. *They have an aura of command that helps them convince their prospects that they can deliver—and deliver well—whatever they say they'll deliver.*

Set your mind so resolutely, so definitely and with such determined expectations toward the sales results you desire, that nothing on earth can sway your purpose. You will then draw to yourself the literal fulfillment of the promise: "For unto everyone that hath shall be given, and he shall have abundance."

MAKE UP YOUR MIND TO GIVE THE IMPRESSION OF SUCCESS AND CONFIDENCE

Make certain you look as if you *are* successful and as if you're accustomed to influencing people and closing sales. When you do, you will have something going for you the minute you face your prospect. Your prospect's natural reaction will be: "This individual must have a good idea or service, and maybe I should listen." All it takes to acquire such professional presence is careful attention to a few simple details.

From every point of view, it pays to dress well. It builds belief. Always look and dress like someone prospects would go to for advice. The first things prospects observe are your facial expressions, your voice and your teeth. These are all they have to go on until they get your initial message. Also, you owe it to yourself to maintain proper body weight. Make it a habit to check your weight on the scales frequently. Watching your eating habits and exercising regularly can be a mental tonic, too.

Observe the salespeople you think are the most outstanding. Don't you agree that they look successful? In selling, Shakespeare's advice is especially true: "The apparel often proclaims the person."

MAKE UP YOUR MIND TO GUARD MORAL VALUES

Few salespeople in any field ever reach the top without a strong sense of morality. The occasional sales rep who does gain a position of prestige without an honest character will eventually be uncovered. There is wisdom in the old adage, "Truth is the daughter of Time."

You are either honest or you are not. You cannot be a "little bit dishonest." If you are going to be a professional salesperson, then honesty has to become a way of life.

A reputation for honesty often pays off in dramatic ways. Donald Douglas built an aircraft company on his reputation for honesty and integrity. At one time, Donald was competing against Boeing to sell Eastern Airlines its first big jets. Eddie Rickenbacker, who headed Eastern, is said to have told Douglas that his specifications for the DC-8 were close to those of the Boeing 707 except for the noise suppression. He then gave Douglas one last chance to out-promise Boeing on this feature.

After consulting with his engineers, Douglas reported back that he didn't feel he could make the promise. Mr. Rickenbacker is said to have replied, "I know you can't. I wanted to see if you were still honest! You've got yourself an order for one hundred and sixty-five million dollars! Now go back and see if you can silence those jets anyway!"

A strong and sincere sense of morality is a prerequisite for winning in selling.

Make up your mind

- ***about what it takes***
- ***to give an impression of success***
- ***to expect great things***
- ***to act as though it were impossible for you to fail***
- ***honesty is not the best policy, it is the only policy***

MAKE UP YOUR MIND TO BE A SOUND FINANCIAL MANAGER

Learn to keep your financial house in order. Most people entering selling must be taught to be money managers. However, it has been our experience that the faculty for being a good financial manager is much like that of being a good golfer—it is not so much *taught* as it is *caught.*

A Louisville consultant, Ken Lutz, recommends to clients, "Form the habit early in your business life of living on 50 percent of your gross income. Sound money management dictates that you set aside 10 percent for church and charities."

Lutz goes on to say, "Next, pay yourself by saving 10 percent. Thirty percent of your gross income is to be earmarked for city, county, state, federal and social security taxes no matter what you do. Fifty percent is all that's left."

You've heard some say, "This sounds good, and the minute I get my bills caught up, I'm going to start the program." That won't get it done. Embrace the "Lutz Formula," learn to live on 50 percent of your gross income. You may not achieve this goal each year, but without a plan, you have no chance at all. Start this practice today and reap the benefits throughout your career. *The condition of your financial balance sheet is generally a reliable measurement of the balance you are achieving in your life.*

MAKE UP YOUR MIND YOU FEEL BETTER WHEN YOU FEEL FIT

Dr. O. Carl Simonton, M.D., is the director of the famed Cancer Counseling and Research Center in Fort Worth, Texas. Dr. Simonton has spent years teaching patients to use their minds to alter the course of their malignancies. In his best seller, *Getting Well Again,* Dr. Simonton writes about the power of a made-up mind. He says, "The results of our approach to cancer treatment made us confident of this conclusion—*a positive mental participation can influence the onset of disease, the outcome of treatment and quality of life."*

Dr. Kenneth Cooper, author of the best-selling book, *Aerobics,* says he wishes more people would be as fresh at five o'clock in the afternoon as they were at seven in the morning. Dr. Cooper says, "I would like to see fewer hospitals and rest homes for curing illness and diseases and more conditioning centers for their prevention." The great scientist Thomas Edison predicted Cooper's approach when he said, "The doctor of the future will give no medicine, but will interest the patient in the care of the human frame, in diet and in the cause and prevention of disease."

Dr. Cooper offers the following advice for anyone who plans to embark upon an exercise program:

1. Have a complete physical and make certain that your doctor approves your program.
2. Regularity is the most important element of your program. Try to maintain a frequency of five workouts a week. Four is adequate, though not ideal; three is a bare minimum. Therefore, choose an activity that you will do regularly.
3. For running, obtain a good pair of running shoes. Each shoe is structurally different, so you may want to try a variety to find the best fit for you.
4. If you are just beginning a program of exercise, start slowly and comfortably. This helps prevent muscle and joint injuries. Also, do not hesitate to reduce your workouts should you sustain an injury or illness or for some other reason have an enforced layoff.
5. Adequate warm-up and cool-down is also important. Simple stretching exercises to loosen muscles and help prevent injuries are helpful prior to exercise. Never sit or lie down immediately after exercise or go directly to the whirlpool, steam room or shower. A slow cool-down for about five minutes

will allow for adequate readjustment of your cardiovascular system.

The aerobics point system is a method of quantifying the cardiopulmonary benefits of various types of exercise. Studies show that 25-30 points per week are necessary to achieve and maintain an acceptable level of fitness. Examples of a 30 points per week program are:

- Run two miles in less than 20 minutes four times a week.
- Swim 800 yards in less than 20 minutes four times a week.
- Walk three miles in less than 45 minutes five times a week.
- Cycle five miles in less than 20 minutes six times a week.

The significance of keeping physically fit was demonstrated in a fitness program conducted in cooperation with the U.S. Public Health Service. After one year in the program, participants were given physical examinations and filled out questionnaires concerning their health, attitudes and behavior. Eighty-nine percent thought that they had greater stamina. But, just as importantly, 60 percent indicated that they had a more positive attitude toward their jobs and that their work performance had improved—and *half* felt less strain and tension!

Why is physical fitness so important for salespeople? In preparing this book, we were privileged to study many top performers, and one characteristic stood out above all the others—this characteristic was *energy*. *Energy*—the ability to work hard and long—isn't possible unless your body is in top condition.

Lynn Hutchings is an example of what energy combined with dedication can mean to a professional in selling.

Lynn earns over $200,000 a year in selling in Rock Springs, Wyoming (population about 35,000)! To do it, Lynn started on the ground floor, working 15 to 16 hours a day, seven days a week.

"I loved it, and I can say I still do," Lynn told us. "Frankly, I love every minute of it. I try to take more time off now for the family, but I still work long and hard." Lynn has shattered every company record—in spite of the fact that he's in a small market.

Roger, of course, is a person with a high energy level. Roger's fitness has equipped him to perform not only on the field but in the office as well. Roger never really knew when an injury might end his football career, so right after his Navy discharge, he began preparing for a dual career—football and selling.

Roger went to the Henry S. Miller Company's new insurance division. He attended insurance schools because he wanted to sell the best product possible. Roger found an annuity policy that he really believed in. He studied that policy and every policy it competed with. It took a lot of hours, a lot of study and a lot of cold calls—a lot of energy. Yet Roger sold over $1,000,000 in only four months—including a substantial key-man policy to a Dallas executive.

Roger's accomplishments as a quarterback are well known. A lesser known fact is that, during his first three years with the Dallas Cowboys, he made more money *selling* than he did playing football!

That takes energy, both mental and physical!

MAKE UP YOUR MIND THAT LEADERS ARE READERS

Newton D. Baker, nationally known attorney and member of President Woodrow Wilson's cabinet, said, "The person who graduates today and stops learning tomorrow is uneducated the day after." Feed your mind as you would feed your body—regularly and with a balanced diet.

There are two types of knowledge you should acquire from reading: *people* knowledge and *product* knowledge. To do this, you should read *at least* one book every month to improve your mind. Charlie "Tremendous" Jones once said, "Chances are you'll be about the same person in five years as you are today—except for the people you meet and the books you read." Charlie also points out that the person who *won't* read really isn't much better off than the person who *can't* read!

Keeping abreast of changes and staying well informed is far more important in sales today than ever before. It's also more difficult than it's ever been because changes occur so rapidly. Your prospects are both sophisticated and demanding. They expect you to have a working knowledge of many subjects. There is more to know and more to read—and more things competing for your time.

Power Reading is a self-instructional program developed by Bill Munn and Dr. Gene Davenport of the Kinder Institute in Dallas. It has a proven success record for improving both reading speed and reading retention. Since good reading skills are a must for today's salesperson, we suggest that you investigate *Power Reading* if you wish to improve your own reading skills.

What should you read? Trade journals and publications, of course. But, also form the habit of reading books that teach you to think, work, sell and live. Study books that will help you be more effective in dealing with yourself and others. Make it a habit to read the *Wall Street Journal, Business Week, Fortune, Nation's Business, Reader's Digest* and *Success Unlimited.* If you are a religious person, or if you want to learn about "the book of books," read and study the Bible. There's no end to its treasures.

As T. B. Smith wrote, "Books extend our narrow present back to the limitless past. They show us the mistakes of those before us and share with us the recipes for human success. There's nothing to be done that books will not help us to do better." That's the reason *sales leaders are readers.*

MAKE UP YOUR MIND TO KEEP YOUR FAMILY LIFE IN ORDER

Obviously, your family is the primary social institution in your life. Along the way, you're sure to discover the importance and the difficulty of scheduling time with them. When you're new in selling, you must spend a lot of time on the job. You have to arrange interviews at times when prospects will see you. This means you will be working many evenings and weekends, until you become established and have built a clientele. This makes it especially difficult to find "the right time" to spend with your family. That's why we urge you to schedule time for them.

It is not always the quantity of time spent with your

spouse and children, but the quality of time that will make the big difference. Plan, schedule and spend quality time with your family on a regular basis. Plan family vacations and outings. Sunday is a good day to devote to your family. It is a time when you can worship together or plan other activities as a family. It is the only day that everyone can be at home together. *You cannot separate your family responsibilities from your personal development.*

As Roger says, "Having your family life in order really helps your confidence in other areas of your life, too. If you find you just don't have *time* for your family and your business, then you're too busy. You need to either reschedule your business or redirect your career paths. When I sensed that I wasn't able to put in the quantity or quality of time I wanted to with my family, it helped to move up my decision to leave professional football."

Your family can be your biggest career booster. Unfortunately, we find that too many salespeople only tell their families the negative things about their business—never the positive. When Roger was quarterback for the Dallas Cowboys, he was always careful to never let doubt or disappointment show on his face—because he knew that discouragement is a contagious disease among football teams. Take care to spread positive thoughts and share successes with your family. Talk freely about your accomplishments and goals and demonstrate a positive attitude toward your selling job and its future.

You'll find that your family is your biggest booster, your cheering *section—if* you consider them in your decisions and invite them to be a part of your success team!

MAKE UP YOUR MIND IT'S THE SPIRITUAL THAT DETERMINES THE MATERIAL

The first and perhaps most important area for seeking personal excellence is in the realm of the spiritual. "Our greatest need is for a spiritual improvement in ourselves," says the well-known author Arthur Toynbee in his book *Surviving the Future.* Toynbee says, "There is an ultimate spiritual reality which gives the universe its meaning and value." H. G. Wells said it this way: "Until a person has found God, he or she begins at no beginning, he or she works to no end." The spiritual life is the base from which every other area of one's life evolves.

Your own spiritual life is quite a personal matter and we would not presume to tell you what you should or should not do. However, we do know you can't separate what you do from what you are. We became convinced at an early age that daily prayer and regular church attendance help immeasurably to keep one's spiritual life in balance.

When Roger was working for the Henry S. Miller Company, Henry S. Miller, Jr., had a sign on his desk that said simply, "INTEGRITY." Because he *lived* it, it meant something to every employee that he met. We need to keep a mental image of that "INTEGRITY" plaque before us at all times. If you have a spiritual undergirding, it is easier to live up to—because those of us with spiritual convictions have an absolute standard to live up to. If you don't, then there is always the temptation to make moral and ethical compromises—and time has a way of uncovering all shortcomings.

We never will forget the Watergate hearings when someone asked Jeb Stuart MacGruder, "How could an intelligent, outstanding young man like you get involved with this mess?" MacGruder thought a moment, hung his head and said, "I don't know. I guess I just lost my moral compass."

We're reminded of Robert Burns who, as he lay on his deathbed, turned to his nephew and, patting his well-worn Bible, said, "Read the book and be a good man and when you come to the place in your life where I am now, you'll know that's all that is important."

Make up your mind

- ***to be a student***
- ***to stay physically fit***
- ***to be a sound financial manager***
- ***to keep your family life in order***
- ***to stay spiritually strong***

THE POWER OF THE MADE-UP MIND ILLUSTRATED

When Roger graduated from Annapolis, he had a four-year stint to serve with the United States Navy. Everyone doubted that he could come back after a tour in Vietnam and ever play pro ball—except for Roger and the Dallas Cowboys.

Yet Roger threw the football to anyone who would catch it while on duty. And while he was at his last duty station, in Pensacola, Florida, he was quarterback for the base football team, the Navy Goshawks.

When he was discharged, he went to the Cowboys and

got his first real chance in the fifth exhibition game—and led the team to victory. In the next game, against Baltimore, Roger ran 118 yards, threw four interceptions and Dallas lost 23-7. Bubba Smith, Baltimore's defensive end, said, "I never ran so much in my life chasing anybody. I don't ever want to play against that cat again."

Yet, Roger still had a made-up mind that he could not only make it in the pro league, but that he could become starting quarterback. Sometimes, the power of Roger's made-up mind wasn't transferable. The evening before the next game, against the St. Louis Cardinals, he told Coach Landry, "Do you realize just a year ago today I was the starting quarterback for the Pensacola Navy Goshawks against Middle Tennessee State in Murfreesboro, Tennessee? And just think, Coach, now I'm starting in the Cotton Bowl for the Dallas Cowboys against the St. Louis Cardinals!"

Roger remembers that Coach Landry just got a sick look on his face and walked away without replying.

The Cowboys defeated the Cardinals 24-3. After the game, Landry told Roger, "You'll do all right in this league. Don't worry about it."

Jack Kinder's favorite story about the power of a made-up mind concerns his close friend, Tommy John, who won 20 games pitching for the Los Angeles Dodgers in 1977. He went on to pitch the winning game in the National League playoffs and finished second in the voting for the coveted Cy Young award. The next season, he was signed as a free agent by the New York Yankees. In June of 1980, Tommy earned his 200th career victory against the Seattle Mariners—a victory that caused Seattle Manager Darrell Johnson to say, "The man was outstanding, that's for sure. John knows what he's doing. He's a master craftsman."

This record alone is enough to earn Tommy John a permanent place in the record books—but there's more. Back in 1974, Tommy approached the All-Star break with the best record in the National League. While pitching against the Montreal Expos, he felt a sudden tearing sensation in his arm, as though his arm had been ripped from its socket and was flying off at right angles to his body.

In surgery, it was revealed that his ligament was completely torn and unrecognizable, that the muscles that arose from the inner side of his arm above the elbow were torn loose and had slipped two inches toward the wrist. The doctors transplanted a tendon, saying that there was only 1 chance in 100 that he would ever pitch again.

Tommy did pitch again, but lost feeling in his fingers. Another operation seemed to help, but Tommy's pitching stubbornly refused to come back—two fingers were paralyzed.

One day, Tommy overheard a teammate say, "What's he trying to prove? He's finished. Why doesn't he face up to it?"

In church one Sunday, Tommy prayed for a miracle—and began working as if the miracle was on its way. Slowly, painfully, with no doubt that he would not only play baseball, but play winning baseball, Tommy worked and exercised and asked to be shifted to the Instructional League. Again, Tommy John struck out batters. He had climbed another rung back on the ladder to success—the ladder that's grounded on a made-up mind!

Roger Staubach's favorite story about the power of the made-up mind concerns a high school nose guard who was born with one leg. The youth's name is Carl Joseph and he attended Madison High School in

Madison, Florida. Although Carl was born with one leg and doesn't even have a thigh on the left side, he never thought of himself as handicapped. In Madison's 5-5 season of 1979, Carl played both offense and defense, blocked two punts and deflected two passes. He also fought his way through blockers to down the opposing quarterback in varsity competition.

Carl only has one leg, but he's worked and built that leg into a tree trunk. His upper body is so strong that he can keep blockers away from him—and he can literally *hop* so fast that he was not only a threat on the football field, but in basketball and track! He was a high jumper on the track team and threw discus and shot. He won dual meets with high jumps of 5′10″.

Carl's power of the made-up mind enabled him to do the "seemingly impossible." Yet, he *does* have a handicap—in spite of the fact that the state of Florida removed him from the welfare rolls. "Anyone who can play football can't be handicapped," they said. Madison Coach Frank Yannossy says, "He never used his handicap as an excuse. He did everything in practice. He took part in every drill. He just threw his crutches aside and went at it."

Yannossy doesn't like to exaggerate. "I don't think Carl will play in college," he says. "It would just be too tough. But, he's been an inspiration to our teams and our schools. He's very religious; he gave the blessing at our pre-game meals. He's the type of kid I wish my own son would grow up to be like."

Another story that illustrates the power of the made-up mind that we all like is the story of Raul Jimenez, owner of Jimenez Food Products, Inc., who has grown from being a migrant worker to a millionaire.

Raul began in a 17′ × 14′ room making Mexican

sausage, tamales and hot sauce back in 1953. Today, his company grosses about $14 million a year and his operation spans most of Texas. His *customers* span the globe.

When Raul began, they mixed everything by hand—because they couldn't *afford* electric mixers. He had never had a bank account and, when asked by a supplier for a "financial statement," he had to turn to a friend to find out what the man was talking about!

What makes Raul's story even more exciting is the fact that he began his business at age 21—and only had a *seventh-grade education!*

In a recent article in *Southwest Airlines Magazine,* Raul was quoted as saying, "I learned a lot of things the hard way. You have to have drive and a goal. Anyone can make it, if you're determined and persistent, with a faith in God. That's my formula for being successful."

Never be a quitter. Quitters never win, and winners never quit!

Excellent advice! It's another way of saying what W. W. Clements, Chairman of the Board of the Dr Pepper Company, is fond of saying. "Foots," as Mr. Clements' friends call him, began has career with the Dr Pepper Company as a route salesman, driving a delivery truck in Tuscaloosa, Alabama, in 1935. It was under his leadership that Dr Pepper became a national soft drink in 1970 after 85 years as a regional beverage. Today, it ranks in the top four soft drinks in America. "Foots" says, "Success is never final—and neither is failure—unless *you* let it be!"

Quitters never win and winners never quit. Or, if you

prefer, success is never final and neither is failure—unless you let it be.

This brings us to Garry Kinder's favorite power of the made-up mind story. It's a negative kind of story that points out the antithesis of a made-up mind.

The boxer with the quickest hands and the fastest feet became the world's heavyweight champion. Many have called him the greatest boxer of all times.

In our opinion, he became that kind of performer not because of his quick hands and fast feet, but because of his positive mental attitude. Muhammad Ali was so positive in his approach that he would even predict the round in which his opponent would fall. Interestingly enough, his opponents seemed to cooperate willingly. This continued for many years, until his featured match with an able contender, Joe Frazier. Sports writers asked Ali, "What is your feeling about this important championship fight?" Ali responded, "If Joe Frazier wins, a lot of people will be glad. If I win, a lot of people will be sad." Notice the word *"if"*—it was the first time ever that there was a crack in Ali's positive-approach armor. As you will remember, Frazier captured the heavyweight crown by upsetting the unbeatable champion. This is another example of the power of the made-up mind—or lack of it!

Perhaps the greatest of all stories on the will to succeed—the power of the made-up mind—centers on Pete Strudwick. Pete, a 50-year-old Californian, had an ambition to be a marathon runner. A marathon is 26 miles, 385 yards. This determined competitor has run and completed more than 40 marathons, including the Boston Marathon—*and he has no feet.* No feet! Pete runs on stumps.

Someone asked him, "Pete, how do you run 26 miles

with no feet?" He replied, "You don't lean backwards!"

In order for *you* to realize your full potential in selling, you must develop the kind of persistence that comes only from a made-up mind. A favorite quotation of ours is this one by Calvin Coolidge: "Nothing in the world can take the place of persistence. Talent will not; nothing is more common than unsuccessful people with talent. Genius will not; unrewarded genius is almost a proverb. Education alone will not; the world is full of educated derelicts. Persistence and determination alone are omnipotent."

We often hear it said of a salesperson: "Everything he or she touches turns to gold." We sometimes think of these high achievers as being lucky. The fact is, their selling success is the result of a made-up mind—their willpower. By the force of their convictions they wring success from the most adverse circumstances.

Coach Tom Landry wrote a great statement entitled *Willpower:*

> "Intellect tires, the will never,
> The brain needs sleep, the will none,
> The whole body is nothing but objectified will,
> The whole nervous system contributes the antennae of the will,
> Every action of the body is nothing but the act of the will objectified."

THE POWER OF THE MADE-UP MIND SUMMED UP

Your power to persuade others originates from your philosophies and beliefs. Your selling philosophies determine the attitudes you develop and the habits you form. The principles of selling and living that you adhere to will move you up to join the salespeople who get to the top and stay there. *Make up your mind* to live by these principles.

Make up your mind that you are your most important customer. You must be sold on your job, your products and your ability to perform.

Make up your mind that your product or service, properly sold, is of considerably more value to your buyer than any commission you can possibly earn.

Make up your mind that time is money and that learning to manage your time productively will be one of your most profitable achievements.

Make up your mind to believe in the law of averages and the wisdom of knowing the dollar value of each of your primary activities.

Make up your mind that honest, intelligent effort is always rewarded.

Make up your mind that a selling interview is *never* to be considered a contest between you and your prospect. It is always to be a "win-win" encounter.

Make up your mind that the power of your sales presentation will always lie in its simplicity.

Make up your mind that the purchase must be "helped along" and is most often made because you guide the prospect's behavior in an effective, organized manner.

Make up your mind that people buy today, not nearly as much because they understand your product thoroughly, but because they feel and believe that you understand them, their problems and the things they want to accomplish.

Make up your mind that almost all development is, in

fact, self-development—that personal growth is the product of practice, observation and self-correction.

Make up your mind that vigorous physical conditioning is a prerequisite for maintaining a high level of energy.

Make up your mind that sales leaders are ordinary people with the extraordinary determination to make every occasion a great occasion.

Make up your mind to believe in the truth; that it is the spiritual that always determines the material.

Make up your mind that there is great power in holding a high ideal of the products and services you are selling. The model your mind holds, your lifestyle is certain to copy.

These are the kinds of philosophies you find held by those salespeople who have warranted pride in their accomplishments. Study them. Digest them. Make them a dominant part of your selling strategy and you will find yourself among those pros in selling who not only "make it to the top," but *stay* at the top.

THE POWER OF THE MADE-UP MIND REMINDERS

- Spectacular achievements in selling are always preceded by unspectacular preparation.
- Selling is the art of assisting your prospects to buy intelligently.
- In selling, the result is always your final judge.
- Selling achievements never rise higher than the expectations.
- The condition of your financial balance sheet is

generally a reliable measurement of the balance you are achieving in your life.

- Readers become leaders.
- Personal growth is the product of observation, self-correction and practice.
- Sales leaders are ordinary people with an extraordinary determination to make every occasion a great one.
- It's the spiritual that always determines the material.

CHAPTER 2

PLANNING AND PROSPECTING: THE CORNERSTONES OF WINNING SELLING

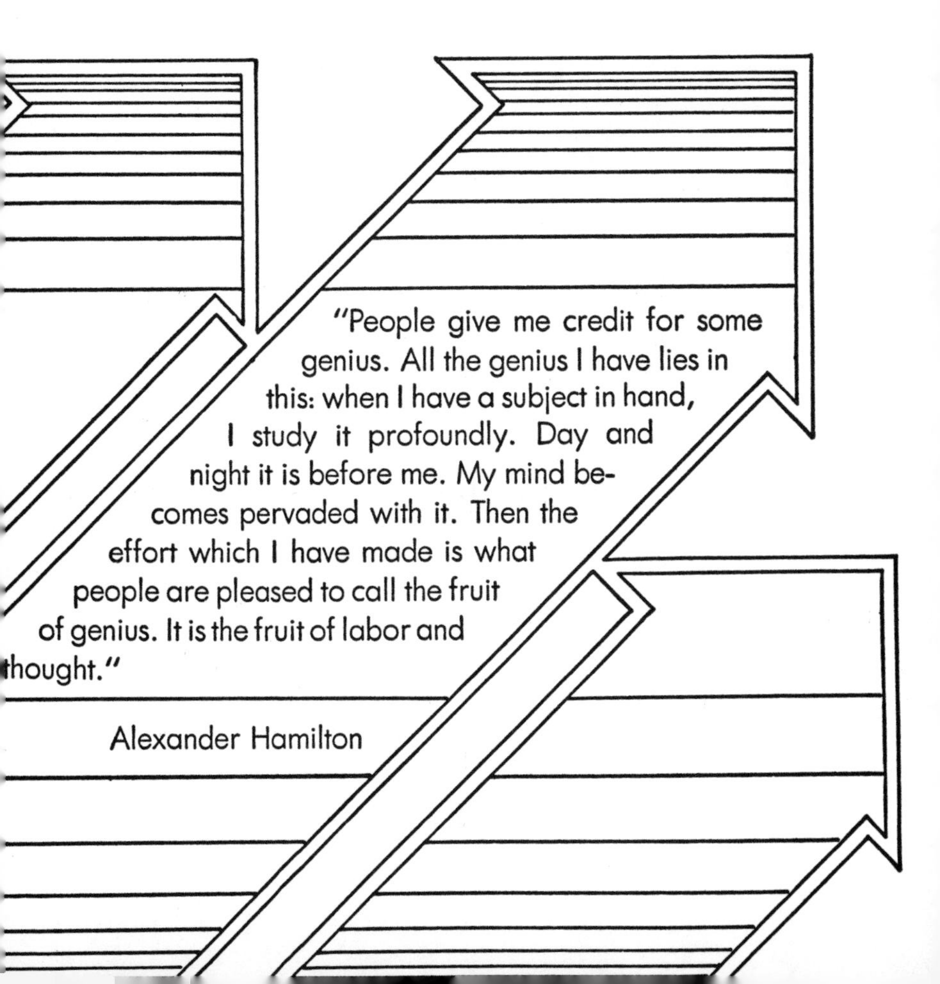

EXAMINING THE SELLING SPECTRUM

Regardless of the "position they play," professionals have a strong belief in the basics. In selling, the professional keeps returning to the basics of planning and prospecting until they become knit with habit.

Before looking at these basics, let's examine an array of positions which comprise the selling spectrum. Think particularly of your job and of the creative skill required in each of the following:

"Suppliers." This salesperson's job is to deliver the product, such as fuel oil, milk, bread, soft drinks. Selling responsibilities are secondary. Efficient service and a pleasant manner will enhance customer satisfaction, leading to more sales. Not many sales are originated by suppliers.

"Interceptors." This salesperson's job is pretty much being an "order taker." Examples are the clothing sales clerk or a furniture store clerk. Here, the prospects have already made up their minds to buy. The salesperson's job is to serve the customer. The salesperson's aim may be to use suggestive selling and upgrade the merchandise purchased. Opportunities to do more than that are limited. Also, interceptors sometimes work in the field as order takers, such as for soap, beverages, perfumes.

"Educators." This salesperson is called upon to educate or to build goodwill with the potential user. Examples are the medical detailer representing a pharmaceutical house or a university representative.

"Generators." These are positions that demand the creative sale of tangible products, such as automobiles, real estate and encyclopedias, and intangibles such as life insurance, advertising, stocks and bonds. Generators must make the prospect dissatisfied with his or her present situation, then begin to sell their product. Intangible products are generally more difficult for the prospect to comprehend. Intangibles are less readily demonstrated and dramatized.

Each type of sales position requires its own unique configuration of traits, attributes and qualities. *However, the basic habits of planning and prospecting are prerequisites to success in each of the described positions.*

THE WAY IN IS EASY— THE WAY OUT IS HARD

Psychologists tell us that we are governed by habit. They say every salesperson develops habits of thought and action that are good or bad, effective, regular or spasmodic. Dryden said, "We first make our habits, and then our habits make us." This is especially true in regard to your sales career. *Your habits determine your behavior and your style.* It's obvious that you can attain real success only if you consciously develop habits that are sound, effective and regular.

One time we came across a truly great thought on

habit building. It went like this: "The way in is easy—the way out is hard." Think about that one. Haven't you found the "way in" to poor dieting, exercising and living habits to be easy, *really* easy? But, haven't you found that the "way out" of those habits is extremely hard?

If you are a follower of competitive Olympic swimming matches, you know that most of the title holders are comparatively young—young men and women considerably under twenty. You know also that almost invariably these title holders are registered in the name of an athletic club, which means that from childhood they have been swimming under supervision. From their first day in the pool, breathing, stroke, rhythm and coordination have been carefully coached and checked.

These young athletes become gold medal winners before they are old enough to vote because they learn good habits from the beginning. They never have to take time out to *unlearn* bad habits and to replace them with good habits. They discover at the very start the "way in" to good habits is easy—the "way out" is hard.

It is the same with the planning and prospecting habits that you build. The "way in" to sound habits will be easy if you follow the procedures developed in this chapter.

THE PLANNING FUNCTION

Planning is just as important as doing, and adequate planning should always take place before doing.

Many salespeople confuse *activity* with *accomplishment*. As far as effort is concerned, an individual running around in circles can be working as hard as the person running down the street, but certainly not getting as far. To maximize your results, you should recognize that planning and doing must work together, with planning always preceding doing.

Planning is the base upon which all future action should take place. Planning awakens you to opportunities and shows you the way to their realization—it is the link between desire and realization.

Planning is ongoing; it is a never-ending activity. In Chapter 12 we will examine in-depth the annual planning process we recommend. But, for now, let's look at planning your day, your week and your month.

PLAN TO WAKE UP EMPLOYED

Form the habit of planning each day's calls and activities the previous day. Plan at the same hour and at the same place. You will be amazed at the creative thoughts that will begin to flow to you during this "planning hour."

Henry Doherty, the great industrialist, said, "I can hire people to do everything but two things: *think* and *do things in the order of their importance.*"

On Normandy Boulevard in Jacksonville, Jim Tatum gets his thinking and priorities right each day. Jim Tatum has earned the reputation for selling more men's suits each year than any other clothing salesman in the United States. "It's the 90-minute planning habit I established 20 years ago that has made it all possible. I have the Holy Bible in front of me and legal pad for planning the priorities. It's my most important discipline. The dividends it has paid me are enormous."

The daily plan habit assures you of waking up each day employed. First, you decide what is to be done. Then, you decide upon priorities. This daily discipline boils down to the trite but effective principle, "Plan your work and work your plan."

SUBSCRIBE TO THE "BOX TIME" THEORY

The "Box Time" theory is an approach used by successful salespeople to focus on the priority jobs. Purchase a daily planning calendar, one with a box or space for each hour of your work week. Plan your time so that you're always either in front of a prospect or endeavoring to be there.

The "Box Time" discipline keeps you focused. It reduces the times when other people or things can disturb your momentum or crowd your day with nonproductive activities.

PLAN A MONTHLY SELF-ORGANIZATION DAY

It's always easy to throw a number of prospect cards together as you start the month and think you are prepared. That doesn't take much time.

However, to plan the upcoming month carefully, to prepare proposals, write letters, schedule calls in their proper order, requires an intensified effort. We recommend setting aside a half day at each month's end and thinking of it as "Self-Organization Day." You'll find it pays you big dividends.

Two key planning benefits:

1. ***desired results are defined and***
2. ***deadlines are clearly established***

THE BEST KEPT SALES SECRET

The best kept sales secret is this: *Do the most important things first.* And, in selling, the most important things are the few factors that make the big difference in obtaining results. When you learn to focus your time, thinking and energy on these, your success is virtually assured.

Tom Tierney is a master salesman—one of the best we have ever known. Here is one of the reasons. Tom says, "I remind myself often that I'm paid for the *results* I produce and not the *work* I do." Tom has formed the habit of recognizing priorities and staying focused on them.

Of course, interruptions will come—learn to anticipate them. Plan a certain time each day to deal with interruptions like phone calls and return them all at that time. You'll only get frustrated trying to "work your plan" if you don't allow for interruptions.

One of the great satisfactions in life comes from being productive, getting things done. If you are having trouble getting organized and being at your best, remember there is only one way: Take more time to think and to do things in the order of their importance. *The secret to improved effectiveness generally lies not in working more hours, but in making the hours work more for you.* You do this with proper planning of your sales time.

THE PROSPECTING FUNCTION

Prospecting successfully on a consistent basis boils down to two things: paying attention and using memory "ticklers" to bring things to mind when you need them. Both are necessary to be successful in any type of sales—but if you're in a business where you must generate all or part of your own prospects, they're absolutely vital!

Let's look at "paying attention" first.

Paying Attention

"You see," Sherlock Holmes admonished Dr. Watson, "but you do *not* observe!" Opportunities come our way each day. We "see" them, but we do not "observe." To put it another way, we see opportunities, but we don't examine them closely enough to get any real value from them.

Successful salespeople *observe.* They keep their eyes and ears open. They make notes. They develop an alertness and a probing, inquisitive attitude.

When Roger was quarterback for the Dallas Cowboys, they studied game films of the team they were to play days in advance. They didn't just "see" the film, like a person would say, "Yeah, I *saw* the game!"—they *observed!* They took notes. They watched key plays over and over until they knew how the other team acted and reacted and, as nearly as possible, they knew how they *thought.*

When Roger was off the field and in his real estate office, he applied the same powers of observation to prospects. He learned what kind of properties each investor was interested in—what his or her buying motives were. He learned to try and think like the prospect would think—and built a successful business!

Paying attention can become one of the greatest factors in your sales success story! You don't just see with your optic nerves, you see with your mind. Paying attention is a powerful mental process. It keeps your mind on the material that your eye brings it, considering, forming opinions, planning, estimating, evaluating, weighing, balancing and calculating.

Paying attention is a key to increasing your production. It prompts you to learn as much as possible about the prospects you're calling on—their reputation and capacity, from whom they are buying now, and what value they are getting from their dollar.

Paying attention helps you do your homework and plan each call in advance. It makes it possible for you to evaluate prospects' problems carefully and to decide upon the best ways to help them solve their problems.

Mona Biscamp pays attention. Mona has sold over $100 million in residential sales in the nine years she has represented the Henry S. Miller Company. "*You prospect 24 hours a day,*" Mona advises. "I make it a practice to ask everyone I come in contact with two questions. Are you thinking about listing your home or buying a new one? Then, who do you know who is?"

"Alertness is the key to the success I've enjoyed," Mona adds. Learn to pay attention—it will pay you substantial dividends throughout your career—*if* you organize the data so that it's available to you whenever you're ready to use it. That brings us to "ticklers."

The "Tickler" System

A "Tickler" system is merely a formal program for bringing bits of data to your mind and to help you locate information you need. A prospecting "tickler" begins with a simple 3 × 5 file box with tab cards—the kind available at any office supply or stationery store.

Into this file you'll place the names of clients and prospects and any other important follow-up information. The primary purpose of the file is to provide you with a system for bringing the names of prospects to your attention at the time when it's most logical to see them. Your "tickler" box should be divided into two sections: an alphabetical section and a "when-to-see" section that you'll arrange by months.

Make every effort you can in every call to get enough information to enable you to know the best time and the strongest reason for seeing your prospect at a future date. Enter the important information on your prospect card and file it in the proper month. Obviously, you want a build-up of qualified prospects in your "when-to-see" reservoir. Effective field work produces a constant movement of prospect calls from the alphabetical section to the "when-to-see" reservoir.

Don't develop a hope chest. It's not a sign of success to have a bulging box of ticklers if your box is full of dead wood. Determine as early as possible whether the person is a prospect for you and whether or not you can make a sale with a reasonable amount of follow-up. If you can't, then eliminate the card from your system. *The only tickler system that works is one that contains bona fide prospects—the kind you can see and sell!*

A large file box made up of dead wood is an impediment. It gets in your way. It fools you into believing you're doing a good job of prospecting when all you're doing is a good job of filing. A box of dead wood invites you to spend idle hours sorting and resorting cards. It's better to have a tickler box with a hundred "prospects" than one with a thousand "suspects."

The good prospector with a well-organized, active tickler system must work hard to find enough time to see all of the prospects he or she has.

We live and sell in a generation of hustle-bustle. "Time out" for thinking and organization is sometimes considered idling your motor when you should be racing out to meet someone. At one time, prospecting may have been thought of as taking time out from selling, but for today's successful sales professionals prospecting is number one on their list of priorities.

All of us keep our tickler file boxes right on our desks where we can get at them. Roger has formed the habit of carrying a notebook in his pocket at all times. Whenever he gets information he can use, he jots it down and then transfers it later to his tickler box. "It's so easy to forget things," Roger says. "It may be a name, it may be data on a deal that might work out for me. It might even be information that won't be ripe to use for two years—in that case, I transfer it to a central file."

You'll also want to add names to your tickler box that didn't work out the first time you tried them but might later. Maybe a prospect got up on the wrong side of the bed the day you called, but you know that you have something he or she needs. You put that person in the tickler file and try again later.

Roger says, "I've run into people who just had a dominant type of personality and, maybe the first time you met, you just approached them wrong. If later you decide that your approach should be to fight dominance with dominance, then you make a note of that. Three months later, you can come back to the same client and you know how to deal with him or her—you've got the product or service he or she wants and now you know how to present your case—and you've made a sale!"

"All good selling starts with a prospective buyer who can make a decision."

EXAMINE THESE SIX PROSPECTING STRATEGIES

Someone has suggested that prospecting is the search "for needers who can be changed first into wanters and then into buyers." *To get more buyers you must discover more prospects.* The vital importance of getting names of people who might be needers is so well recognized that six key strategies have been worked out to assist you in becoming more effective as a prospector.

We've made no effort to list these in order of importance because, quite frankly, none of us *exactly* agree on the ranking. Their relative importance will vary with individuals and, of course, with professions, but all six are vital and none of the six can be neglected.

They are:

- the personal observation strategy
- the endless chain strategy
- the center-of-influence strategy

- the junior associate strategy
- the direct mail strategy
- the cold canvass strategy

Let's examine them in more detail.

1. The personal observation strategy. This consists of being constantly on the alert for prospect leads no matter where you are or with whom you are. Prospects are everywhere and, once you become prospect-minded, you'll develop a "nose for business" just as keen as a reporter's "nose for news," or a hound dog's "nose for game." It's another way of saying that you form the habit of *paying attention.*

To fully utilize this strategy, you must constantly be on the lookout for bits of information of value to you. These surface in your office, waiting to interview a prospect, talking on the phone, at lunch, and at home listening to a conversation or reading the newspaper.

2. The endless chain strategy. This is predicated upon the theory that from each interview or each buyer you should be able to secure the names of other prospects.

In employing this strategy, attempt to get from each person interviewed information about and/or introductions to two or three of their contacts who possess the need for your product or service. Naturally, this strategy is more effective in instances where you have been successful in selling the prospect just interviewed. New buyers are generally sufficiently enthusiastic about their purchase to believe that some of their friends and contacts will likely want to consider the same proposition.

The term "endless chain" is applied to the process of securing an endless number of qualified sales links from a single source. When you employ this strategy, you can, in fact, make it a never-ending chain. Each introduction carries with it an element of recommendation. Your new prospect realizes that unless their friend had been helped by you, they would never have provided the introduction. This constitutes a "referred lead." It is the best kind of prospect, because a level of trust and common interest has been established between you and the prospect.

3. The center-of-influence strategy. In using this strategy, you develop a number of people who will serve as feeders. In some cases, these people will be customers and clients; in other instances, they may be influential friends who are willing to cooperate.

An illustration of the manner in which this strategy might be applied is the "Board of Directors" developed by the late Dick Reed, one of the life insurance industry's top performers. We watched Dick move his production from $1 million to over $25 million in a *single year* as a *direct result* of organizing his center of influence.

Dick picked 10 prominent citizens to serve on his personal "Board of Directors." Each month, he called the board together for a regular luncheon meeting. Insurance ideas were discussed and prospects were developed that propelled him into the big league in selling! It can possibly do the same for you.

When you employ the center-of-influence strategy, it is important to make an effort to repay the services of your contact group by regular reminders of appreciation and goodwill, such as gifts at Christmas, cards on important occasions and frequent calls to thank them personally for their assistance. Remember, no one is going to give much thought to helping you unless you can establish yourself as a knowledgeable professional and a skilled representative.

4. The junior associate strategy. Batman has his Robin, Holmes has his Watson and great actors and actresses have understudies. Many professional salespeople have found that there is value in having a Junior Associate. This person acts as a "bird dog" and points out contacts that the more experienced sales professional will call on and sell. *This strategy is employed in those selling situations that require both contacts and technical information.* Your "bird dog" sniffs around and locates prospects and then signals to the "experienced hunter" who brings them in. This strategy enables you to use your time more efficiently and makes it easier to "bag your limit."

5. The direct mail strategy. This strategy is used effectively for products that are bought repeatedly, especially when used in connection with previous buyers and present users.

To employ this strategy, you send a prepared announcement with the idea of calling first upon those who respond and invite you to call. Ultimately, your plan should be to get around to the rest. Frequently, direct mail makes your prospect conscious of a need not realized until the message is received.

The "lead service letters" of many companies today are excellent examples of direct mail generating live prospects who have not previously perceived any need for their product or service. As a result of a well-structured letter, recipients respond and ask that you come to see them. If they don't respond, you still have made them aware of you and your service and have a natural lead to follow up on.

6. The cold canvass strategy. This strategy assumes that you know little or nothing about the person being called upon except perhaps his or her name. The law of averages is supposed to result in a satisfactory number of good prospects and, hence, sales being developed simply through the volume of cold calls made.

Many salespeople today contend that this prospecting strategy is no strategy at all—that it lacks professionalism. *Obviously,* the nature of the product being sold has a great deal to do with the strategies you use. Cold canvass may be a sound approach to use in the sale of a generally used tangible product. It is more debatable in the case of intangible services which are sold largely on the basis of confidence and contacts. The cold canvass strategy is much better adapted to selling those products and services that are almost essential—such things as automobiles, home appliances, fire and auto insurance, since every prospect approached either needs them or will need them at some future date.

PLANNING AND PROSPECTING SUMMED UP

Nothing in selling is more important than planning and prospecting! It always pays to "plan your work and work your plan." More important than how *much* work you do is what *kind* of work you do. It's more important to "work smart" than to "work hard."

Just as you wouldn't begin a day of driving without a clear idea of where you were going, you shouldn't begin a day of selling without having prepared a "road map" to follow.

There are basically four types of salespeople: suppliers, interceptors, educators and generators. These are listed in *ascending* order, going from the easiest and least well paid to the most difficult and most profitable. While planning is necessary in all four fields, it is increasingly important as your job increases in importance.

Good planning means that you:

- subscribe to the "box time" theory,
- plan to wake up employed,
- plan a monthly self-organization day,
- and know the best kept sales secret!

Good prospecting means that you:

- learn to pay attention
- use a "tickler" system
- know the six basic prospecting strategies
    1. Personal observation
    2. Endless chain
    3. Center-of-influence
    4. Junior associate
    5. Direct mail
    6. Cold canvass

PLANNING AND PROSPECTING REMINDERS

- Planning is just as important as doing and should take place before doing.
- The daily planning of priorities provides an intelligent course of action to be followed.
- The planning discipline keeps you focused.
- Your success in selling depends, in large measure, upon your ability to recognize priorities and to stay focused on them.
- Prospecting successfully on a consistent basis boils down to paying attention.

- Prospecting is the search for needers who can be changed into wanters and then into buyers.
- The personal observation strategy calls for you to form a habit of alertness.
- An introduction to a prospect carries with it an element of endorsement.
- The junior associate strategy works best in those selling situations that recognize both contacts and technical information.
- Remember, a good prospector is almost sure to outsell the salesperson who may be strong in closing sales but who lacks prospecting skills and strategies.

CHAPTER 3

HOW THE BUYER BUYS AND HOW THE SELLER SELLS

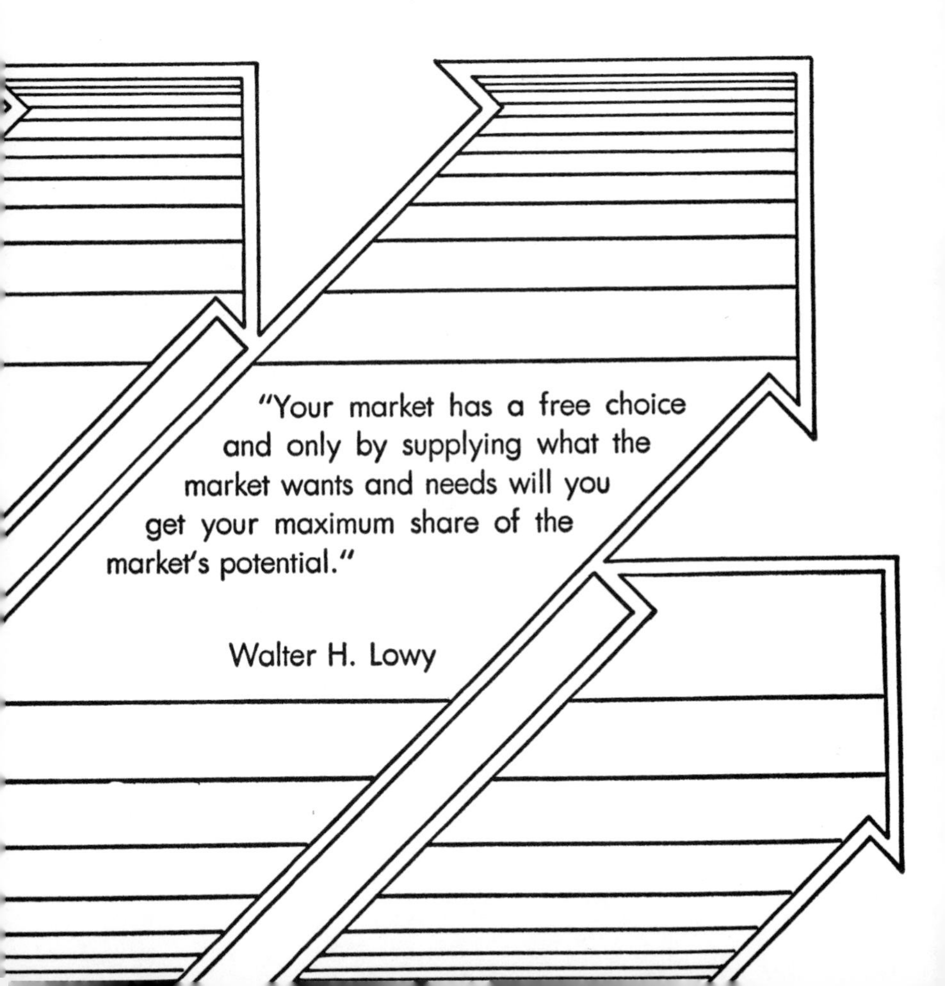

"Your market has a free choice and only by supplying what the market wants and needs will you get your maximum share of the market's potential."

Walter H. Lowy

NOTHING HAPPENS UNTIL SOMEONE MAKES THE DECISION TO BUY SOMETHING

This all-important buying decision is the "trigger" of the marketing cycle. Everything in a company depends on the salesperson pulling that trigger—assisting the buyer in buying. Your success, and that of your company, is tied to your skill in selling. Remember, the secret of success in selling is forming good sales habits. That means you are willing to do things failures won't do. Successful salespeople are motivated by the desire for pleasing *results*. Mediocre salespeople are influenced by the desire for pleasing *methods*.

You are a creature of habit just as a machine is a creature of momentum. *Every single qualification for success in selling is acquired by habit.* You discipline yourself to form right habits and those habits shape your future. If you do not deliberately form good habits, then unconsciously you will form bad ones.

You are, and will always be, the kind of salesperson you are because you have formed the habit of doing those things unsuccessful people don't like to do. The only way you can change yourself is by changing your habits. Habit formation and habit alteration are the result of discipline.

"Success is an inside job."

HOW SUCCESS IS EARNED

The success habits in selling which require daily discipline can be divided into five main groups.

1. thinking right
2. working right
3. selling right
4. studying right
5. living right

Let's examine each of these briefly.

1. Thinking right. *"You become what you think about most of the time."* Thinking right requires you to form the habit of thinking greatly of your function. See its significance. Consider your sales job to be most worthwhile, important and necessary. Don't sell yourself short. Make every occasion a great occasion. Remember, it's *always* too early to quit.

2. Working right. *"Honest, intelligent effort is always rewarded."* Establish the habit of starting your selling day at a specific time. Form the daily planning habit that assures you of staying focused on priority activities. Developing a regular routine permits you to accomplish much more and leads to a consistent effort.

3. Selling right. *"Be a professional client-getter—not a client-visitor."* Selling right boils down to three basic fundamentals: paying attention, staying in front of decision-makers and having a good sales strategy.

4. Studying right. *"An individual who doesn't read and digest information or learn from cassettes is no better off than one who cannot."* Long ago, you formed the habit of feeding your body regularly—remember to feed your mind too! The learning process is a continual one. You wouldn't quit eating when you turned 30 just because you had eaten regularly for the first 29 years of your life; never quit feeding your mind, either! The learning process is a continual one. Studying right means forming the habit of learning as much as possible about your product, your prospects and your performance.

5. Living right. *"You are what you repeatedly do. Excellence, then, is not an act but a habit."* Living right requires you to balance every area of your life. Success escapes many talented people because of their unwillingness or inability to develop this habit.

Success is learned best by those who learn quickly to form the habit of thinking right, working right, selling right, studying right and living right.

"Nothing builds self-confidence like successful experiences."

THE FIVE BUYING DECISIONS

Discipline comes first. Discipline builds right habits that reflect themselves in right actions. Right actions, when accompanied by strategy, always produce right results.

Let's turn to our study of selling strategy. It begins with an understanding of how the buyer buys.

You must assist the prospect in making certain decisions, one decision at a time. When your prospect has made them all, he or she has bought your product or service. How does the buyer buy? The buyer buys by making the following decisions:

- I will see and then listen to this salesperson.
- I realize and recognize a need.
- I will evaluate a possible solution to my problem.
- I approve the proposition offered. I'm convinced.
- I will act now.

These five different, important decisions must be reached in a logical, orderly manner.

STEPS IN THE SELLING PROCESS

Throughout your career, you must be learning more and better ways of assisting your prospects in making each of these buying decisions. In a sense, you play the role of "assistant buyer." To play your role effectively, you must master the five steps in the selling process.

- **Step one:** *Pre-approach*—The aim here is to get the prospect's attention. You sell the prospect on *listening* . . . giving you an appointment on a favorable basis.
- **Step two:** *Approach*—This has two chief objectives: First, to make a favorable impression. Second, to gain positive interest in learning more about your product or service.
- **Step three:** *Probing*—The primary objective of this step is to assist the prospect in *recognizing a need,* then arousing an interest in evaluating a possible solution.
- **Step four:** *Presenting*—Here you create desire by

showing the advantages now being missed that will be gained by *accepting* your sales proposition.

- **Step five:** *Closing*—Few prospects are ready to accept a sales offer even when interest has been aroused and desire has been created. You must add a closing motivation of a logical and/or emotional nature.

WANT-CREATOR VS. NEEDS-SATISFIER

Frank Bettger once said, "I am convinced the most important secret of selling is to find out what the prospect wants, then help him or her find the best way to get it."

In order to sell people effectively, you must form the habit of putting yourself in the prospect's place.

Charley McCann, a leading diesel engine salesman in Montreal for 35 years, said this to us: "The day I began to consider myself a want-creator, rather than merely a needs-satisfier, was a red letter day in my selling life."

"Do unto others as you would have them do unto you" and you will be utilizing the strongest tool yet developed for carving out a successful career in selling.

Remember, the golden rule is always golden in selling.

HOW THE BUYER BUYS AND HOW THE SELLER SELLS SUMMED UP

Remember that no one really wants to be *sold* anything—their stimulus, in their mind, comes because *they've* decided to *buy*. Until they decide to buy, nothing can happen—it's up to you to help them make that decision!

Acquire the habit of thinking right, working right, selling right, studying right and living right. Then remember that there are five steps on the ladder of decision. First, a prospect must decide to *see* and *listen*, then to recognize a *need*, then to *evaluate* your solution, then to *approve* the solution and then to act *now*. If you don't skip any rungs on the way up, your career will be on the way up too!

HOW THE BUYER BUYS AND HOW THE SELLER SELLS REMINDERS

- Nothing happens until someone makes the decision to buy something.
- Success comes to those who form the habit of doing things that failures don't like to do.
- Successful people are influenced by the desire for pleasing results, not pleasing methods.
- Habit forming and habit changing are the result of discipline.
- You become what you think about most of the time.
- Honest, intelligent effort is always rewarded in selling.
- You assist the prospect in making certain decisions—one at a time.
- The prospect must realize and recognize a need.
- The prospect must be convinced of your proposition's value and benefits.
- You play the important role of being an "assistant buyer."

- Probing arouses interest.
- Presenting creates desire.
- Most sales do not close themselves. You must add the motivation of a logical and/or emotional close.
- Be more than a needs-satisfier, be a want-creator.
- A secret of successful salesmanship is staying in front of decision-makers with a selling strategy.

CHAPTER 4

MAKING CONTACT: WINNING PRE-APPROACH STRATEGIES

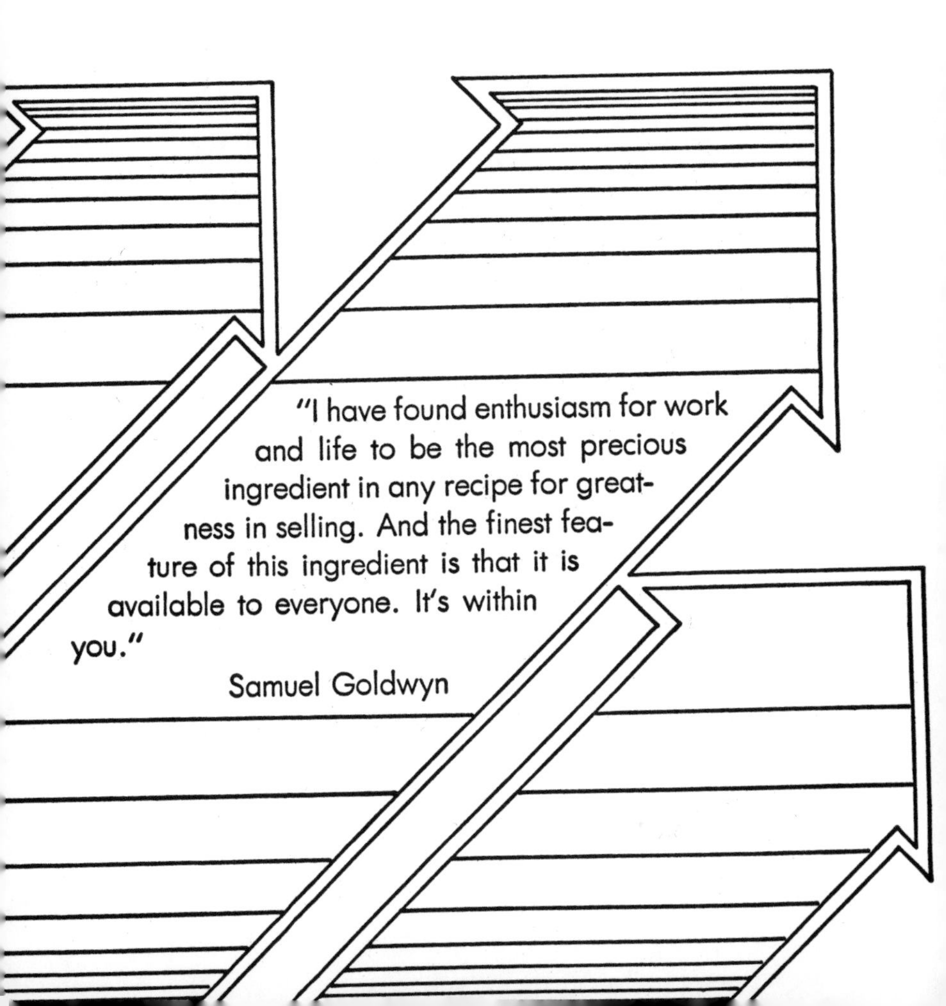

WHERE THE "BALL GAME" IS WON

Football games are won at the point of initial contact—the line of scrimmage. Sales are won at the point of initial contact—the pre-approach. Fred Novy, a great and successful salesman in Chicago, says, "Making a great many calls will do almost anything that super-salesmanship can do—and many things it can't."

People remain names on cards and only become prospects when they are contacted and interviewed under favorable conditions.

IT'S A SERIES OF DECISIONS

Again, the sale you make is always a series of decisions in favor of your proposition. Be reminded of this fundamental truth.

The purpose of your pre-approach is to assist your prospect in making the first decision—to give you an appointment under favorable circumstances. A pre-approach can be made using a telephone call, a personal visit, a letter, or a combination of these methods.

PREPARING FOR THE INITIAL CONTACT CALL

After the prospect is identified, but prior to your initial contact, you assume an important role. You become, for all practical purposes, an investigator. How extensive this kind of preparation is varies with the nature of your sales position and the kind of products you sell.

In most selling jobs, the investigative work and the subsequent use of this information can make or break the setting up of an appointment.

Sales do not just happen. Most often, they're the result of planning and the application of strategy in the "get ready" phases. The investigative work you do in preparation for the initial contact will contribute to both your effectiveness and time management.

This pre-planning is vitally important. In his days as a quarterback, Roger studied game films of the team he was to play against next. He learned their moves, their formations, their favorite plays. He tried to learn how they would respond to different approaches and circumstances. Correctly sizing up the other team *before* they came together was a vital part of the whole success story, because once the game began, they followed a pre-determined game plan on every major play!

In selling, we have all found that this same attention to detail, *before* that initial contact is made, is very, very vital to the success of the game—whether your game is football, baseball or selling!

OBJECTIVES OF PLANNING THE INITIAL CONTACT

The following objectives of the investigative planning phase, when accomplished, will help you function at your best during your initial contact. These objectives are to:

- accumulate any special information that can help you present yourself in the strongest possible manner
- discover what the prospect's dominant buying motive will most likely be
- gain insights on how you can best establish a good relationship

To become proficient in obtaining the information you require, you must sharpen your questioning and observation skills. Generally, finding out what you want to know is a matter of asking the right people. Most people will want to help, if properly approached. Here are the important things to do:

First, seek out information about the prospect:

- Personality characteristics
- Special interest, sports and hobbies
- Family ties and marital status
- Business aims, ambitions and objectives
- Business needs
- Special personal or business problems

Second, gain information about the prospect's company:

- Comparative growth in industry
- Most pressing needs

- Specific business problems
- Experience with similar products
- Objections likely to be raised
- How they are doing now
- How your product or service will help them do better

Finally, secure an introduction and/or endorsement of you and your product or service. You gather this important information and these helpful insights in a variety of ways.

First, listen to:

- existing clients
- other salespeople
- receptionists
- assistants and secretaries
- the prospect's associates and employees

Second, read:

- local daily papers
- technical journals and trade papers
- special surveys, reports and bulletins
- magazine articles

Next, talk with:

- trade association members
- other experienced salespeople

Finally:

- Assemble your findings.
- Coordinate information and insights.
- Analyze the facts and your feelings.

THE MOST IMPORTANT THING

After you've done your homework, the next most important thing is to make the *right* contact and then *get in!*

One of America's top salesmen is Cleveland's Corwin Riley of the Kirby Company. Once we asked him what he considered the most important thing in selling and he replied with two words: *"Get in!"*

Corwin went ahead to explain how important he feels it is to assist the prospect in wanting your product or service, and how essential it is to keep your thinking right. "However, these are to no avail," he added, "if you fail to *get in!"*

To see how important this is, look at the final result you want and work backward. What is the final result you want? A satisfied client and a sales commission, of course.

But:
You can't secure a client and collect a commission until you make a sale.
You can't make the sale until you've written up the order.
You can't write the order until you get an interview.
And, you can't have an interview until you *get in!*

Making the contact and getting in is the foundation of success in selling.

One of the most dynamic sales organizations in the history of American business is Amway. Amway sales surpass the $1 billion mark annually. We have always felt that one of the reasons for the Amway success story lies in the philosophy professed by its co-founder and president, Rich DeVos. Here is what he has to say:

> **The most important thing in selling is selling.**
> **It is not talent, for many people with little talent make it.**
> **It is not product knowledge, for many with limited detail knowledge make it.**
> **It is not singly enthusiasm or persistence or all the other good things that make up the whole.**
> **After 30 years of watching and working with winners (and some losers), I'm convinced it all comes down to action.**
> **Nothing will take the place of doing something now.**
> **Get the body in front of the prospect and sell.**
> **That's what it's all about, and that's the pay-off point.**

Estrella Lynch is a great inspiration for women entering sales—especially those who have the feeling that it takes years of diligent study and experience to become a steady producer.

Estrella led her company, The Prudential, during her *third* year! She's a $10 million a year producer in Los Angeles!

"I tell them with my eyes that they are the most important people in my life at the time of the interview. I listen for clues to help me decide the thing that is most important in their lives. I work hard to come across to the prospect as an understanding, unhurried, conscientious agent. *I want the time the prospect spends with me to be a high spot of his or her day.*"

What makes *you* feel important—that someone wants to sell you something? No, of course not. What makes you feel important is the fact that someone recognizes you as an individual, as the special person that you are. When you take time to do your homework on prospects, you're letting them know they were important enough to research.

We asked a buyer for a large Mexican restaurant chain what irritated him most about salespeople, and he replied, "When they haven't taken time to do their homework! I've had people come in and want to sell me white bread, fruit pies and all of the other things *most* restaurants use, but we don't. That tells me that we weren't even important enough for them to stop and look at one of our menus. A salesperson like that is not only wasting my time, but his—and certainly puts himself in a bad light if he *should* happen to have some products we could use!"

DON'T TELL YOUR STORY FOR THE PRACTICE

One of the most important strategies in making contact calls is to make the right one. You may have researched the contact, the company and know all there is to know about them, but if your contact doesn't have the authority to *buy,* then you're wasting your time!

If we had a dollar for every hour wasted each year by sales reps who tell their stories to the wrong person, we would be on Easy Street. It is important to see the right person *first.* The only people worth talking to are the people who have the authority to give you the order when you have convinced them that they should buy.

Trying to sell someone who does not have the authority to buy is a double mistake. First, you waste your time. Second and perhaps even worse, the individuals interviewed are apt to become obstacles because they do not want you to realize their lack of authority.

Be careful not to be fooled by titles. They are often misleading. The rule to follow is this: When in doubt, go to the top. When you start at the top, you generally get action and decisions. Often, the top person will take you to the right person and introduce you. This can be construed as "an approval from the boss."

You seldom go wrong when you start at the top. When you start too low on the ladder of authority, you are dependent upon someone else to relay your story. No one can tell your story with the power you can—so, when appropriate, eliminate the "middle person." You can't expect the buyer's assistant to do your selling for you.

The same things hold true in direct consumer selling. Whether the interview is conducted in an office, a home or a business, it is still important to talk directly to the decision-maker. In nearly every family group, there is one member who decides upon most family expenditures. Find out who the decision-maker is and direct your selling efforts toward that individual. You can increase your selling effectiveness by making sure that you tell your story in your way to the right person.

TAKE THIS PLEDGE NOW

Before you move ahead, stop and take this pledge. Feed it into your mental computer so that you can recall it instantly for the rest of your selling career.

> **"I will never make contact with a prospect until I have written out my script, practiced and learned my lines so that they can be expressed naturally, conversationally and sincerely."**

Taking the pledge assures your effectiveness for three reasons. First, it allows you to say the right thing, not occasionally, but every time. Second, it allows you to say the right thing in the fewest possible words. Finally, it gives you confidence, because you know what you are going to say.

As Frank Sullivan says, "Ad-libs are for amateurs. In selling you must prepare much like a professional in acting—going over the lines a hundred times or more."

Many successful salespeople owe their selling success to the fact that they "took the pledge"—why not join in?

FACING THE IMPORTANT FOUR-MINUTE BARRIER

Dr. Leonard Zunin, a Los Angeles psychiatrist, says the first four minutes of your initial contact are the crucial ones. He says, "It is the average time, demonstrated by careful observation, during which the prospect decides to continue or terminate the discussion." Dr. Zunin goes on to say, "All salespeople must be reminded they constantly face the four-minute barrier during which a favorable impression must be established."

It's human nature to make quick decisions based upon "feelings" and "hunches." *The more positive the feeling prospects have toward you, the more they will tend to hear and accept what you say.*

The following is a list of "do's" and "don'ts" to review often:

- *Do be prompt for the appointment.*
- Don't mispronounce your prospect's name.
- *Do make the object of your call clear immediately.*
- Don't show impatience.
- *Do give a warm greeting with a firm handshake.*
- Don't chew gum.
- *Do put a smile on your lips and in your voice and eyes.*
- Don't smoke, even if your prospect does.
- *Do find something to praise.*
- Don't compliment unless it's believable.
- *Do watch your posture and look your customer in the eyes.*
- Don't pull at your glasses, tap with your fingers or use other distractors.
- *Do avoid conversation relating to politics, race and religion.*
- Don't use profanity.
- *Do stay enthusiastic. It's contagious. It attracts a favorable response.*

FIVE WAYS TO COPE WITH CALL RELUCTANCE

Call reluctance will plague you throughout your career. You can learn to cope with call reluctance in five ways:

1. *Saturate yourself with positive, upbeat feelings.* This produces a commanding posture and attitude. Dorothy Sarnoff, the well-known New York City consultant, taught us a powerful attitude conditioner. Dorothy recommends feeding your mind and body with stimulants she calls "my million-dollar energizers."

   "I'm energetic, enthusiastic and effective. I'm prepared, poised and persuasive."

   With this kind of mental conditioning, you key yourself up to trigger favorable responses.

2. *Prepare yourself technically.* No matter how long a show plays on Broadway, the actors continue to study. They must know exactly what they are selling. They must understand the response and reaction that they must generate from their audience. Knowing your product and your lines gives you a competitive edge. It builds your confidence in selling the prospect.

3. *Focus on the rewards of success,* never the penalty of failure. The very next call can have results that change your entire week or month. Imagine how you'll feel after such a sale! You can never control your *feelings,* but you can control what you *imagine.* Feelings follow thought. Keep your thoughts optimistic. Act the way you want to feel.

"Focus on the rewards of success—not the penalties of failure."

4. *Remember that most people are nice.* Most of the people you'll call on will be nice people—just like yourself. If you go in with a mental chip on your shoulder, thinking, "This buyer will really be tough," it will show in your attitude.
5. *Remember that most people may not show they're nice right away.* These nice people you'll be dealing with may not show their true colors during the first couple of minutes of the interview. They may be tense and nervous and act "abnormal"—as though they aren't *really* nice at all. This is even more reason for you to stay in control as a poised and prepared professional. *Let them key off your attitude—don't you key off theirs!*

To be a success, you must develop call courage. You build it in these five ways and by pumping into your bloodstream the motivational suggestion, *"Do it now!"* Psychologists teach that the surest way to develop courage is to act courageous—to do the thing you fear.

If you fear making calls, then begin making them now. Call courage can be developed. Start now!

Your Aim Is to Gain an Appointment

In making this all-important initial call, keep it concise, simple and to the point. Put yourself in the prospect's position and view your pre-approach through his or her eyes.

Never imply anything about buying your product or service during this period. In a sense, you are not trying to "sell a solution" or "sell a product" on the initial contact. Your sole aim is to "sell an appointment!"

Make the Object of Your Call Clear Immediately

Don't ask for "just a few minutes of your time" and hope to stretch it into a longer session. Ask for what you need and give your honest assurance that everything you have to offer can be described in that length of time, unless he or she *wants* more information.

Plan to Sell the Prospect on Listening

You will get your prospect's favorable attention in any one or more of these ways:

- Promise a benefit.
- Offer a service.
- Appeal to curiosity.

Never take for granted your prospect will want to listen. Instead, launch your pre-approach with reasons why he or she will want to listen.

Your pre-approach plan should be memorized and repeatedly rehearsed. It must be conversational in tone (not rote!) and instinctive if you are going to be consistently effective in setting appointments.

Practice in a small room so that you can hear yourself and improve your voice quality. Practice in front of a mirror. Put your pre-approach lines on a cassette tape to critique and improve your technique. Practicing the right lines makes for perfection. Knowing exactly what you are going to say and how you will say it gives you confidence.

Of course, the manner in which you pre-approach your prospect is important too. Make your initial contact show a poised, positive attitude. Be certain your prospect senses by your entire manner that what you have to say is important. Remember, Dr. Zunin says that relationships are made or lost in the first four minutes of that initial contact! It's important that your prospect's initial impression of you is favorable!

"The prospect's first attention is focused on you—not your proposition."

Making Contact by Telephone

In many selling positions the telephone call has replaced the personal visit in making the initial contact with prospects. The telephone is the one business tool that helps budget time, qualify prospects and enhance your professional image.

The peculiar advantages of the telephone are:

- The number of calls can be increased.
- Cost per call is reduced.
- Effectiveness may be improved. It is often possible to gain the ear of a busy prospect when you couldn't gain a face-to-face interview.
- Brevity is encouraged. It encourages concentration on both ends of the wire.
- You can work rapidly over the telephone and concentrate your personal calls on large buyers or those who require a visit.
- Opportunity is provided for you to obtain an immediate decision.

Ken Miller at Phoenix says, "In my business, 10 cold sales calls resulting in one appointment can take a *full day.* Ten phone calls resulting in one appointment takes only one hour." This is quite an advantage when you are measuring time investment versus return.

Telephone contacts have their weaknesses too:

- The opportunity to present a complete message is often lacking.
- Some regard the telephone as an intruder.
- Appeal is to the sense of hearing only. You can't show samples, use visual aids, or impress with your personal appearance.
- It's easier to say "No" over the telephone.

Basic Telephone Strategies to Employ

The situation requires you to develop telephone effectiveness. You'll find it helpful to review these basic strategies often.

1. Choose a private spot to make your calls and avoid any interruption.
2. Build and use a script. Know exactly what you are going to say before you call.
3. Introduce yourself and your company, and state the purpose of your call quickly.
4. Verify the name of the prospect to whom you are speaking. Make sure of its pronunciation. Use the prospect's name frequently.
5. Courtesy, sincerity and clarity of speech are essential to your success. Use "thank you," "may I ask" and other expressions that demonstrate good manners. Put a smile in your voice. A mirror in front of you helps you smile.
6. Be aggressive without seeming to be so. Using questions that invite "yes" answers is the best

strategy for driving through without giving your prospect the opportunity to cut off the conversation.

7. By all means, avoid an argument. No matter what the response from the prospect is, ask for the appointment—give the prospect a choice.
8. Sell your name. Ask the prospect to write it down.
9. Take frequent breaks if you are calling over an extended period of time. Telephone calling is an exhausting activity.
10. Thank your prospect and always let the prospect hang up first.

Whether your pre-approach is made in person, by telephone or letter is usually dictated by the situation (your territory, the nature of your product or service, local business customs and other pertinent factors). However, the theme remains consistent. Many of the words will be identical. The objective is always the same—gaining an appointment.

RECOMMENDED TIMES TO TELEPHONE

Accountants	April 16 to December 31
Attorneys	11 am to 2 pm; 4 to 5 pm
Bankers	Before 10 am; after 3 pm
Builders	Before 8 am; after 5 pm
Business Owners	Between 10:30 am and 3 pm
Clergy	Between Tuesday and Friday
Dentists	Between 8:30 am and 9:30 pm
Druggists	Between 1 pm and 3 pm
Engineers/Chemists	Between 4 pm and 5 pm
Executives	Before 8:30 am; after 4 pm
Homemakers	Midmorning; Midafternoon

Manufacturers	Between 10:30 am and 3 pm
Physicians	Before 9:30 am; after 4:30 pm
Retail Merchants	Between 1 pm and 3 pm
Sales Managers	Afternoons
Salespeople	Weekends
Stockbrokers	Before 10 am; after 3 pm
Professors and Teachers	After 4:30 on weekdays; anytime on weekends or holidays

Working customs in your locality may vary but these are generally effective guidelines.

One other good idea relative to the telephone comes from Jay Lewis, a top producer in Chicago. "I started reaching and surpassing my goals the day I made the decision to install a toll free number," Jay says. "I put in a toll free line at a cost of $40 per month and it increased my earnings $2,000 a month almost immediately."

CRUCIAL FACTORS

Selling successfully is generally based on two fundamental activities:

- Consistently obtaining a sufficient number of qualified prospects
- Contacting these people in a manner which leads to them granting you an appointment

The foundation for selling success lies in getting interviews. The secret of getting good, attentive interviews is in setting appointments. That's why we say the pre-approach, the selling of an appointment, is the crucial factor in selling success.

When carefully planned pre-approaches are made to a sufficient number of prospects each week, enough interviews will be arranged and enough sales produced to reach your personal objectives. It's as simple as that! Honest, intelligent effort is always rewarded—and it all starts by making the contact call correctly!

MAKING CONTACT SUMMED UP

The first rule of selling is, "*Get in.*" If you don't get in, it doesn't matter how good your presentation, how good your product, or how superior the service is that you offer.

You can't score if you're not on the field during the game—and you can't score in selling if you aren't where the prospects are!

You *get in* by planning, by learning as much as you can about your prospect and your prospect's company. You're not merely looking for idle chit-chat items, you're looking for "handles" that might help you motivate the prospect.

Knowledge and an appointment alone won't sell the prospect. You can't score unless you're playing in the right ballpark. You can't sell unless your prospect has the *authority to buy*. If you aren't certain, *ask!* Say, "Pardon me, Mr. Wilson, but are you the person with the authority to buy running boards here at the Antique Refinishers Corporation? Oh, you're *not?* Then perhaps I should see Mr. Johnson instead, so that I won't waste *your* time."

Don't tell your story for the practice—tell it where it'll do some good!

Once you've got the appointment made, be prompt, polite, personable, posture-perfect, poised and persuasive. That's a mouth full of "p's" that add up to "profits!"

A tightrope walker doesn't look down at how long the drop is or how narrow the rope. He or she looks steadily at the goal—the other side. Don't *you* concentrate on the penalties of failure—fasten your mind on the rewards of success. As the old song goes, "You gotta accentuate the positive, eliminate the negative, don't mess with Mr. In-Between!"

If you keep your mind positive, you'll remember that most people are nice—just like you. It may just take them a few minutes to show it.

Learn how to make the telephone work for you. Make a well-written, well-rehearsed telephone presentation part of your success story.

Finally, learn the best times to call. However, a call at almost *any* time is better than no call at all. After all, remember:

> **You can't collect a commission until you make a sale. You can't make the sale until you've written up the order. You can't write up the order until you get an interview. And you can't have an interview if you don't *get in!***

MAKING CONTACT REMINDERS

- Sales are won at the point of contact.
- The sale of your product or service is always a series of sales.
- The purpose of your pre-approach is to sell an appointment.

- One of the advantages of using the telephone is that it encourages brevity.
- A disadvantage of the telephone is that it appeals to one sense only.
- When calling, introduce yourself and your company, and state your purpose quickly.
- Clarity of speech, sincerity and courtesy are essential to your success on the telephone.
- As you plan your pre-approach, you want to gain insights on how you can best establish a good relationship.
- Also, you want to learn as much as possible about the prospect's buying habits.
- Secure an introduction whenever possible. It builds credibility.
- "Taking the pledge" assures you of speaking conversationally.
- Be prompt for the appointment.
- Make the object of your call clear immediately.
- Don't compliment unless it is believable.
- The prospect can be expected to act "abnormally" during the early minutes.
- Stay enthusiastic; it's contagious.
- On the initial contact, you are not trying to sell a solution.
- You get the prospect's favorable attention when you promise a benefit, offer a service and/or appeal to curiosity.
- Be certain the prospect always recognizes that what you have to say is important.

CHAPTER 5

PROBING: HOW TO GAIN POSITIVE INTEREST IN YOUR PRODUCT

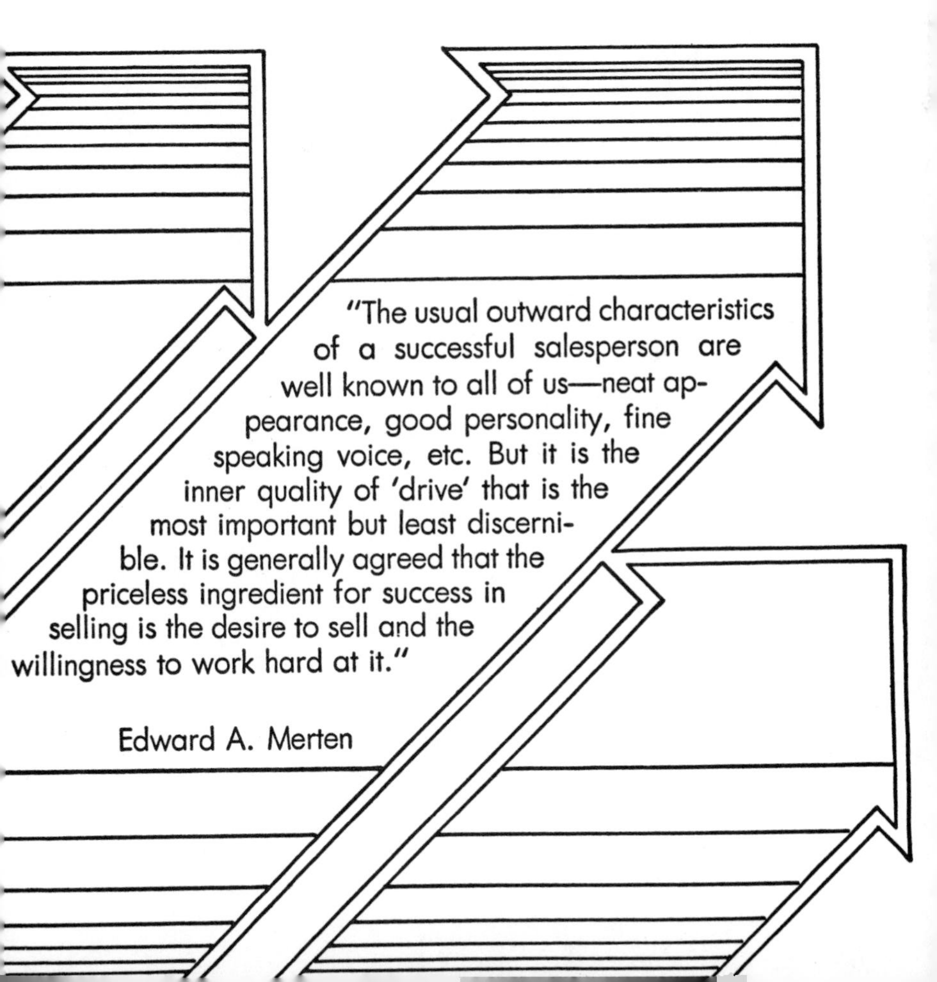

"The usual outward characteristics of a successful salesperson are well known to all of us—neat appearance, good personality, fine speaking voice, etc. But it is the inner quality of 'drive' that is the most important but least discernible. It is generally agreed that the priceless ingredient for success in selling is the desire to sell and the willingness to work hard at it."

Edward A. Merten

THE APPROACH AND ITS OBJECTIVES

Selling is leading your prospect to make certain decisions, one decision at a time. A most important decision has already been made—the decision to grant you an appointment. The prospect has made that decision; you have made the first in a series of sales you'll have to make before you're ready to write up the order.

The *approach* is the name given to the second stage of the selling process, presumably because it is the first actual meeting between you and your prospect. The approach has two chief objectives:

- To make a favorable impression upon the prospect and secure favorable attention
- To gain positive interest in the product or service you came to talk about

During the approach, build an atmosphere of trust so that your prospect will be open to your ideas. Get your prospect to listen. Condition the prospect to logically consider your service, your product and your recommendation.

PROBING—ITS OBJECTIVES

Robert Hutchins, when Chancellor at the University of Chicago, said, "One of the biggest things you get out of a college education is a questioning attitude, a habit of developing and weighing evidence—a scientific approach." The objective of probing is to assist the prospect in making two important decisions:

- To recognize a need
- To become interested in evaluating a possible solution

The best way to get your prospect to think and recognize a need is to ask questions—*relevant* questions. In many cases, it's the only way you will get the prospect to think.

People do not buy something unless they feel it is in their interest and benefit to do so. The "interest" may be on the part of themselves, their family, their company, their charity or their community. The point to remember is that probing questions provide you with pertinent information.

One of the surest ways to increase your selling effectiveness is to learn more about what your prospects want. Strategic questions develop this kind of information.

PROBING—ITS ADVANTAGES

There are a number of things you gain by developing a questioning strategy:

- It helps your prospect discover a need.
- It helps you avoid talking too much.
- It helps avoid arguments.

- It helps crystallize the prospect's thinking—the idea becomes his or hers.
- It helps give your prospect a feeling of importance when you show respect for his or her opinions; he or she is more likely to respect your opinions and recommendations.

KNOW WHERE THE SALE IS MADE

A sale is not made in your mind or over the counter, but in the mind of your prospect. Every word, every question, every gesture you make during the first face-to-face meeting should have only one objective: assisting the prospect in discovering a need.

This is merely another way of saying you must cultivate the habit of viewing yourself and your acts through the eyes of your prospect. This habit makes you a more agreeable person and more highly regarded as a friend. It assures you of making more sales.

LEARNING IS LISTENING

Learning about your prospect and his or her needs is largely a listening process. *Learn to listen. Listen to learn.*

Listening wins favorable attention. It helps you focus on the needs of your prospect as revealed in the answers to your questions.

Effective listening habits include the following:

- *Stop talking*—You can't listen if you're talking.
- *Show your interest*—Look and act interested.

- *Empathize*—Put yourself in your prospect's shoes.
- *Put the prospect at ease*—Help the prospect find it easy to answer your questions.
- *Never interrupt*—Let your prospect interrupt you, but never interrupt the prospect or complete his or her sentences.

It's imperative for you to show your prospect that you are genuinely interested in his or her situation. You assist the prospect in recognizing a need and in evaluating a possible solution for that need. The key, of course, to the prospect making these two decisions in your favor lies in the quality of your probing and listening.

> ***"Prospects don't care how much you know—they want to know how much you care."***

Shirley Meyer is a national sales leader for the Metropolitan Life Insurance Company at Eugene, Oregon. Shirley is a student and a listener. Shirley's market is the logging industry. "I started by talking to the log truck drivers. I gathered all the information about them I could, including their problems. I *researched* all of their government, group and personal insurance. I rode in a log truck to the loading ramps—up and down the mountains on old logging roads. I studied to know everything possible about their business and personal insurance needs. I found out where they spent their money, how they spent it and why. Because I learned everything about their business, I gained their confidence and built an important rapport. *I listened to them—in turn they listened to me and acted on my recommendations.*"

Shirley was a participant in one of our Portland Sales

Clinics. She told the salespeople in attendance, "What it comes down to and what I truly believe is that *it is not what you know about your business that makes the sale, it is what you know about the prospect's business!*"

"Good listeners generally make more sales than good talkers."

FINDING THE FACTS

The right questions to ask depend upon the product or service you sell.

You will want to ask yourself what kind of information you must develop to prepare for your presentation.

- What specific need is recognized?
- To what degree is price a factor?
- What is the potential volume?
- Who is the decision-maker?
- What is the buying philosophy?
- How is the competition rated?

Ask confidence-building questions. These open your prospect's mind to possible needs. Examples would be, "Did you know more than 5,000 companies now use this service?" or, "Did you know we now provide an international service?"

Ask questions that will help you later key your presentation to your prospect's specific needs. You'll find that you'll get more favorable attention.

Ask questions that emphasize the benefits you offer. This technique can be learned easily. Instead of generalizing by saying, "We can bring you more profit," emphasize the specific benefits you offer. Then sum them up by saying, "As you can see, the bottom line means more profit for you."

Learn to put benefits in the form of questions. For example, few prospects would fail to show interest if you asked, "Would you be interested if we could show you how to improve your safety record and reduce your insurance costs?"

Ask questions that encourage your prospect to take an active part in the interview. Many times it's easier and more effective to gain understanding through the prospect's eyes and hands. "Can you *feel* the difference?" "Can you *see* our superior workmanship?" "*Taste* it—don't you agree it's delicious?"

Master the questioning technique to assist prospects in making the decision to study your proposition.

DISCOVER THE DOMINANT BUYING MOTIVE

Behind every purchase is a buying motive. You can test the validity of this claim from your own experience as a buyer. What caused you to buy your last car? Last TV? Last book? Last dress or suit? Perhaps you had several reasons or motives for each purchase—but *one* was the *dominant* motive, wasn't it?

There are six basic motives which move your prospect to action:

- Desire for money gain (profit)
- Fear of loss (security)
- Pride of ownership (status)
- Interest in doing it easier (efficiency)

- Desire for excitement (pleasure)
- Interest in self-improvement (effectiveness)

Buying motives vary among individuals and products. Some of them are fairly obvious. For example, a merchant who buys a new line of merchandise is motivated by the desire for profit. The individual who buys an accident policy is motivated by fear of losing security. A young person who buys a new sports car may *say* that he or she is buying it because it's needed. Actually, it is probably his or her vanity or pride of ownership at work.

So it is with everything that is bought from you. You appeal to the right motive or motives. As the old saying goes, "Everyone has two reasons for doing something—the *real reason* and one that sounds good." You need to discover the *real* reason behind each potential purchase.

Speaking of dominant buying motives, Baltasar Gracian wrote in his book *The Art of Worldly Wisdom,* published in 1653, "First guess a man's ruling passion, appeal to it by word, set it in motion by temptation, and you will infallibly give checkmate to his freedom of will. Find out each man's thumbscrew. You must know where to get at anyone. All men are idolaters; some of fame, others of self-interest, most of pleasure. Skill consists in knowing these idols in order to bring them into play. Knowing any man's mainspring of motive well, you have, as it were, the key to his will."

How do you find a prospect's dominant motive? *By asking a lot of questions—and doing a lot of careful listening!* Ask yourself what you would do and how you would react if you were the prospect. Probe well enough and long enough to get inside the prospect's mind with your questions.

When you decide on the main buying motive, be sure to record it. Don't overlook secondary or minor motives. These six forces are what motivate prospects to buy. Learn to discover the motive most likely to move each prospect to buy. Throughout your presentation, learn to concentrate on the key motive, or motives, much as a boxer concentrates on landing the perfect jab.

Each of us could give you thousands of examples of how probing on our parts enabled us to read the prospects' minds and make the sale. But probably you'll remember this example best:

It is the Superbowl game of 1978, the Dallas Cowboys versus the Denver Broncos. Each team has "probed" the other well—studied their game films, learning not only their plays, but their tendencies. From this probing, Roger has learned that Bernard Jackson, the Broncos' weak safety, tends to watch the quarterback's eyes and fade where he's looking.

The Cowboys set up a play to go to the fullback on the right side. Roger fades back to pass and looks to the right. Bernard Jackson begins running in that direction. But Roger had told Butch Johnson that instead of running end route he should go ahead and run post, and he gets behind Bernard Jackson. Roger lays the pass over Jackson's head and Johnson catches it—touchdown!

You'll score time after time if you take the time to study your prospect's "game plan" and tendencies!

PROBING SUMMED UP

The purpose of probing is to find out enough about your prospect and your prospect's situation to enable you to make intelligent recommendations. You are searching for facts and feelings that will be helpful to you in making a sale.

Your primary objective is to assist your prospect in making two important decisions:

- To recognize a need
- To become interested in evaluating a solution

When you ask questions, you develop additional facts and feelings such as:

- Understanding the prospect better as a person
- Understanding the prospect's needs as they're related to your product or service
- Understanding why it is important for the prospect to meet these needs
- Strengthening your relationship with the prospect
- Creating a more professional image
- Determining the prospect's buying power
- Determining whether the prospect is the decision-maker
- Establishing or reinforcing the prospect's decision to move forward
- Triggering in the prospect's mind mental images of what it would be like to solve the problem
- Determining the prospect's dominant buying motive

Many a prospect, thoroughly persuaded that he or she has a need, still does not buy. They are persuaded, but not convinced.

In the next chapter, you will discover presentation techniques that can bring about a state of mind that will condition your prospects for the close.

PROBING REMINDERS

- A chief objective of your approach is to make a favorable impression.
- During the approach, build an atmosphere of trust.
- Assist the prospect in recognizing a need.
- Arouse the prospect's interest in evaluating a possible solution.
- The sale must always be made in the mind of the prospect.
- Learn to listen and listen to learn.
- An important listening habit to cultivate is to never interrupt.
- Good listeners make more sales than good talkers.
- Ask questions that emphasize the benefits you can offer.
- Discover the dominant buying motive.
- Determine who the decision-maker is.
- Work hard to strengthen your relationship with each prospect.

CHAPTER 6

PRESENTATIONS THAT HELP THE PROSPECT BUY WITH CONFIDENCE

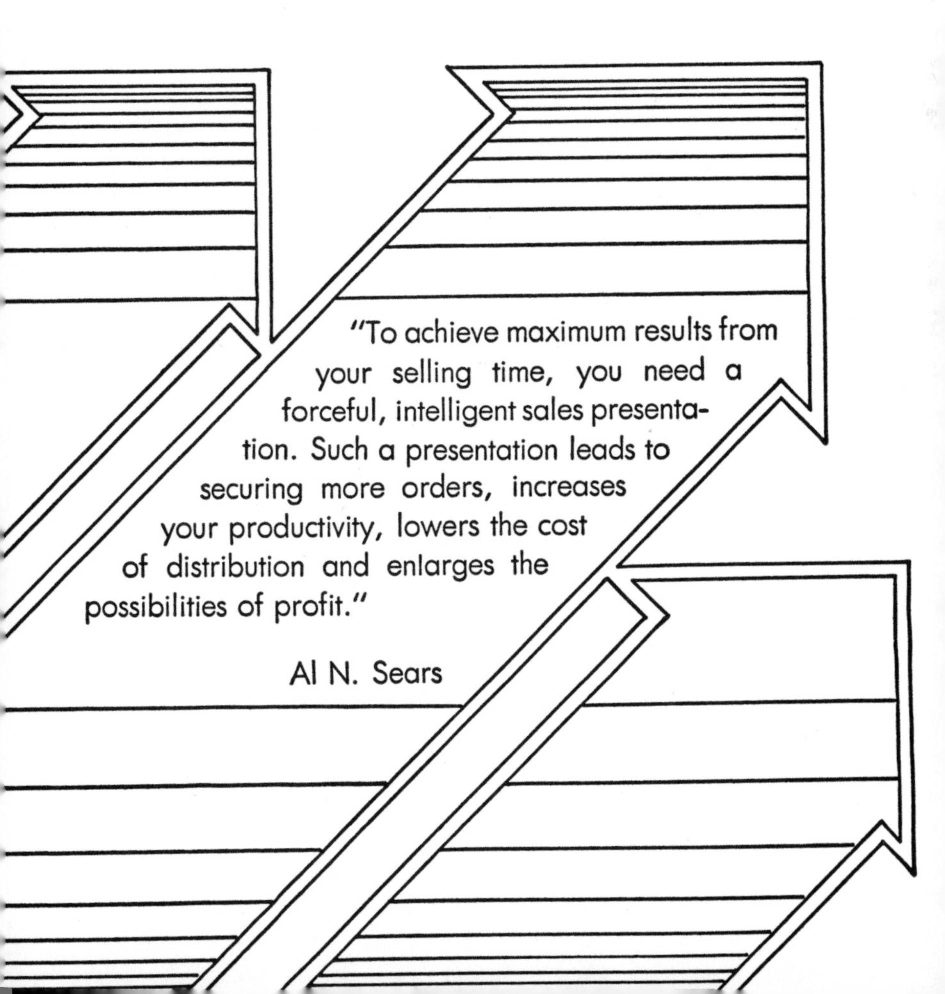

WHAT A GOOD PRESENTATION MUST DO

Many salespeople owe their six-figure incomes to the fact that they prepare and present their sales talks with maximum impact. *Your presentation must be believed, agreed with and acted upon. It must be designed from the buyer's point of view.* In other words, it must give the kind of information your prospect wants and needs to have before he or she is willing to buy.

Knowing how to develop and deliver a convincing presentation is one of the surest and quickest ways for you to reach the top in selling.

> ***"Every successful sales interview begins with a well-planned presentation."***

FOUR ESSENTIALS OF A GOOD PRESENTATION

Your company may have given you a prepared sales script and insisted that you learn to give it verbatim.

At the other extreme, there are firms that leave it up to you to plan and develop your own sales talk.

Whatever the practice of your company, it is necessary for you to thoroughly understand the four essentials of a result-producing presentation. No matter what your presentation is designed to sell, it must meet these four requirements if you are to sell successfully.

- It must capture the prospect's instant and undivided attention.
- It must arouse interest by describing buyer benefits and their advantages to the prospect.
- It must create desire by winning the prospect's confidence.
- It must motivate the prospect to take action *now*.

HOW TO GAIN INSTANT ATTENTION

The first requirement is unquestionably the most important. Get instant and undivided attention. Unless your prospect hears what you say, you cannot expect to get satisfactory results, no matter how well you know your lines. Your presentation, right away, must gain attention. It's not always easy to gain attention. Your prospects are not exactly waiting with bated breath for you to make your presentation. To get and hold attention, you must earn it.

How do you do it? There are two ways. One is to appeal to the senses—sight, touch, taste, hearing and smell. "*See* the superior workmanship." "You can *feel* the difference." "*Taste* it, it's delicious!" The second way to capture attention is to say or do something that relates the prospect's needs to your product or service. "We can show you how to have a better safety record and reduce your insurance rates as much as 20 percent." "We can reduce costly turnover the very first year." "Your overhead expenses will be cut in half—immediately!" *Remember, there are two reliable ways to gain attention:*

- Get the prospect into the act.
- Dramatize the value of the product or service.

In dealing with one or more people who make buying decisions, we have found the use of visuals in the form of original and creatively prepared transparencies or 35 millimeter slides to be very effective.

Here's what Bill Harmelin, a master salesman in New York City, has to say about this type of aid: "In talking to prospects without the use of these aids, frequently they will accept telephone calls or permit other interruptions; whereas my experience has been that one has their undivided attention when using transparencies or slides. I have very successful businesspeople listen for as long as 3½ hours uninterrupted. The slides or transparencies have a kind of hypnotic effect which is not present without such aids."

It is impossible to know how many sales we lose because we cannot hold the prospect's attention.

Bill Harmelin goes ahead to say: "When one uses visuals of the type described above, prospects are willing to spend more time with the salesperson and are less inclined to permit anything to interrupt the discussion. In one instance, a business prospect's secretary came in to say, 'The man with whom you have your next appointment is here.' The businessman said, 'Let him wait!' Such things never happened to me before I started to use transparencies and/or slides."

Bill concludes: "My investment in the equipment, which is available at any audiovisual supply house, came to about $600. It paid for itself after the first sale. The equipment consists of a portable overhead projector, which can be plugged into any outlet, and a transparency maker which is easy to use. There's no need to carry a screen because the projector can show clear images on any light wall."

HOW TO AROUSE INTEREST

Converting attention to favorable interest comes next. The big question you must always answer in your presentation is, "What's in this for me?" Benefits are what prospects buy. You must know which benefits will get the greatest response from your prospect.

You must ask yourself, "What is it this prospect wants or needs that is best satisfied from my proposition? What are the owner benefits he or she will buy?"

There are two types of benefits—plus benefits and minus benefits. The plus benefits are those your prospect gains through buying financial, physical, mental, social, emotional or spiritual improvements. The minus benefits are the risks or losses he or she avoids by buying from you, such as financial loss, loss of health, or loss of prestige.

You arouse interest by focusing on the owner benefits that appeal to your prospect and that he or she will buy.

"Your presentation produces orders when it is built around buyer benefits."

HOW TO CREATE DESIRE

The sale is seldom closed unless your prospect has a degree of confidence in your proposition. This confidence may depend upon your product or service, your company or you.

The colorful, capable Ralph Carlisle of Lexington, Kentucky, said to us, "One statement in a sales presentation which your prospect finds reason to doubt is like a single drop of ink in a glass of water—it colors the entire contents!"

The winning of the prospect's confidence is a vital part of your presentation. One reason: the prospect has been taught, perhaps by experience, that you can't believe everything you hear, especially when you hear it from someone who is selling.

Roger began selling shortly after he joined the Dallas Cowboy football team in 1969. In the early seasons, he was relatively unknown so that the name didn't help him get interviews. On the other hand, once the prospect found out he was a professional football player this sometimes worked against him. The buyer thought, "What can *he* know? He's really just an off-season football player." This meant that Roger had to work extra hard to win each buyer's confidence!

You, too, have to win each buyer's confidence. Frankly, the *better* the offer, the more skeptical they'll be! In order to win their confidence you must be mindful of two things:

- *First, the winning of the buyer's confidence is of no avail unless he or she has been made to want your product or service first.* Your prospect may be convinced that your product is the finest of its kind, but still not buy until and unless he or she has been made to see the need for the product and to want it. It is the *want* that makes people buy. A person may need a computer and yet may not want it because he or she doesn't know what it will do for the business. That person will not buy until he or she wants it, even though the need may have existed for some time. On the other hand, how often have you watched people buy something they do not actually need, just because they wanted it? *Your job is to arouse a sense of want before you spend too much time gaining confidence.*

- *Second, spend only as much time as is needed in the winning of confidence.* Too many facts, figures, charts and proofs of various kinds may bore a busy prospect and a bored prospect begins to lose interest.

"The best way to convince a buyer is to make it his or her idea."

HOW TO GAIN THE BUYER'S CONFIDENCE

Paul Hutsey of Pittsburg, Kansas, says the key thing to develop today in sales is not salesmanship but "buymanship." We believe Paul is exactly right. Today, you must learn to function as an assistant buyer. You must demonstrate your knowledge of "buymanship" skills.

You apply "buymanship" skills in the following ways:

- *Use of testimonials.* This is based on the principle that a satisfied customer is your best single advertisement.

  In advertising, testimonials are used to gain attention rather than create desire. We listen to well-known personalities like Roger on television as they promote certain products and services. In selling, you introduce the testimonial for the purpose of inspiring confidence. Your testimony will carry more weight when the individual is known to the prospect and is known to be reliable.

Testimonials in a sales presentation are best used when selling to a relatively inexperienced prospect. He or she relies heavily on the experience of others. Often, experienced buyers are not all that impressed with testimonials. They feel competent to make their own choices.

- *Speak the prospect's language.* Being able to speak the language of your prospect is one of the best ways to gain his or her confidence. The natural tendency is to speak in the jargon of your particular industry—avoid that—speak the *prospect's* language.

  Remember the "KISS" principle—Keep It Simple, Stupid!—don't try to impress a prospect with your command of your industry's jargon or the result of your latest reading of the dictionary.

- *Research results and evidence.* This method includes test results, reports from authorities and/or product sample approval by a well-known governing body. The bigger the name of the person or organization developing the evidence, the more believable the proof.
- *Guarantee.* This is a convincing sales aid, particularly when selling a new product. It is always a big advantage when you can tell your prospect that what you are selling is so good it will be guaranteed.
- *Company reputation.* This talking point carries a lot of strength when your firm has earned a reputation

for quality products and superior service. Sales reps for such companies need to spend little time convincing their prospects that their product claims are true.

"Produce in your prospect the confidence to buy."

HOW TO MOTIVATE TO ACTION

This is the aim of every presentation you make. The single most important attitude for you to carry into this final step is this one:

"I will take the initiative and assist my prospect in making the buying decision. The prospect will seldom ever close the sale. *I* must supply the motivation."

It is vital for you to have a well-organized procedure for providing the motivation on the part of your prospect to act on your proposition *now.*

Professional selling dictates that you start the motivation by summarizing the key buyer benefits. Remind your prospect of the reasons he or she should act now. Frequently, the prospect forgets some of the reasons for buying. Your summation recalls to the prospect's mind the important things that dictate acceptance of your proposition. *Remember, one of the best ways to convert desire into action is to present the key buyer benefits in rapid-fire summation.*

It's like the elderly minister who explained that the secret of his powerful sermons was this: "First, I tell them what I'm going to tell them. Second, I tell them.

Third, I quickly tell them what I told them." Don't rely on the prospects to remember all the key points of the presentation—act as assistant buyer and remind them!

Next, ask for any questions the prospect wants answered. Assuming you have answered your prospect's questions, you should then move to questions of your own. Your strategic questions should assist the buyer in making minor decisions in favor of your proposition. These minor decisions should direct the buyer to make the important decision to buy from you now.

We like a little children's book by Dr. Seuss called *Green Eggs and Ham.* In this book, a wacky character is trying to get someone to try green eggs and ham. Obviously, the prospect isn't the least bit interested, but the salesman is persistent and begins asking questions like, "Would you like them *here* or *there*? Would you like them in a house? Would you like them with a mouse?" You might want to read this little book because in the end persistence pays off and the prospect not only tries the product but loves the product. More than that, he *appreciates* the salesman's taking time to act as assistant buyer. He is sincerely thankful.

We mention this because, after you have done all of the rest, it is now time to *ask for the order.*

"Assume the prospect is going to buy from you **now."**

Many buyers say it is amazing how many sales reps seem unable to bring themselves to ask for the order. Keep constantly in mind that you may have to ask the prospect for the order several times before the order is obtained.

The important thing is having an established strategy—a strategy that enables you to effectively function as an assistant buyer in motivating prospects to action; a strategy you employ with any type of prospect; a strategy you use with confidence because you know it will be result-producing.

PRESENTATION POINTERS

The stronger your presentation, the more sales you'll make. *An effective presentation is always a planned presentation.* It is planned and developed to fit your particular product or service and your prospects.

Review these presentation pointers often:

- *Personalize your presentation.* Make it tailor-made. You will have a much more receptive listener.
- *Review the minutes.* Before you begin your presentation, review everything that has been previously discussed. Tell the prospect what you intend to show.
- *Plan to get your prospect involved.* The best presentations are those that give the prospect an active part. You can always manage to give your prospect an active role, no matter what you sell.
- *Slant your presentation to your prospect's self-interest.* Your presentation produces orders when it is built around buyer benefits. Jim Beveridge, a well-known marketing consultant for the defense industry, says, "Everyone feels a little bit confused, a little bit incompetent and a little bit insecure. Your presentation, while never stating these things, should show the prospect how purchasing your product or service will make them feel less con-

fused, less incompetent and less insecure. It's natural someone would want a product or service like that."

- *Choose impact words.* Words and expressions are the raw materials out of which you construct your sales presentation. Some can trigger emotion. They cause immediate action. Some words almost automatically have impact, no matter how they are used.

  As a professional, you should become a student of words. No matter what product you wish to describe, there are image-making words that will stir your prospect's imagination. Discover these words. Put them into sentences that will show them off to their best advantage.

  Our study of words tells us your list of impact words should include the following:

Let's	Discovery	Wealth
Guaranteed	Proven	Please
Flexible	Secure	You
Why	Scientific	Safety
Must	Time-Saving	Positive
Help	Economical	Health
Loss	Quality	Value
Advantage	Courtesy	Popular
Easy	Status	Excel
Wise People	Up-to-Date	Sympathy
Truth	Tested	Necessary
Fitness	Tasteful	Growth
Death	Thank You	Recommended
Life	Home	Durable
Profit	Beauty	Modern

  How many of these words can you tie to the sale of your product?

In addition, use "agreement," not "contract." Use "invest," not "buy." Use "arrange," not "pay." It may sound strange, but it *is* true that certain words have positive power—and other words have negative power.

Certain words and phrases can have a negative effect on your prospects. You will want to eliminate these from your selling vocabulary. Always avoid profanity and slang even if used by your prospect. "Do you understand?" and "Do you follow me?" are expressions to be eliminated. Prospects do not appreciate the implication that they are incapable of following your line of thought. Stay away from the word "obviously"—it might not be so obvious to the prospect. The word "deal" has a negative connotation with most prospects (although it is acceptable in selling real estate). Most prospects today are offended by the salesperson who starts sentences with "honestly" or "truthfully" or "believe me." Also, you will want to regularly check your selling style to eliminate distractors such as "you know?" and "Do you see what I mean?" These can become habit forming and will distract from even the most persuasive sales talk.

- *Gain understanding*. The confused prospect seldom buys. Keep it simple. Your aim is to show the prospect what your product can do for him or her. Tell the prospect what it does—not what it is. You sell the product of your product.

  The great real estate salesman, Hank Dickerson, once told us, "If you can't write your idea on the back of my calling card, you don't have a clear idea of what you are selling."

- *Stop—look—listen*. Fish for feedback. Give your prospect many chances to express himself or herself. This is your opportunity to learn how the prospect reacts to your presentation.

"TALK LESS– DEMONSTRATE MORE"

Let the prospect interrupt you, but never interrupt the prospect. Know who you are selling. Prospects react and buy differently. When interrupted, start all over again. Should you be interrupted by another individual, make the appropriate introductions. Quickly determine the interest of the new party. If it is important to do so, do not hesitate to terminate the interview and reschedule. In all likelihood, this will strengthen your case by placing the prospect under further obligation. However, if you decide to continue, it is imperative that you start all over again. Go back to the beginning and bring everyone up to the same point.

- *Achieve credibility*. Bring on your evidence and testimonials.
- *Help your prospect sell himself or herself.* The best way to convince the buyer is to make it his or her idea.
- *Use emotion and logic*. The strongest appeals are to the emotions rather than to the mind. However, the ideal presentation is a composite of appeals to the head as well as to the heart. Almost every prospect wants to be, or at least appears to be, rational in arriving at the decision to give you the order.
- *Summarize strategically*. Remind your prospect of the reasons he or she should buy now.
- *Be an assistant buyer*. Build the trust level and

then assist the prospect in taking action on your tailor-made proposition.

- *Ask the prospect to buy.* Be prepared to ask more than once.
- *Powerful presentation expressions to use.*
    - "I would appreciate *your courtesy* in giving me the time to explain our service."
    - "I want to *make certain I understand* how you feel."
    - *"May I ask* why you feel that way?"
    - "I would like very much for you to buy from me and my company. We're in a position to do a good job for you."
    - *"In addition to that,* is there any other reason for not moving forward on this matter now?"
    - *"Let's* move forward on this basis."
    - "Now here is what *I would like to do."*
    - "I would like very much for you to *help me."*

Learn to use these expressions in your presentations. They are confidence-builders and resistance-chasers! They will boost your effectiveness greatly.

ONLY THE BEST IS GOOD ENOUGH

The motto of a prominent Chicago advertising agency reads, "Where only the best is good enough." What a motto this would be for you to "carry into" each presentation you make. Why not adopt it as yours? Display it in your office. Carry it with you in your wallet. Weave it into the texture of everything you do and your presentation is sure to become what you want it to be—a masterpiece.

There is an indescribable superiority added to the character and fiber of the salesperson who consciously puts the trademark of quality on his or her presentation. The mental and moral effect of doing things accurately, painstakingly and thoroughly can hardly be estimated because the processes are so gradual, so subtle. Every time you obey the inward law of doing right you hear an inward approval. On the contrary, every half-done, careless, slipshod job that goes out of your hands leaves its trace of demoralization behind and excellence becomes impossible. You will like yourself much better when you have the approval of your conscience.

There is no other advertisement for the professional salesperson like a good reputation. Many of America's greatest manufacturers have regarded their reputation as their most precious possession, and under no circumstances would they allow their names to be put on an imperfect article. When Ben Hogan was trying to create a golf equipment manufacturing company back in 1953, he lovingly did each operation by himself, trying to make a set of golf clubs as near perfect as he could make them. In spite of advice from friends to go ahead and put a product Ben felt was inferior on the market, he destroyed $150,000 worth of golf clubs before he perfected his operation enough to put his *reputation* on each club!

Never allow *your* name to appear in connection with an imperfect article and success is yours. Large sums of money are often paid for the use of a name because of its reputation for integrity, reliability and excellence. Your presentations are opportunities to build this sort of a reputation.

Your Life magazine said this when talking about Walter Hoving, the retired president of Lord and Taylor and the youngest department store president in New York City: "Walter Hoving took the trouble to know many hundred times as much about his product as he would ever use in a sales talk. Perhaps that is one reason why he became top man at Bonwit Teller's and Tiffany's in New York City." Take *time* to know your product.

There is nothing like being in love with excellence. No other characteristic makes such a strong, lasting impression upon prospects. When it comes to your sales presentation, never be satisfied with "pretty good" or "that's going to be O.K., I think." Accept nothing but your best every time. Someone is watching. Someone will notice . . . and that someone may become a valuable customer.

In Italy during the early part of the eighteenth century, Stradivari put his stamp of excellence on the violins he "made for eternity." His workmanship was superior. Not one of his violins was ever known to break. Stradivari did not need any patent on his violins because no other violin maker would pay his price for excellence. Every Stradivarius in existence is still worth thousands of dollars.

In selling, you can make your own "Stradivarius." Every sales presentation can bear your personal trade-mark of excellence. Never has the demand been stronger, the supply shorter or the rewards greater!

PRESENTING SUMMED UP

If your presentation is to be believed, agreed with and acted upon, it must be designed and presented from the buyer's point of view. The *only* benefits the buyer is interested in are benefits to him or her. To be successful you must capture your prospect's instant attention, arouse his or her interest by describing benefits, create desire through winning confidence, and motivate the buyer to take action *now*.

You gain attention by appealing to the senses or by relating your product to your prospect's needs.

You arouse interest by answering your prospect's unasked question, "What's in it for me?" You answer this by showing plus and/or minus benefits.

You create desire by making the prospect *want* your service or product. You do this by obtaining the prospect's confidence, through testimonials, by knowing your product and your prospect's need, by keeping your presentation simple, and through research, guarantees and company reputation.

You motivate to action by first summing up your major points. You then ask if the prospect has any questions and answer them. You then ask *your* questions, questions that fit in with your strategy to take the prospect step by step to the conclusion you want him or her to reach.

All of this works best, of course, when you *personalize* your presentation, use positive words and phrases —and avoid negative words and phrases.

The presentation is the climax of a lot of work on a salesperson's part. As Roger says, "The presentation is where it all comes together—probing, asking for the interview, researching. In football, the presentation is the Sunday afternoon game. A lot of unspectacular preparation has gone into this presentation but, once you're out there, everything is based on the game plan you agreed on beforehand. You learn about the other team while you concentrate on the basics of football. You go into the game with a good feeling about what you're going to do and what they're going to do.

"Sometimes, when you get in a game, however, you find that unusual opportunities open up. Then you have to be flexible enough to move to take advantage of those opportunities.

"In selling, it's the same way. You should know the buyer you're playing against and know his or her team. You should have a well thought-out game plan based on basic salesmanship. But, once you're in the 'game' or presentation, you've got to be able to shift with the prospect. You may have decided beforehand that this buyer needs a formal presentation and, once you're in, find that they would really prefer an informal presentation. You still follow your basic game plan, but you change the emphasis a bit to keep the buyer comfortable.

"Then, remember that only the best is good enough. Do your best each time you represent your company. Play your best each time you're on the field. The Cowboys have to know all the plays in the playbook . . . all the signals. You should know all about your product or service and a *lot* about the buyer's company. You should know more than you'll ever use; be able to answer questions frankly and accurately. Of course, if you don't know the answer, *admit* it—never try to 'fake it'—they'll know and lose respect for you."

Make each presentation your "Stradivarius" and you'll be a success!

PRESENTING REMINDERS

- Your presentation must be believed, agreed with and acted upon.
- One way to gain the prospect's attention is to dramatize the product value.

- Your presentation produces orders when it is built around buyer benefits.
- The sale is seldom closed unless your prospect has a degree of confidence in your proposition.
- Speak the prospect's language. It's a sure way to build confidence.
- In motivating the prospect to take action and give you the order, you must take the initiative.
- The important thing in getting orders is to have an established strategy you can use with confidence.
- Personalize your presentation.
- Slant your presentation to your prospect's self-interests.
- Choose impact words with motivation strength.
- You sell the product of your product.
- Be willing to let the prospect interrupt you.
- Achieve credibility. Bring on your evidence and testimonials.
- The ideal presentation uses both emotion and logic.
- Be an assistant buyer who stays in front of decision-makers with a strategy you believe in.

CHAPTER 7

STRATEGIES FOR CONTROLLING OBJECTIONS AND CONVERTING THEM INTO SALES

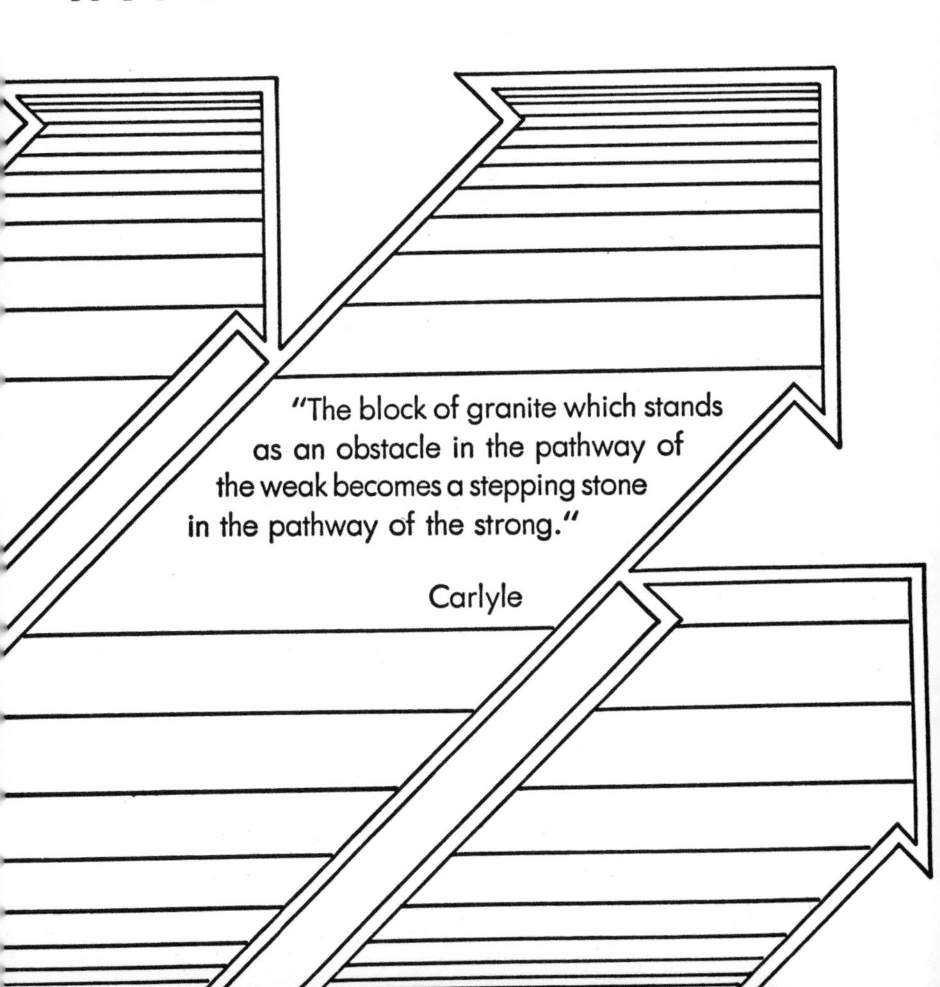

"The block of granite which stands as an obstacle in the pathway of the weak becomes a stepping stone in the pathway of the strong."

Carlyle

HOW YOU STAY IN CONTROL

If you want to stay in control throughout the presentation, *write your presentation out before the appointment.* The advantage of writing out and using a standardized presentation is that it gives you complete control, no matter what your prospect says or does. Many things can and often do happen during the presentation. The prospect can interrupt. The prospect can—and generally will—interject resistances or objections. You must learn to handle these.

Your sales presentation must allow for resistances, objections and interruptions. Expect them. Prepare to meet them even before they occur. You do this by planning and writing out your presentation in advance. Knowing all that you must say and do in advance will enable you to:

- Present your facts clearly so they will be understood.
- Include the relevant points that you believe your prospect will want to know.
- Include answers to common objections you feel may be raised.
- Remember where you were in the presentation before the interruption occurred.

ALWAYS ASSERT

Study the great sales leaders in your company or in the country. They assert. These leaders are so charged with conviction that they present their conclusions as ultimate truths. They speak as individuals having authority. *Never weaken your conclusions by suggesting a doubt.* Your job is to persuade, and effective persuaders always assert. This is the principal reason they are able to overcome objections before they come up.

OUR ATTITUDE TOWARD OBJECTIONS

How should you regard objections? The inexperienced sales rep often considers an objection as a refusal to buy. To this person, an objection is viewed as a major obstacle to making the sale. *The prepared professional welcomes the objection. He or she knows it can help along the sale and not hurt it. The toughest prospect to sell isn't the one who objects but the one who shows no interest at all.* If a prospect sits in stony silence it's hard to tell where you stand. Faced with a prospect like this, you'd be praying that he or she would give you a clue. An objection is a clue to the prospect's thought processes. The antithesis of this is the prospect who *agrees* with everything you say. He or she usually doesn't buy either—because you don't know what he or she is really thinking. Again, an objection gives you a "handle," an insight.

As a skilled salesperson, objections give you the best clues to your client's reactions. Early in your sales presentation you fish for feedback to determine what the prospect's thoughts are about the points being presented. As your prospect learns more from your presentation, he or she then begins to interject objections. These objections serve as guides. Your attitude should be to welcome and expect them.

CLASSIFYING THE OBJECTION

To effectively handle an objection, you must understand what kind of objection it is. Objections fall into two general categories:

- Genuine objections
- Insincere objections

Genuine objections can be answered. Insincere objections cannot. One of the first things that will set you apart as a professional salesperson is learning to distinguish between the genuine objection and the fake.

What are the characteristics of these two kinds of objections? The insincere objection generally has the characteristic of being illogical. It is expressed through alibis, excuses or stalls. The prospect gives fictitious reasons to hide the real, genuine objection.

The genuine objection has the characteristic of truthfulness. Here the prospect feels there is a valid reason for not buying at this time. This is the easiest kind of objection to handle. In fact, it is the *only* kind of objection you *can* handle.

WHY DO PROSPECTS OBJECT?

When a prospect objects, he or she is saying, "I'm not sold . . . yet." They generally object for three reasons:

- *There is something not understood.* Your presentation has not gained understanding. You must do a better job of stating your product or service in relation to the client's need or want.
- *There is something the prospect doesn't believe.* Your presentation has not yet achieved credibility. You haven't produced enough evidence to convince the prospect of the value and owner benefits.
- *There is something the prospect is trying to cover up.* When you sense this, you must try to be considerate and build confidence.

WHEN TO ANSWER

In determining when to answer an objection, you must consider whether it is genuine or insincere and why it has surfaced. You can handle an objection before it comes up if you anticipate it. This gets easier as your experience grows. Like an actor in a long-running play, you soon not only know all of *your* lines but the lines of all of the other actors and actresses as well! Experience will teach you that there are only so many objections to your particular product or service and soon you will have heard them all. As soon as you've heard them, of course, you've also learned how to deal with them. As you've learned how to deal with them, you've learned how to anticipate them.

ANTICIPATE OBJECTIONS

Suppose, for instance, you've found a common objection to your product is that the cost is far below competition. You can anticipate that and bring out in your presentation something like, "I've had dozens of people ask me, 'How can you sell it so reasonably?' And the answer is really quite simple. Our company *invented* this process and, consequently, we've been doing it longer than anyone else. Our high volume has enabled us to retail the item for little more than other firms wholesale theirs."

IGNORE OBJECTIONS

Another way to handle an objection is to ignore it. Occasionally, you'll find it best to manage initial resistance by ignoring the response completely. In your initial contact with prospects, their resistance is likely to be high. Most people tend to react abnormally when they are in a buying situation. How many times have you noticed people shopping in a store with the idea of making a purchase? A sales clerk approaches and asks, "May I be of help?" The customer often replies, "No, I'm just looking." Generally, customers do not mean that at all. It's just a vocal pause, a defense mechanism. What they probably mean is, "I haven't lowered my resistance yet. Be patient with me. Let me learn more about what you have to offer."

In his fine book, *Meeting Objections,* Dr. J. A. Stevenson says, "The tendency to raise barriers undoubtedly originates in the same instinct which causes animals to assume a defensive attitude when brought into contact with strange objects or animals, or even familiar objects if they encroach on their domain. This resistance or defensive attitude as displayed by a prospect probably originates in the same instinct which causes a dog to bark if a stranger approaches what he considers his territory. The dog may have no real antipathy for the stranger, or the prospect any actual objection to the proposal. They both raise a sort of a barrier, however, because they are afraid of the disturbance which this unfamiliar idea or strange person may cause."

The "I don't want it/I don't need it/I can't afford it!" which so often greet you are, in reality, more often mere "barks" on the part of the prospect. "Barks," as the old saying goes, "are often worse than their bites."

ASK PERMISSION TO ANSWER THE OBJECTION LATER

One of the strategies successful salespeople have used for years in managing objections is merely to delay them. The strategy is that if you can delay a resistance, you can rob it of some of its strength. You may handle it permanently simply by delaying it. The prospect may become so wrapped up in what you say about your product or service that he or she will forget the resistance. He or she may never mention it again.

ANSWER THE OBJECTION NOW

If you feel the objection is genuine and would hinder the sale if not given a satisfactory answer, you should meet it when the prospect brings it up. To hesitate or evade may cause the objection to magnify in the prospect's mind and block the sale.

MASTER THE SIX-STEP STRATEGY

You must master a definite strategy for handling objections. You must develop an ability to react naturally, with a maximum of poise and effectiveness, whenever an objection appears to block your path.

This ability is one of the critical keys to your selling success. The sense of personal selling power derived from the confidence of having a strategy for handling objections is an invaluable asset.

These six steps should be learned and instinctively followed in any sales situation where there is an objection:

1. Hear it out.
2. Ask the prospect to repeat it.
3. Restate.
4. Isolate.
5. Use an example or story.
6. Stimulate action.

HEARING THE PROSPECT OUT

Don't evade or resent the objection. Never interrupt. Be glad it is being voiced; it shows someone is listening! It shows you've a bit more selling to do before you close, and it shows you in what area that selling must lie.

An automobile tire will gradually go flat once it has a puncture. *In somewhat the same way, your prospect's objection is likely to deflate itself once it is expressed.* When he or she gets it off his or her mind, it loses much of its steam. Listening is the basis for handling objections. How you listen is important. Lean forward. Let your facial expression register an "I'm taking your objection seriously" look.

"Let them complete your sentences, but never complete theirs."

ASKING THE PROSPECT TO REPEAT

Take the objection seriously. Treat it with respect. *Return the ball to the prospect's court.* Often, when you ask the prospects to repeat, they will answer their own objection, or will define it in such a way that it is easier for you to handle.

RESTATING

This says to the prospect that you are listening and have understood what was said. It makes it clear you do not accept the objection as being final. Then, too, it gives you more time to think out your answer.

This restating step puts you in step with your prospect. It takes him or her off the defensive. It can help you avoid an argument. Remember, there is probably more inclination on your part to indulge in arguments when answering questions or objections than in any other part of the interview.

Few prospects are ever really convinced by argument. The members of college debating teams are always of the same conviction following the debate as they were before the debate. The members of the losing team did not have their opinions changed by the superior arguments of their opponents. In the televised presidential candidate debates (between Kennedy and Nixon, Ford and Carter, Carter and Reagan) none of the debaters switched to the opposing view as a result of the other's rhetoric.

Dr. George W. Crane, the essayist, believes that argument is poor sales strategy. He says, "Don't argue. Suggest. An ounce of suggestion is worth a ton of argument. When you suggest, it means that you get me to arrive at my own conclusion. When you argue, it means that you force me to arrive at yours. And what you want to do is to make your conclusion mine and lead me to it.

"Guide me deftly to the decision you wish me to make. Don't shove. Let my mind amble along at its own gait. I have known few men to be convinced by argument. And no women!"

The familiar philosophy, "A person convinced against his or her will is of the same opinion still," reiterates the necessity of staying on the prospect's side. We once saw a poster that said simply, "You have not converted a man simply because you have silenced him."

Let's assume that you're a sales rep for a large, well-known company and the prospect raises an objection such as, "Yes, but I'm concerned about service *after* the sale!"

You lean forward, drink it all in and restate the question. "Let me see if I understand you, Ms. Jones—you're concerned about our service *after* the sale, is that correct?" She nods and you say, "I can understand your concern, but I'm sure you'll agree that it's our *service* as much as our *products* that have made us the giant company we are today! I can assure you that service will *never* be a problem—our service department is available night and day . . ."

ISOLATING THE OBJECTION

There are always two reasons a prospect has for not deciding upon your proposition: the one that sounds good and the real reason, the genuine reason and the insincere reason. You must "smoke out" the real reason!

You do that by asking, "In addition to that, what *other* reasons do you have for not acting on this proposition today?" You must uncover the *real* reason to progress.

As you learned in the word list earlier, one of the strongest words in the English language is that little three letter word "WHY?" This powerful word can help you isolate the *real* objection. It also helps you to stay out of arguments.

For example, when your prospect says, "I can't afford it right now," restate the question and ask, "Would you mind telling me why?" The real or hidden objection will often surface.

"Locate any real obstacle and remove it."

USING AN EXAMPLE OR STORY

More objections are overcome by emotional responses than through intellectual appeals. You can educate prospects in the soundness of your proposition, you may get them nodding vertically at every point— but unless you stir them emotionally, there is no action. Almost every student of behavior will assure you that most of us engaged in selling have too much reverence for facts. We should equip ourselves better with fresh, relevant examples and stories.

The purpose of an example or story is to help the prospect see himself or herself in the light of another person's experience. Its success lies in the fact that each of us is imitative. We will follow if relevant examples are held up in front of our eyes.

Jesus taught with parables so that people might see themselves more clearly. Lincoln used this example to explain how he felt when Douglas defeated him in the Illinois senatorial contest: "I feel like the boy who stubbed his toe. He was too big to cry and it hurt too darned much to laugh."

Carefully chosen examples and stories exert a tremendous power over the mind of the prospect.

Develop the skill of choosing and telling yours well.

STIMULATING ACTION

The only reason for answering an objection is to make the sale. The first five steps, if done properly, have moved your prospect into a position where it is more reasonable for him or her to say "yes" than to say "no."

The most important factor in stimulating action is your attitude. Always assume your prospect is going to buy now. Proceed as if all you must do is settle the few questions of minor detail.

Your attitude makes closing the sale easy and natural.

Don't be objectionable. This is not the first time the importance of avoiding arguments has been mentioned. Remove the objection without being objectionable. This is not always an easy thing to accomplish, especially when your prospect clings to an objection.

Wendell White, in his book *The Psychology of Dealing with People,* treats this subject well:

> **"The removal of objectionable ideas is a very delicate procedure. It can entail the danger of wounding the individual's pride. The slightest injury to another's self-esteem may become an insurmountable barrier to dissuading him or her from a committed position. To succeed in getting a person to give up an idea you must proceed in a manner that will safeguard the person's pride. There are several ways in which you can disparage an idea expressed by another person without offending."**

White then offers these resistance chasers:

1. To exonerate the prospect from any blame for expressing an objection:

- "I see I have not made that point clear" or "You may feel differently with this added information."

2. To make a concession before taking exception:

- "Under normal conditions you would be correct but . . ." or "Your suggestion has much to recommend it. On the other hand . . ."

3. To reveal a deliberate attitude:

- "This is really worth considering" or "Perhaps you should secure an opinion from another before making a final decision."

Getting into arguments with prospects is one of the easiest things you can do and one of the most disastrous. There is generally a tactful, diplomatic way to remove the objection without being objectionable. Your job is to always find and employ it.

YOU DON'T HANDLE EVERY OBJECTION

The prospects you deal with have their own viewpoints, desires and prejudices. They won't respond favorably every time to what you want them to do.

Prospects will follow your advice willingly on those things that happen to be in accord with their own desires. However, they must be directed, assisted and persuaded to get the action and cooperation you desire.

There is just no sure-fire strategy for handling all prospects' objections, all of the time. There are far too many variables in each selling situation to ever formulate a guaranteed answer to all objections.

Some people who seemingly should buy, simply will not be a prospect for you. Moreover, you will find some prospects who will buy in spite of having objections. Why? They discover a reason for buying that exerts more pressure and influence than any of the negative reasons.

When the prospect really *wants* a product or service, logic goes out the window and emotion takes charge. This is human nature. Someone once observed, "People would rather have one good, solid and honest emotion in making up their minds than a thousand facts." Their motivation may be *said* to be facts when it is the emotional appeal that really lures them. This causes good salespeople to stress buyer benefits and, especially, buyer motives.

"Be an assistant buyer."

FUNCTION AS AN ASSISTANT BUYER

Throughout the book we've said, "Function as an assistant buyer." We can't say it often enough or stress it too strongly. Today's prospects are more sophisticated and informed than ever before. They consider themselves to be very knowledgeable.

By the same token, product lines are far more complex and services far more sophisticated than ever before. The most knowledgeable prospect cannot expect to stay abreast of all the changes. There is too much to know about the products and service he or she must buy.

These prospects look to you for information and guidance. Today, they are much more sensitive to the insincere and poorly informed salesperson or anything that "smacks" of manipulation. Today, prospects see through the old high-pressure techniques and gimmicks. When anything resembling high-pressure techniques, gimmicks or insincerity is detected, they immediately become suspicious. They become defensive. Their buying resistance shoots upward!

The moral is this: Stay on the prospect's side. Help him or her remove and overcome the real obstacles. This kind of attitude is essential if you are to develop an effective procedure for handling objections.

As Betty Potts of Louisville says, "The basis of every sale I make is the absolute belief on my part that my client needs my product and will profit by deciding to buy it now."

HANDLING OBJECTIONS SUMMED UP

To handle objections, you have to stay in control. You stay in control by writing out your presentation ahead of time and by memorizing it so that you can give it naturally.

Writing out all you must say enables you to present your facts so that they will be understood, to include relevant points, to include answers to common objections and to remember where you are when interruptions or objections come.

When objections come, you'll have confidence because you're prepared. Because you're prepared, you'll *welcome* objections—they show that your prospect is still alive and listening. The first thing you want to do is classify an objection. Is it genuine or insincere? *You can only do something about genuine objections—insincere objections are hopeless.*

Prospects object because there's something they don't understand or believe, or because they're trying to cover up something.

You can deal with objections by anticipating them, ignoring them, asking permission to handle them later or by answering them now. Which strategy *you* use depends on your overall game plan and the nature of the objection.

To master objections, master six steps: Hear it out, ask that it be repeated, restate it, isolate it, use an example or story, and then stimulate action. Once the objections are out of the way, there's no reason why you shouldn't move swiftly toward the close.

You'll know where you are at all times, thanks to having taken the time to write out your presentation.

Because you have confidence, you view objections as "opposing blockers" who are trying to block your winning pass play—because to win the sale, you must pass over all these opposing objections.

In the 1979 thriller between Dallas and Washington, the Cowboys were "up." They knew their game plan, they knew their opponent, and they felt they knew what obstacles would be put in their way. They exuded confidence. They were prepared. They were ready.

As Roger puts it, "There are occasions when you might luck out and win when you're not prepared—but that's rare. Confidence doesn't count unless it's based on solid preparation."

In spite of this confidence, Dallas fell behind 17-0. But they still had confidence that they could come back. Then they went ahead 21 to 17. Then Washington bounced back and Dallas trailed 34 to 21!

Only a little over three minutes were left to go and it looked like the Cowboys were dead ducks—even some avid Dallas fans began filing out of the stadium, thinking the game was over. Dallas needed two touchdowns in three minutes!

Roger and the entire team had confidence—confidence based on preparation and an honest assessment of their ability. There were 11 objections to their making two touchdowns on the opposing team—but they were prepared to overcome those objections and win.

Dallas *did* come back and Dallas *did* win with the final score at Dallas 35, Washington 34. It went down in the books as one of the best regular season games in the 1970s.

But the game wasn't won *just* on the field, or *just* in practice, or *just* in making up the game plan. The game was won in the *minds* of each of the Dallas Cowboys and the coaching staff!

Roger had all the basic ingredients for success—he watched for the right opportunities and moved over the objections to win.

Roger has done the same in real estate. One time, he put hours into preparing what he felt was a dynamite presentation for a group of investors for an apartment complex in Tyler, Texas. He had done his homework. He had assembled potential buyers. He had put together a program that he felt would appeal to these buyers because he had prequalified them as people who needed a moderate cash flow and an extensive tax write-off.

He went in with a good game plan and played the game according to the plan. The game ended with no score.

Later that same day, Roger met another individual and, in talking with him, realized that he too met the investor profile. Using the same game plan, he went on to close the sale—and that one man purchased the entire complex!

Was Roger discouraged when he lost the first game? Certainly he was disappointed, but Roger has taught himself to be a percentage player, just as we all have to be. He knew that there was nothing wrong with the product and nothing wrong with the presentation. He was willing to continue to play the game until he scored—and he did.

He overcame objections and proceeded until the game opened up and he had an eligible receiver down field—and won.

HANDLING OBJECTIONS REMINDERS

- You stay in control in selling by having a planned presentation.
- Sales leaders speak as individuals having authority.
- Objections offer important clues. Welcome them.
- Objections are either insincere or genuine.
- Prospects raise objections when they don't understand, don't believe or are trying to cover up.
- Common objections can be anticipated. Handle them before they come up.
- Objections can be ignored or they can be deferred.
- Asking the prospect to repeat an objection shows your sincerity.
- Restating the objection shows you are listening and gives you an opportunity to think.
- Isolating the objection smokes out the real reason.
- More objections are overcome through emotional responses than through intellectual appeals.
- The most important factor in stimulating action is having confidence in a strategy.
- Don't argue. Handle objections without being objectionable.
- When the prospect really wants a product or service, logic slips away.
- Prospects look to you for information and guidance.

CHAPTER 8

LEADING THE PROSPECT TO THE BUYING DECISION

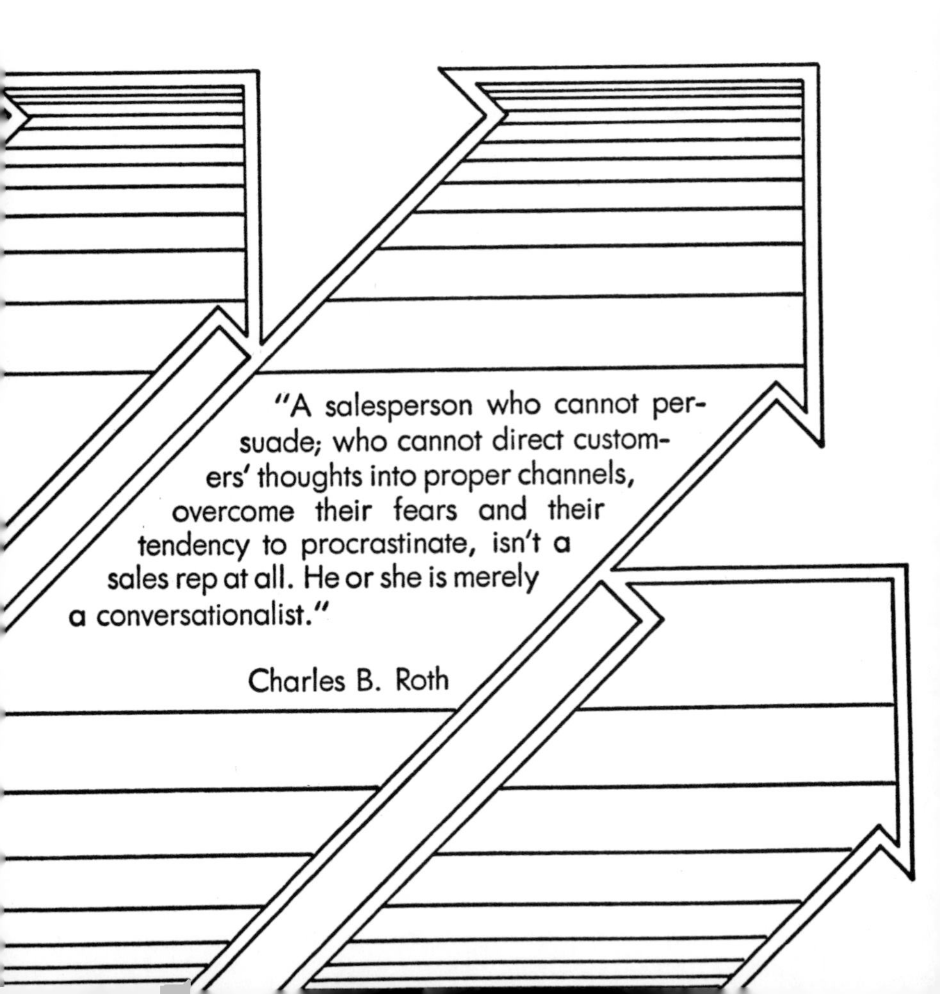

AN EFFECTIVE SALESPERSON CLOSES

An effective salesperson closes, and a poor closer is *always* an ineffective salesperson. *The close is the main event which the entire selling process aims toward.*

"The entire selling process is a closing process."

Everything that has gone before—planning, prospecting, making contact, probing, presenting, handling objections and all of the other activity and effort—has been focused on this main objective. The sales rep who cannot close is like the football team that rolls up impressive yardage but lacks the punch to move the ball across the goal line.

You may hear someone described as "a pretty good salesperson but not a strong closer." Since closing does require strategy, there may be some truth in this analysis. However, the problem generally lies throughout the selling process. The sales rep who is strong all the way through the selling process will not ordinarily become weak at completing the sale.

Drive into your mind this truth: The entire selling process is a closing process. Closing, when properly done, is a natural and rather obvious experience.

FIVE CARDINAL RULES OF SELLING TO REMEMBER

Every person has a personality that is different from all others. We see successful sales reps who are bold and aggressive. They have little difficulty asking prospects for anything. We see effective salespeople who are sensitive and somewhat quiet. They have to muster courage every time they ask for an order.

Regardless of what type of personality you have, you can become a stronger closer. You can turn the toughest prospect into a willing buyer, ready and eager to do business with *you—if* you regularly use these five cardinal rules of selling:

1. *If you would win a prospect to your cause, first convince him or her that you are a genuine friend.*
2. *Help the prospect recognize a need.* Uncover the basic need and stick with it.
3. *Keep in mind the prospect is best convinced by reasons he or she discovers.* There is only one way to get anybody to do anything; that is, by making the other person want to do it.
4. *Always plan to demonstrate the value and benefit your product or service provides.*
5. *Make it easy for the prospect to buy from you.* You do this by getting your prospect into the position where it is more reasonable to say "yes" than "no."

DEAL WITH DECISION-MAKERS

As a professional salesperson your time is valuable. Make certain you don't waste it by telling your story "for the practice" to someone who can't make a buying decision.

Frank Calari, Sr., of Los Angeles has consistently ranked at the top of his company's production honor role. Frank feels that you'll improve your closing ratio by as much as 100 percent if you're firm in your resolve to only make a presentation where a decision-maker is present! Frank says this is especially important in dealing with husband-wife situations or partnerships. "Their response is altogether different when they are alone, and this weakens your position. If you don't have both together, wait until you can!"

THE TWO VITAL CLOSING FACTORS

The most important factor in closing is not your proposition, your price or business conditions. The most important factor is *you.*

Since you must do the closing, *your mental attitude and your method are more important than anything else.* To be a successful closer, you must develop a closing consciousness—and then, you must have a closing strategy.

Closing Consciousness

This is an attitude of expectancy. It is your absolute belief that you will close the business. This feeling will perform for you. It will be transferred to your prospect naturally, without conscious effort. Your prospect will begin to feel as you do. He or she will expect to buy.

"The most useful sales tool I have ever found is *imagining a desired outcome,"* says Joe McKinney. This has proved consistently reliable for Joe, a former securities broker and investment banker who is now the chief executive officer for Tyler Corporation.

Joe says, "Visualize the outcome in Technicolor, three dimensions and high fidelity. See yourself executing a document, writing the order and shaking hands with a sold prospect. Do it with as much vivid detail as your imagination can develop. *Feel the pressure of the handshake and experience the elation that engulfs your entire being as you receive the expected news that you have the order."*

Steve Stone became the top winning pitcher in Baltimore Oriole baseball history. In the process he won the coveted Cy Young Award. Steve was asked how he made such a dramatic change in his performance. Like Joe McKinney, Steve credited his remarkable success to *"the mental practice I have on the day I am pitching."*

Steve says, "I see myself pitching masterfully to each hitter. I am using the pitches they can't hit. I sense the scene which follows the final out—the roar of the crowd—the congratulations of my teammates and manager. I see myself reading the morning newspaper account of my victory. I capture the winning feeling all the way."

This winning feeling never makes itself known in so many words. You never insult your prospects by implying you know their needs better than they do. Your expectancy works through your manner and actions. It is always there—in your expressions, your responses, the way in which you handle the order blank, in the ways in which you demonstrate or explain your product or service. You expect the prospect to buy now. *You engender qualities in the prospect's mind like those you display.*

"Believe in your product, believe in yourself— belief produces behavior."

Closing consciousness takes planning and finesse. It pays off in sales.

Closing Strategy

You must learn to create your own closing opportunities. Most of the sales you make will not close themselves. You must guide and direct the prospect's behavior. Here again, you play the role of an assistant buyer.

Let's say your prospect has been attentive but indicated no strong interest to move forward. There has been no nodding of the head, no handling of the product, no asking of particularly revealing questions. It is a common error for you to assume that because no interest has been expressed, none exists. In most cases, you must do more than watch passively for indications of interest. You must create the situation in which interest can reveal itself.

We recommend you adopt a four-step strategy for closing:

- Summarize.
- Ask for your prospect's questions.
- Ask your questions.
- Stimulate action.

Summarize. Emphasize the buyer benefits. Benefits and features are blended together in such a manner that your summation accomplishes its purpose of refreshing the prospect's memory. In this step you assure by affirmation and create understanding by repetition.

Ask for Your Prospect's Questions. You are probing for any major objections. You don't ask for objections; it wouldn't sound right. Instead, you ask for questions. The end result is the same—it smokes out any objections.

> *"Questions uncover closing opportunities."*

Ask Your Questions. Take the prospect's mind off the big decision and put it on the little ones. Obviously, the big decision in every sale is, "Will you buy now?" Develop a series of little questions you can ask that gain agreement on minor points. If your prospect is not quite ready to buy, your questions will merely seem a part of your normal routine. If the prospect is ready to buy, he or she will cooperate by answering your questions easily and naturally. Develop the feeling that it is the prospect's decision to move forward. You strengthen the close in this step by recording on the order blank the prospect's responses.

Stimulate Action. This final step is one shared by all the effective closers we have ever observed. You must start to do something that the prospect must stop you from doing if he or she wants to avoid giving an order. You must follow through to the end.

Getting your prospect's approval and signature is the logical conclusion. The confident manner in which you proceed to gain action provides leadership for the prospect. Your strongest weapon in combating reluctance and fear is your manner in this step. More than ever you must be sure you are confident, self-assured and poised.

"Make it more reasonable for the prospect to say 'yes' than 'no.' "

GAUGE THE PROSPECT'S PACE

Every person has his or her own pace. Your ability to gauge it can be an important asset.

Judging a prospect's pace is not all that difficult when you understand its importance. Study each prospect closely. Does he or she comprehend your presentation quickly? Does his or her mind seem to "jump" to conclusions? If so, he or she will probably make the decisions to buy in the same way. On the other hand, if the prospect seems to hesitate, if he or she pauses, asks many questions, and mulls over the answers, the chances are you're dealing with a slow, methodical buyer. He or she will be a deliberate decision-maker.

It is important to form an estimate of each prospect's rate of thinking because you must follow his or her pace to make the most sales. If the prospect is always thinking ahead of your presentation, he or she is going to become impatient. If you move too quickly, the prospect is going to feel he or she is being rushed. In either case, you will not be effective.

You must walk at the prospect's pace if you're going to guide him or her to your destination—a sale.

"Sell at the prospect's pace."

A LANGUAGE YOU MUST LEARN

Every creature sends out signals about its feelings and attitudes. The cat purrs when contented and arches its back when angry. The dog growls when angry and wags its tail when it wants to be friendly. The baby signals wants by laughing or crying.

These reactions are caused by certain pressures within the mind and body, which respond almost automatically to given situations. In selling we refer to similar reactions on the part of prospects as "buying signs."

You will improve your selling effectiveness by studying the response reactions of prospects. Theirs is a language you will need to master. Learn to observe the common signals prospects flash that can be valuable progress reports.

Knowing how to read the buying signs of prospects provides you with a competitive edge. Nearly every buyer will show some signal when he or she is ready or almost ready to make a decision.

WHEN TO STOP SELLING

Much has been written about the "psychological moment" to make the close. Today most students of selling believe that "the moment" can be created several times throughout the selling process. They advocate to close early, to close late . . . to close anytime the prospect gives you the indication that he or she is ready to buy.

In the typical sale, there probably is a rising interest level that turns to desire. *By staying alert, you can learn to "feel" the prospect's attitude.* Although you may not be able to describe precisely how you know, you will feel it through a sort of sixth sense.

BUYING SIGNS TO WATCH FOR

Learn to watch for these indications:

- **Words and Questions.** These are some of the most important buying signs. What your prospect says and how he or she says it can be very meaningful. Questions should almost always be interpreted as buying signs. Some examples include, "What discount do you allow for cash?" or "How long would it take for delivery?" Questions of any kind indicate interest. Questions as pointed as these tell you your prospect is waiting for you to bring the interview to a close.
- **Prospect's Attention.** The prospect's attitude often betrays his or her interest. The prospect leans forward, rubs his or her chin, pulls an ear or scratches his or her head. These actions are revealing an "almost persuaded" attitude. Likewise, when a prospect reexamines the product or contract, the time has arrived for you to close.
- **An Act of Hesitation.** When your prospect hesitates just for a moment over one article or item, this is an important signal.
- **Tone of Voice.** Even a slight raising or lowering of the tone of voice will give you an indication of interest.
- **Facial Expressions.** Most people betray their thinking in their expressions. Watch your prospect's eyes for a look of interest. Many feel that eyes tell you more than words.

Emulate the successful pros in selling. Stay alert—pay

attention. Be able to recognize and read your prospects through the body language and other indicators we have described. Whenever you are reasonably sure of your "feel," then act—attempt a close.

SEVEN AND ONE-HALF STRATEGIES FOR CLOSING THE SALE

There are at least seven and one-half strategies for closing the sale. The selection of the particular strategy for a certain situation is up to you. It depends on the type of prospect you are selling, the timing, your judgment and your selling style.

What we are giving you now are the basic strategies. Become thoroughly familiar with each of them. Then, put your imagination to work. You will create many variations that will make these strategies even more effective.

1. **Closing by Assuming.** When you use this strategy, you are taking it for granted your prospect will buy. *Let the prospect see and feel your undoubting attitude about his or her buying from you now.*
2. **Closing on a Minor Point.** It is easier for anyone to make a minor decision than a major one. Using this strategy, you make it easier for the prospect by avoiding the major decision.

   You use this strategy whenever there is a choice between two appeals. The choice is given to the prospect. It might be a simple question like, "Would your investment be registered as an individual or as tenants in common?" or "Should we ask our legal department to prepare the contract papers or will your lawyers draw them up?" or "Would you prefer white or blue?" or "Would you prefer to have someone pick them up or have us deliver?"

Take the prospect's mind off the big decisions and put it on the little ones. You will make more sales.

"Make it easy for the prospect to buy."

3. **Impending Event.** Psychologists tell us the fear of loss is an especially strong motivating force. Using this strategy, you tell your prospect of some impending event that necessitates immediate action if the prospect is to avoid losing something of value.

   People usually want what is difficult to get. It is contrary to human nature to let an opportunity slip. It is an inborn trait.

   This "last chance" strategy is a favorite of life insurance agents. For years, they have closed many sales because of an impending age change. Real estate brokers remind prospects, "At this price, this property won't last long." Salespeople remind prospects that products will be more expensive in the future or that the "sale ends Saturday."

   The prospect is made to feel that he or she must buy *now* to avoid a loss.

   Use this strategy to rout procrastination. You'll find it is one of the best weapons in your closing arsenal, *if* you're honest. Don't tell a prospect, "This offer is good only if you buy *now*—I can't make it tomorrow." It's usually not true and almost never believable.

4. **Closing with Physical Action.** It pays to *do* something as well as *say* something when attempting to

close. *Action is a most persuasive language.* Many times action without words will serve the same purpose, such as clearing a space to fill out the order blank, getting your pen ready to use or just pulling a chair closer to the desk.

The principle of this strategy is this: *Start to do something the prospect will have to stop you from doing if he or she wants to avoid giving an order.* You are sure to discover that most prospects will permit you to go ahead and write up the order. They will then proceed to sign it rather than interrupt the progress of your leadership action. This is a strategy used by almost all strong closers. It produces orders.

5. **Closing with Emotion.** Emotion and impulse influence more people to action than do reason or logic. Most strong closers are master storytellers. They find a story to be a useful motivational tool. It brings a third-party endorsement into play which often becomes the turning point of an interview.

   For example, the pro at your country club talks with you about a new set of irons. You feel your present set is good enough. The timing isn't right—you have a tax bill to pay. Logically, the new clubs must wait. But then, the pro tells you about Danny Reeves. He purchased the same irons last month and has taken three strokes off his score. This emotional appeal moves you into action. Impulse now overcomes reason.

   Equip yourself with interesting stories and examples that appeal to pride, fear and self-esteem. Your prospect will identify with the hero in your story. The prospect sees, point by point, the parallel between your story and his or her own. Emotion wins—plain common sense doesn't have a chance!

The stories you tell must be told well. No matter how busy or distracted the prospect might be, you want to capture his or her attention. Telling stories is an art. Like any other art, you have to practice and work at it to get it perfect.

Examine the stories told by the next really good public speaker you hear. Listen to the stories of professional humorists like Jerry Clower. It isn't the stories *themselves* that are so funny—it's the exciting, dramatic way that they're *told*. Learn some sales stories that illustrate your points. Then learn to tell them well.

6. **Closing by Inducement.** One of the chief enemies to closing sales is procrastination. This strategy recognizes that procrastination operates against you most of the time. An inducement enables you to close in spite of it.

   This sales inducer rests its case on one of the most fundamental of human appeals—the desire to get something for nothing. "During the month of January, we will install your antenna without charge" or "If you can agree to the lease arrangement during June, you will be given free rent until October."

   Your success in using the inducement strategy will depend on *how* you use it. It can be viewed as a high-pressure tactic. Used properly and tactfully, it constitutes an effective closing aid.

   Along this line, form the habit of offering related items. Selling related items and/or selling special low-priced goods is a strategy used by most high-performing sales reps. This helps you sell more than the customer intended to buy. It boosts your average sale and it often gains a new customer for you. Jayne Kinder sells for Xerox. She doesn't stop with just selling equipment. *She keeps probing until she finds a related need.* If she can't sell a copier, she sells ribbons or computer forms. Her new customer receives direct mail catalogs and other Xerox supply incentives. "Now that these prospects have bought something from me," Jayne says, "it will make selling them a copier that much easier." Use it as a closing strategy—any sale is better than no sale.

7. **Closing by Asking Them to Buy.** One way to get an order is to ask for it. Purchasing agents and buyers say that it is amazing how many sales reps seem unable to bring themselves to ask for the order.

   We're reminded of the life insurance agent who was a close personal friend of Henry Ford. The agent read of Ford's purchase of a substantial policy from another agent. He stormed in to see Mr. Ford and exploded, "Why in h--- didn't you buy the policy from me?" Henry Ford's reply was reported to have been, "Why in h--- didn't you *ask* me?"

   Sometimes it is smart to forget the complex strategies and simply ask for the business boldly and frankly.

7½. **Closing with Silence.** A most powerful influence in controlling others is silence. Nature abhors a vacuum and silences must be filled. Many times, an effective close puts the prospect into the role of being the salesperson. In other words, the prospects feel they should *sell* you on why they *don't* need your product or service.

   The toughest person in the world to sell is one who doesn't talk. Now you be that person who doesn't talk! Use silence. The prospect will become unpoised. Few can stand silence. Often, buying signs will surface at this precise time.

Silence requires courage on your part. Practice until you can use it without difficulty. You will discover you can control the buyer with your silence as effectively as you can control him or her with your words. Silence will help you do much to "smoke out" buying signs and close sales.

Silence can be golden.

ASSIST THE BUYER WITH THESE QUESTIONS

Lynn Newman, a fine graphic sales rep, believes there are five important questions the prospect must answer before deciding to buy. We agree with Lynn. Here are Lynn's five vital questions:

- Do I need the owner benefit this product provides?
- Is this the single best answer to my need?
- Is this the right source?
- Is the price right?
- When should I buy?

Whatever your product or service, think of your prospect as having to make these five decisions before giving you the order. Then do your best to assist your buyer in making all of them affirmative.

This practice will strengthen your effectiveness and improve your closing ratio.

ASK YOURSELF THESE QUESTIONS

If you are not closing a favorable percentage of your interviews, refer to this check-up on closing effectiveness. Reviewing these questions regularly will improve your closing ratio:

- Did I make it easier for my prospect to say "yes" than "no"?
- Did I display poise and enthusiasm which showed in my words and actions?
- Was my speed of delivery too slow? The average sales rep talks much too slowly. Most talk at a rate of 135 words per minute. The average prospect thinks at a rate of 1,500 words per minute. Don't let the prospect's mind wander by talking too slowly.
- Did I wear my prospect out with too many facts? Were there too few examples and picture elements in the presentation?
- Were my statements vague and unclear?
- Did I do my homework to enable me to answer questions intelligently?
- Did I focus on buyer benefits?
- Did I embrace the ABC principle—*A*lways *B*e *C*losing?
- Did I listen effectively?
- Did I prepare my summary?
- Did I make it too hard for the prospect to buy?
- Did I ask the prospect to buy enough times?

It's been our experience that a failure to close seldom leads to a sale later on. As Roger says, "When you leave a prospect saying, 'I'll think it over and call you,' don't expect a phone call. It's rare that someone decides to buy later. Usually, if it's a good prospect and you've done your homework and presented it properly and made a strong close, you'll leave the office having made a sale."

CLOSING SUMMED UP

Next to the first four minutes, the most important part of your sales interview is the time when you close the sale.

In a well-planned sales presentation, there should always be several such closing moments. Remember the ABC's of selling—*A*lways *B*e *C*losing!

Each time you drive home one of the important selling points in favor of your proposition, ask for the order. Attempt to close then. If you're unsuccessful, stay with your presentation, driving home the buyer benefits.

You are somewhat like the football team that tries one offensive play after another until it discovers what tactic will score and win.

No one buys anything unless he or she feels that it is in his or her interest. This is why your summary talk is so important. It must convince the prospect of the ways in which your product or service will benefit him or her.

Prepare to make it much more reasonable for the prospect to say "yes" than "no" to what you are selling.

In closing, nothing is more contagious than enthusiasm. Effective sales reps are excited about what they have to sell. Radiate confidence, goodwill and genuine sincerity in what you say and the way you say it.

Finally, remember that the way to close is through your dominant attitude of expectancy coupled with planned strategy. It is *impossible* to close too soon. It is entirely *possible* to close too late! The time to close is whenever it can be done effectively; and the sooner the better!

CLOSING REMINDERS

- The entire selling process is a closing process.
- To win a prospect to your cause, first convince him or her you are a friend.
- Always demonstrate value and benefit.
- Make it easy for the prospect to buy from you.
- An important closing factor is closing consciousness.
- Make it more reasonable for the prospect to say "yes."
- Questions uncover selling opportunities.
- Sell at the prospect's pace.
- Decide that you must stimulate the closing action.
- Learn to read the language that has to do with buying signs.
- When you "take it for granted" you are closing by assuming.
- Put the prospect's mind on little decisions.
- The fear of loss is a powerful motivator.
- Emotion influences more people to action than does logic.
- A chief enemy of closing is procrastination.
- Using silence to close sales requires a courageous attitude.
- A sales rep's job is to sell, and selling means closing sales that don't close themselves.

CHAPTER 9

REMEMBERING SERVICE AND FOLLOW-THROUGH AFTER THE SALE

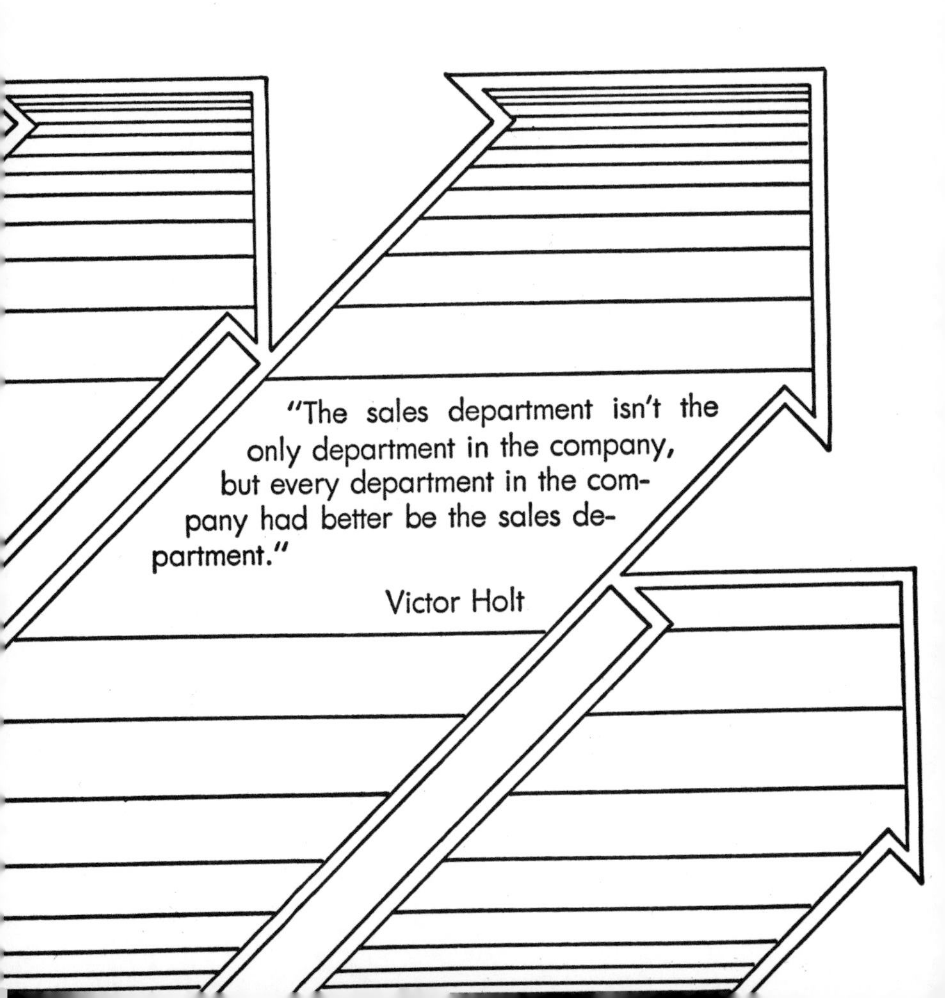

"The sales department isn't the only department in the company, but every department in the company had better be the sales department."

Victor Holt

THE IMPORTANCE OF FOLLOW-THROUGH

The salesperson who stops selling when he or she has the order is destined to stay among the ranks of the mediocre. Your work is by no means ended when you leave after a successful selling effort. *Today, more and more customers are coming to appreciate service and follow-through as a thing of value in making buying decisions.*

More and more companies are emphasizing service not only as a means of keeping satisfied customers but as an added "initial sales value." Life insurance agents are now offering a ten-day free look. Automobile salespeople are stressing longer warranty periods. This same sales psychology is spreading to other fields as well.

If your product will last longer and require fewer repairs, if it is covered by a longer or better warranty, or if your capacity for service is greater or more convenient—point out these values to the prospect. *A reputation for prompt, courteous and reliable service often means more to a buyer than does the price of the product being sold.*

Building customer satisfaction in today's business climate is more and more the result of the personal service you promise and deliver after the sale is made. Customer satisfaction is essential to good business. Make customer satisfaction your "stock in trade."

"There is one thing you can always give which makes your product unique—a better buy than your prospect can hope to find elsewhere." Joe Johnson of Georgetown, Kentucky, said that and he adds, "That one additional ingredient is your personal service." Joe tells his many customers, "Stop for service where service never stops."

We talked to Jerry Griffin, the nation's leading Cadillac salesman four times in the past six years. Jerry's entire approach centers on building a lasting relationship. Jerry tells the prospect, "I want to help you get what you want. I'm not interested in selling a car, I'm interested in building a customer. I want all the cars you buy in the future." We discovered that Jerry ties his buyers to him in many ways. For example, he employs a full-time assistant to provide free delivery service whenever the buyer needs his or her automobile serviced!

Randy Heady, a top real estate salesman, sums it up well when he says, "Quick commissions I don't need—lasting clients I do!"

SHOW THEM YOUR APPRECIATION

All of your customers have one thing in common—each one is hungry for sincere appreciation. Most feel that others do not recognize or appreciate their true worth. Praise and appreciation can work wonders in building long-lasting, viable relationships.

Consider how *you* feel when someone shows you sincere appreciation. Sincere appreciation gives you a lift. It makes your whole day brighter. You develop a feeling of kinship and liking for the person who takes the time to appreciate you. You must create these same feelings in your customers. You might ask, "Why don't more people use this technique?" This is a question that has no logical answer. Properly used, praise and appreciation are strong factors in building and maintaining relationships.

"What can I do to favorably stand out in my customer's mind?"

If you want to become an effective relationship builder, start looking for ways in which you can show genuine appreciation. You have, of course, some natural times when you should always show your appreciation:

1. **Express your appreciation for each order received.** Appreciation for new orders is usually automatic. The following is an example of the kind of expression we recommend:

> Mr. Robert S. Schoder
> 1516 Woodward Avenue
> Detroit, Michigan 75603
>
> Dear Bob:
>
> Just a note to say "thank you" and let Val and you know that we appreciate doing business with you very much. As the years roll on, I assure you that both my company and I will strive to merit your confidence.

Since changes in family and financial conditions make it desirable to review your life insurance plan periodically, I will keep in touch with you and call on you from time to time.

Naturally, I will consider it a privilege to be consulted by you and your friends whenever the subject of life insurance comes up. Bob, I would like very much to have you consider me your life insurance man.

Sincerely yours,

Jack Murray, CLU

2. **Give appreciation to those who assist you.** It is good to give appreciation to those who assist you in any way to reach and sell your new customer. These might include receptionists, assistants, secretaries, etc. They can be most helpful to you in building a relationship.

All of us have made a habit of sending thank-you's to those who have helped us. Roger has carried it a step further and jots down the name of each secretary he talks to and keeps it right beside the boss's name. Then, the next time he calls, he can call the secretary by name. This goes a long way in getting Roger interviews. After all, isn't memorizing someone's name a way of saying, "You're important"?

Now if the boss has been busy and hard to catch, who is going to get preferential treatment—a salesperson who is on a first-name basis with the secretary or one from a competing company who's brisk and businesslike?

Roger says you'd be surprised what a card or a short

thank-you to a secretary will do to your stock in a company too!

3. **Always express appreciation for an interview.** You should always give appreciation to the prospect who grants you an interview, even though he or she does not buy. This is one of the best ways to make an impression and to keep the prospect's mind open to your proposition at a future date. When the need or opportunity arises to consider a change, he or she will be inclined to remember you.

4. **Show appreciation through your manners and actions.** Your manners and actions reveal your appreciation. Let the buyer know where you can be reached whenever you are needed. This tells your customer you appreciate his or her business and want to keep it. Returning telephone calls promptly shows your appreciation, as does being an attentive listener.

5. **Look for opportunities.** Look for opportunities to recognize any special occasions or achievements. It shows your interest. Scout trade papers, local papers and the like for news of promotions or advancements. Be aware of the impending birth of a child. Then send a clipping with a short congratulatory note—it shows you care!

6. **Give thanks for referrals.** Always express appreciation to those customers who refer business to you. By all means, report back to them on your results.

7. **Send prospects to your customers.** If your customers are also in business, send them prospects or supply them with leads. This is an effective way to develop an on-going relationship. It is just natural for a person to respond favorably to you when you show your appreciation and helpfulness.

The basic principle to follow is this one: Never forget a customer and never let a customer forget you.

SERVE WHAT YOU SELL

Your customers will be presented claims and counter-claims from people who offer similar products at about the same price. The competitive edge you want to develop comes from the attitude you project of serving as you sell. You do this in two ways.

First, you do whatever it takes to establish a record of consistent reliability. Earning the reputation of being a 100 percent reliable sales rep whose every word and promise can be depended upon takes application, effort and attention to detail.

Second, you stay determined to be the best-informed sales rep who calls on your customers. This requires a commitment to excellence and a regular program of study.

Once you have established the image of being a reliable, well-informed salesperson, you are in an enviable position.

***"Never forget a customer.
Never let a customer forget you."***

HANDLE COMPLAINTS—FAST!

Customer satisfaction can be evaluated in most companies by studying the company's policy and record in handling complaints. When complaints are handled courteously, promptly and reliably, complaining customers are retained as customers.

Sooner or later, you are going to run into a complaining customer. The complaint may be minor or major. It may be a mistake in billing or shipping. It could be an unwarranted letter from your credit department.

Whether or not the complaint appears to be reasonable, *your objective is to handle the complaint courteously, promptly and reliably.*

There are certain rules you should follow. The first rule is to listen. Do not interrupt—wait until the customer has talked it out. Second, always thank the customer for calling the complaint to your attention. Next, carefully evaluate what action can be taken to rectify the situation. Finally, report back to the customer promptly.

During any period of adjustment, be certain you keep the customer informed. Let him or her know what action is taking place until full restitution has been made or until you have reached agreement.

Your aim is to maintain customer satisfaction if at all possible.

FIVE KEYS TO SERVING BETTER

A team of some of America's most eminent psychologists, psychiatrists, sociologists and financial experts developed five key ways to be happier, healthier and live longer.

Their remarkable recipe for the "good life" will work just as well in achieving and maintaining customer satisfaction. The golden keys are these:

1. Value your relationships.
2. Think of others and how you can help them.
3. Be positive about yourself, your business and your future.
4. Strive for stability in your personal and business life.

5. Work hard to give more than you get out of every relationship.

Make it a practice to follow this recipe. You will serve better. Your customers will feel more secure—and you'll feel better about yourself.

YOU ARE THE FIRM

Always be mindful of your aura of influence. *Professionals in selling always identify themselves with their companies.* They never say "the company," it is always "we." The customer cannot talk about your company without including you. You cannot refer to your company without including yourself. In your customer's eyes, you do more than represent the firm—you *are* the firm.

Here's a quotation we saw at the reception desk of a Dallas hotel some years ago. It describes the influence of a single individual.

> **An institution may spread itself over the entire business community. It may employ all kinds of people . . . but the average person will almost always form a judgment of it through contacts with *one individual.***
>
> **If this person is discourteous, inefficient or ineffective, it will take much time and energy to overcome that bad impression.**
>
> **Each member of an organization who in any capacity comes in contact with the public is an agent, and the impression made is an advertisement, good or bad, which will make an indel-**

ible impression on the mind of the prospect.

As Dr. Albert Schweitzer said:

> **"I don't know what your destiny will be but one thing I know, the only ones among you who will be really happy are those who will have sought and found how to serve."**

Dr. Schweitzer could have been describing you and your career in selling. "The person profits most who sells and serves best." Be determined to deliver better service than your competition. You will profit most!

SELLING AFTER THE SALE SUMMED UP

One of your biggest and best sales tools is service. Successful salespeople soon find, as we have, that most of their business comes from either former customers or referrals from former customers. Today, more and more customers are beginning to appreciate service and follow-through—so much so that it enters into their buying decisions.

If your product has service advantages, whether it is length of life, time between recommended service or speed of service, be sure to point them out.

The world is full of similar products, similarly priced. Your product has one distinct advantage: *your service!* Your service can be the cutting edge *if* you show your clients your appreciation.

How do you show your appreciation? By thanking

them for each order received. By showing your appreciation to those who assist you. By expressing appreciation for an interview. By showing appreciation through your manners and actions. By looking for opportunities to show your appreciation. By giving thanks for referrals.

Service what you sell. Never forget a customer and never let a customer forget you. "*To give real service you must add something which cannot be bought or measured with money—sincerity and integrity,*" wrote Donald Adams. This is something that can't be faked, at least not for long. If you have the best interest of your people at heart, it will show in your actions time and time again. You'll build a reservoir of goodwill.

If you have complaints (and you eventually will!) handle them fast. Let the customer "get it off his or her chest." Learn to listen. Be courteous. Take immediate action and keep the customer advised of what is being done.

There are five keys that unlock the good life and they relate to all facets of life, including service.

They are: value your relationships; think of others and how to help them; be positive about yourself, your business and your future; strive for stability; and work hard to give more than you get.

Remember that *you are the firm.* You are the company in the minds of your customers. If you do a good job, then your company does a good job. If you perform poorly, then your company performs poorly.

We tend to judge ourselves by what we want to be—others judge us by what we are. *Be* the salesperson you want to be—learn to sell with service!

SELLING AFTER THE SALE REMINDERS

- All of your customers have one thing in common—they are hungry for appreciation.
- Praise and appreciation are strong factors in building relationships.
- Express your appreciation for each order received.
- Give appreciation to those who assist you in making sales.
- Your manners and actions reveal your appreciation.
- The basic law, "Never forget a customer," will continue to stand and apply in any age.
- To serve as you sell, establish a record of consistent reliability.
- Be and stay an informed sales rep.
- Handle any and all complaints courteously, promptly and reliably.
- Professionals always identify themselves with their companies.

CHAPTER 10

HOW TO PROFIT FROM TIME MANAGEMENT IN SELLING

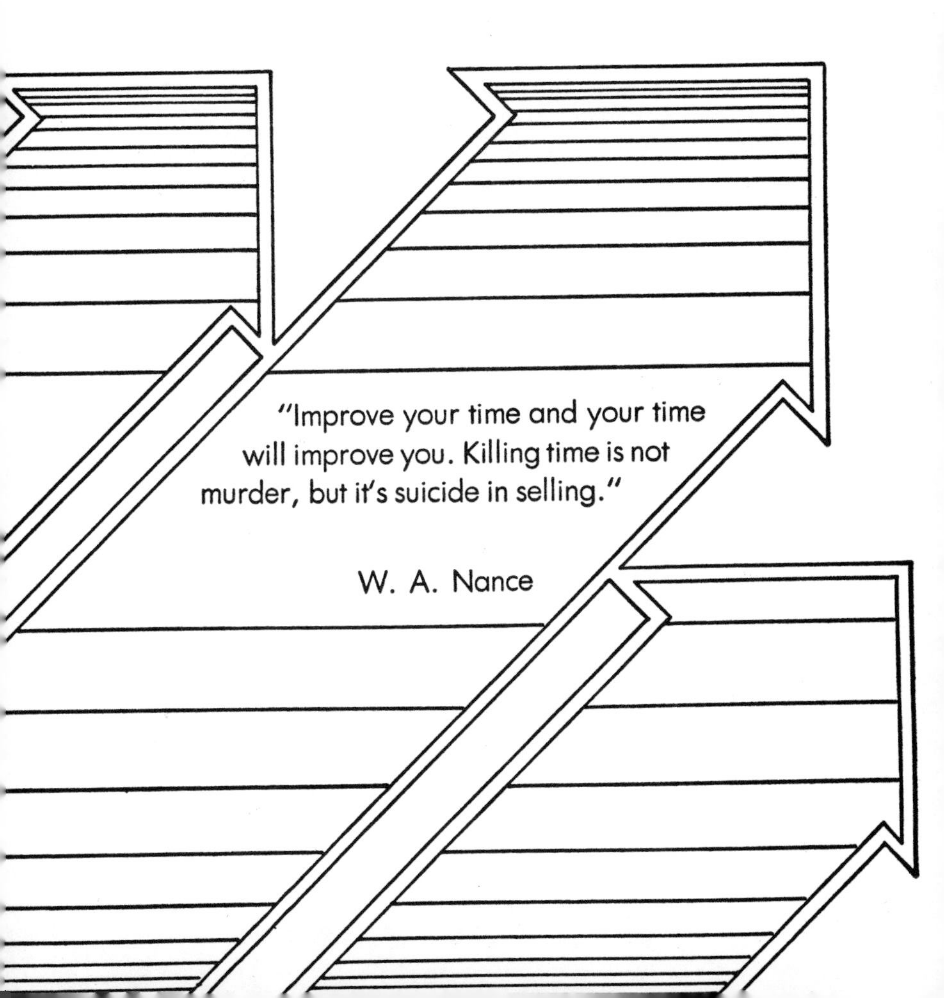

A SLIGHT IMPROVEMENT

In the Kipling Room at the Toronto Library, a plaque reads, "What you do when you don't have to determines what you will be when you can no longer help it!" Quite often those "things you do when you don't have to" will be the important things you do consciously and routinely to manage your selling time.

"Too little time," complain many salespeople today. Too much to do and not nearly enough time to get it done—too many crises, too many interruptions, too many problems, too many changes in plans. How often have you said to yourself, "If only I could add an extra hour or so to my selling day!" Normally, you can be expected to work 100,000 hours during your lifetime. Obviously, often a slight improvement in time management makes a big difference in your bottom-line production.

The urge for more time is nothing new. Napoleon, in the heat of battle, once said to an aide, "Go sir, and gallop! And remember that the world was made in six days! Ask of me anything you wish—except time!"

You *can* have more time, *if* you're willing to plan for it.

YOU CAN GIVE YOURSELF A RAISE

In sales, you are measured and rewarded not by the hours you put in but by what you put in the hours. The quality of selling time is a function of what you spend it doing, where you spend it, how you spend it, and with whom you spend it.

Here's a study we've made ourselves and encouraged many people in sales to make. You'll find it quite revealing.

First, buy or borrow a stopwatch. Be careful which kind you get. You will need the kind used to time athletic events—not the kind that resets to zero after every stop.

Second, take the watch with you every day for a week of normal selling. Keep it in your pocket. Turn it on and let it run every moment you are actually in the presence of a prospect. It goes on only when you are talking to a prospect about your products or service, in other words, *while you are selling.* Don't let the watch run while you are driving around deciding whom you will call. Don't let it run while you are "shooting the breeze," even with a prospect. Don't let it run while you wrestle through paperwork in the office or while you are having coffee. In short, don't let the watch run while you are doing anything but making an actual sales call. Next, don't tell your manager about your experiment. Your manager might ask to read the watch! Don't talk about it to your associates. You can tell them later when they start asking about your improved production records and larger commission checks. Since the stopwatch readings are for you, and *you alone,* there will be very little temptation to cheat. After all, you are trying to bolster your *income*—not your *ego.*

Finally, add up the daily readings at the end of the week. If you find (as most who make honest measurements will find) that during the whole week you spent less than ten hours of new, creative sales effort in front of your prospects, don't be discouraged.

Don't be discouraged even if the readings for the week total less than five hours! It's okay to be *shocked*—but don't be *discouraged.*

After you recover from shock, you'll realize that you have gotten to the heart of your most important problem: time. *The problem is that you aren't earning the kind of money you could easily be earning because you aren't spending enough hours making calls.* Sure, you're putting in the hours! But now you know that few of those hours are productive, selling hours. The other hours are being frittered away!

To increase your productivity and income you won't need to work any *harder*—but you will need to work *smarter.*

Working smarter means you need to spend less time on:

- paperwork during your most productive hours
- expensive cups of coffee
- pleasant but expensive conversations
- unnecessary footwork

Regardless of where those extra hours go, if you have timed your actual selling time, you know exactly what your most important problem is. It's managing your time.

Six most common time problems:

- ***Unplanned meetings***
- ***Lack of organization***
- ***No-shows***

- ***Poor scheduling of calls***
- ***Procrastination***
- ***"Fire-fighting"***

HIGH-QUALITY VS. LOW-QUALITY TIME

To an engineer, lawyer or accountant, time is simply a quantity, a number of seconds, minutes and hours. In the quantitative view they take, every hour is equal to every other hour. This is not so in your case. Clearly, you have high-quality time and low-quality time. One of your hours will be very productive when all other hours are wasted. An hour spent in front of a prospect may produce a very big money-making result for you. An hour spent in filing, which may be necessary, will never make you very rich. *Remember, you are paid for results—not for your hours.*

Because time management is vital to every salesperson's success, we've extensively researched the subject and studied various remedies. You'll find the time management principles developed here to be practical. You can start using them today to make maximum use of your selling time.

In our research we reached a couple of important conclusions. First, as stated above, in any type of sales work a slight improvement in time management produces a marked improvement in bottom-line results. Second, if you condense the many articles written and thoughts developed with reference to time management, you will discover that the most sound approach to sound time management revolves around mastering five principles:

1. Developing a time-conscious attitude
2. Planning your priorities daily

3. Staying effective
4. Establishing and maintaining momentum
5. Developing a sense of urgency by setting deadlines

Let's examine some specific suggestions in each of these important areas.

Developing Time-Consciousness

Like most success factors in selling, time management is largely dependent upon attitude. Shape your attitude so that you become aware of time and the manner in which you use it. Time is one of the major resources to utilize if you achieve outstanding selling success. An outstanding salesman in New Jersey, Mike Fitzpatrick, has discovered a fine tool for shaping his attitude toward becoming aware of time and the manner in which it is used. Mike carries a tiny quartz alarm clock on interviews. "It tells my clients I'm time-conscious. They like the novelty of it and the fact that I'm conscious of *their* time as well as my own."

Make it a practice to ask yourself the question, "What should I be doing with my time right now? What is it that *really* needs doing now?" More than anything else, your attitude determines your success in managing time.

Six tools for effective time management:

- ***Goals***
- ***Appointment book***
- ***Deadlines***
- ***Priorities***
- ***Secretary***
- ***Systems***

Planning Priorities

Planning is decision-making. As Alan Lakein says in his book *How to Get Control of Your Time and Life,* "Control starts with planning. Planning is bringing the future into the present so that you can do something about it now." As a general rule, the more detailed your plan, the better chance that action will follow. Plan your to-do list of priorities for each day the day before. You'll find that it is a good idea to always plan at the same time and same location. Your subconscious mind will respond to this habit pattern and you will find creative planning thoughts beginning to flow. Determine how much time you need for planning each day and put it on your schedule. The "planning hour" will often save several hours of implementing. We recommend using an hour on Friday afternoon for reviewing next week as well as detailing Monday's plan. The purpose of planning is to achieve production, so gear your planning to reach key results.

Staying Effective

The best-kept secret in selling is that unusual success usually follows the individual who determines the few factors that make a significant difference in producing results and who then focuses attention on those key factors most of the time. That's staying effective. There is a difference between efficiency and effectiveness. Efficiency means doing the job right. Effectiveness means doing the *right* job right! *The effective salesperson spends time on the high-payoff activities.*

Your attitude must become one of smoking out the vital tasks and being determined to stay focused on those key factors most of the time. One way of doing this is to make a list of the specific items to be done each day the day before and then decide on the priorities. Sort out those things that must be done. You will discover there is always enough time to do the high-payoff jobs. Ask yourself many times throughout your selling day this key question: "Is this the best use of my selling time right now—am I staying effective?"

Establishing and Maintaining Momentum

You do this best by establishing a daily routine. Decide how to budget your time as you determine hours when you are the most effective. You budget time like you budget money.

Momentum can be safeguarded by finding out what might be wasting your time. Discover your "time leaks." Make a list of "time wasters" you have in a typical day. Study them from the standpoint of how much time they use up. This list will pinpoint activities that need not be done or that could possibly be done by somebody else. Delegate everything possible. It saves time and it develops the roles of others.

Form the habit of avoiding interruptions. Interruptions are momentum stoppers. "The longer I look at time management," said Dr. Kenneth Dunn, Superintendent of Schools in Hewlett, New York, "the more I am impressed with the power of interruptions to kill time."

Remember that your time is valuable. Unnecessary interruptions take a devastating toll. A daily routine that forces productive activity builds momentum.

Developing a Sense of Urgency

Realize the value of deadlines. Imposing deadlines on yourself and experiencing self-discipline in adhering to them aids you in overcoming indecision and procrastination. Give yourself some special reward when a high achievement is reached on time. Stay in a hurry to get things done. Consider these specific "time savers."

- **Become clock-conscious.** Set your watch five minutes fast. It will make you time-conscious and keep you punctual.
- **Don't try to remember everything.** Record appointments and important information.
- **Make every call count.** If you can't make a sale now, determine when you can.
- **Keep your automobile in top condition.** You can't earn commissions if you can't get to your prospect.
- **Become adept at dictating into a pocket cassette recorder.**
- **Make the most of your transition time.** Listen to cassettes during your "in between" time. A remarkable amount of information and inspiration can be obtained during your "scrap time." Turn your automobile into a learning center.
- **Use your secretary as an assistant**—a kind of department head. Besides routine correspondence, phone answering and monitoring of visitors and appointments, a secretary can be invaluable in anticipation and follow-up.
- **Make use of specialists where you lack expertise.** It saves time.
- **Skim books and magazines for ideas.** Learn to skip over unnecessary details and omit copy that's only marginally informative or take a speed reading course. Retain usable ideas and quotations on 3 by 5 index cards.
- **Take advantage of waiting time.** Plan ahead to make this time productive.

- **Generate less paperwork.** Throw away nonessential papers once you have read them.
- **Handle each piece of paper once.** Frequently, a reply to letters can be made on the same sheet of correspondence. Save trivia to be handled on the final day of each month.
- **Avoid "friendly visits."** Many salespeople fall into the trap of looking up friends when they should be making calls.
- **Carry a list of frequently used telephone numbers.** Don't waste time looking up numbers or waiting in line for change.
- **Decide on those responsibilities where you must be accountable and those things that can be delegated.** Then delegate where you can.
- **When you start something, be determined to do it right the first time and do it to a finish.** The old cliché, "If you don't have time to do it right, when will you have time to do it over?" applies today too. Resist the temptation to leave a job unfinished. It takes more time to refamiliarize yourself with a project than to complete it the first time around.
- **Plan unavailability.** Plan a "quiet hour" each day for concentration and creative thinking. It will pay dividends.

Sound principles like those listed above suggest solutions to the time wasters confronting you every day of your selling life.

A MEANINGFUL PARABLE

If you had a bank that credited your account each morning with $86,400, and every evening cancelled whatever amount was still unspent, what would you do? You would draw out every cent every day, of course!

Well, you have such a bank—it's a life bank and it makes a "time deposit" into your account each and every morning. It credits your account with 86,400 seconds. Every night, it rules off as lost any amount you failed to put to a good purpose. It carries no balance forward. It allows no overdrafts.

Each day, it opens a new account for you. Each night, it burns the records of the day. If you fail to use the day's deposit, the loss is yours. There's no going back, no drawing against tomorrow. You must sell in the present on today's deposits. Invest it wisely. Invest it carefully so that you achieve the most return on your investment.

If you'd like to get more value out of your account, reread and restudy this chapter on managing your time. For a quick look at how important your time is, refer to the chart below:

If you earn:	Every hour is worth:	Each minute is worth:	In a year, one hour a day is worth:
$25,000	$12.81	21¢	$3,125
$40,000	$20.49	34¢	$5,000
$50,000	$25.61	43¢	$6,250
$75,000	$38.42	64¢	$9,375
$100,000	$51.23	85¢	$12,500

MANAGING YOUR TIME SUMMED UP

You are paid for what you do—not how many hours you put in. However, of all the hours you spend on your profession, only those actually spent in front of a prospect can make you wealthy. You're able to give yourself a raise (a healthy raise) right now, *if* you can put more selling into the hours you already spend at work.

First, buy or borrow a stopwatch—find out just how little of your time is actually spent in selling. For an entire week, just keep track of your selling time. At the end of the week, reread this chapter—you'll be ready to take remedial action!

Not all of your time is high-quality time. Concentrate your selling into that time—use the low-quality time for routine matters.

Develop a time-consciousness; plan to stay effective, to establish and maintain momentum, to avoid interruptions and to develop a sense of urgency.

When you find out the "routine" or nonproductive things that are costing you time, you will have found the things that are costing you money. You get 86,400 seconds deposited to your account every day—if you don't use them wisely, they're wasted!

MANAGING YOUR TIME REMINDERS

- The quality of selling time is a function of what you spend it doing.
- Develop a time-conscious attitude.
- Plan your priorities daily.
- Stay focused on the essential activities that influence your production.
- Establish and maintain momentum.
- Develop a sense of urgency by setting deadlines.
- A most common time management problem is unnecessary interruptions.

- Make every call count.
- Make the most of your transition time.
- Make use of specialists where you lack expertise.
- Plan a quiet hour each day for creative thinking and self-organization.
- You will discover there is always time to do the high-payoff job.

CHAPTER 11

STAYING UP: KEEP A VITAL SELF-IMAGE AND EXPECT TO WIN

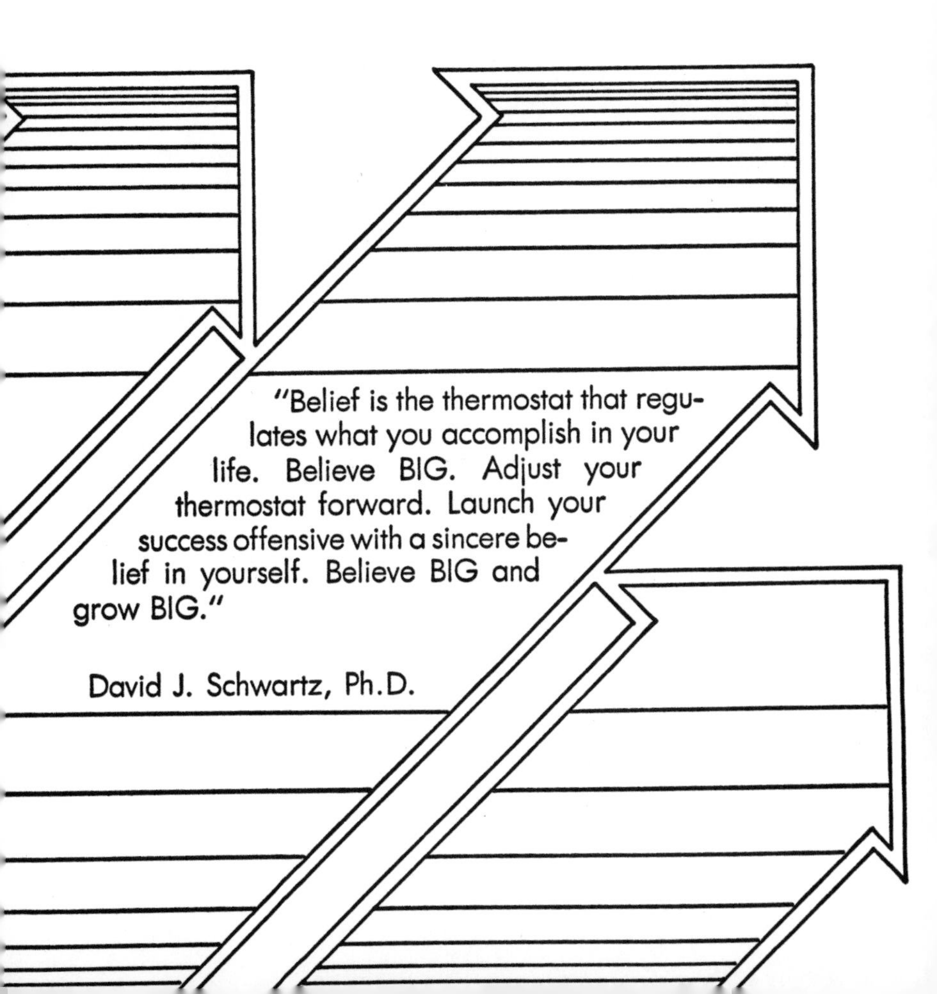

"Belief is the thermostat that regulates what you accomplish in your life. Believe BIG. Adjust your thermostat forward. Launch your success offensive with a sincere belief in yourself. Believe BIG and grow BIG."

David J. Schwartz, Ph.D.

YOUR NEED FOR "UPNESS"

The final gun sounds. The favored team has been upset. Sports writers gather around the dejected coach and ask, "What happened out there today?" The coach struggles for a response and then says, "We were just not up—they were." In the winning dressing room, in answer to the identical question the jubilant reply is, "We were really up—that's the only way to describe it."

The team that finds the way to stay up most of the time is a winner. *Likewise, in selling, upgrading your thinking upgrades your performance, and this produces success.* Your need for "upness" as a professional in selling is just as critical as it is for the professional in any field of endeavor.

We agree with the former all-pro, Bill Glass (now an evangelist and in great demand as a speaker for sales conventions). Bill says, " 'Upness' is a product of self-image and self-motivation. The mind is a most delicate, a most sensitive and amazing mechanism. When your mind works one way it can carry you to outstanding success—when it works another way it can carry you to uninspired performance."

Let's examine ways in which you can build a strong, healthy self-image and stay motivated on a consistent basis.

WHAT IS SELF-IMAGE?

Whether or not you are conscious of it, you carry into every selling situation a rather definite picture of yourself. If asked, you could produce a number of words to describe yourself. It is to be hoped that you think of yourself as an intelligent, informed, competent person. Psychologists agree your self-image is an accurate measure of your personality and your possibilities as a salesperson.

Self-image is how you view yourself. It is how you perceive yourself. Your perception measures the height of your selling possibilities. "A stream cannot rise higher than its source." Nothing else will gear you to accomplish superior selling results as will the belief in your own possibilities. It is here that your selling power originates.

It's important to understand two fundamental principles about self-image:

- **You will be true to your self-image.** You will perform the way you see yourself performing.
- **Your self-image can and does change.**

Since you perform according to your self-image, the key to changing your sales performance lies in changing your self-image.

CHANGING YOUR SELF-IMAGE

Your self-image can be changed by the people with whom you choose to associate. It can be changed by the books you read, cassettes you listen to, TV programs you view. The feedback from all of these things can change your daily performance. Occasionally the change will be dramatic. Most of the time it is gradual—so gradual, in fact, that you may not even notice the change.

A friend of ours underwent a spiritual change in his life five years ago. Some key things changed immediately, others slowly. He told us, "I didn't really realize just how *much* I had changed until I met a man I hadn't seen in about four years. As he began to reminisce about things we had done then, I was mildly shocked. Oh, I had done all of the things he was talking about, but it was so far from my present character that it was as though he were talking about someone else."

The friend paused a moment and added, "I've read that when they make star maps, they first expose a photographic plate, wait a certain length of time and then expose another. Stars move so slowly that it is only by comparing the latest plate with the previous one that you can detect movement. In the same way, my change was so gradual that I wasn't even aware of it."

Dr. Maxwell Maltz, in his best-seller *Psycho-Cybernetics,* talks about the girl who changed her self-image dramatically after plastic surgery on her face. Once her appearance changed, her personality changed. She perceived herself differently. Many people experience change in self-image through religious experiences. Most of the time, however, the changes are gradual. This is why it's important to associate with successful people, read self-improvement books and listen to motivational and inspirational cassettes. As you become more confident, you will gradually perceive yourself as a more effective, persuasive salesperson.

The important motivation you have for changing

your self-image lies in the fact that the great selling results are produced by the perpetual expectation of attaining them. Despite any natural talents, training and education, your selling achievements will never rise higher than your expectations. *The expectant approach, the expectant presentation and the expectant close are what produce the desired results.* People can, who think they can. People can't, who think they can't. This is an unchanging, indisputable law of selling and of life itself.

Through the ages, philosophers have disagreed on many things. But they have had unanimous agreement on one thing: "You become what you think about most of the time." Emerson said, "People become what they think about all day long." In the Bible, we read, "As a man thinketh in his heart, so is he." There's not much question about it—you will perform the way you see yourself performing. You will be true to your self-image.

ONE THING NOT TO SURRENDER

Count as an enemy the person who shakes your expectation of your selling ability. Remember, as a professional salesperson your self-confidence is the one thing you can never afford to surrender. Nothing multiplies a salesperson's ability like faith in himself or herself. It will make a one-talent person into a success—while a ten-talent person without it will fail.

How often have you heard said about some successful person, "Everything he or she touches turns to gold?" We sometimes think of successful people as being lucky. The fact is, their success represents their expectations—it's the sum of their habitual ways of thinking. By the force of their expectations, such persons wring success from the most adverse circumstances.

Expectation brings successful experiences and successful experiences reinforce the power of confidence in selling.

Individuals who are self-reliant, positive, optimistic and assured "magnetize" conditions. They carry in their very presence an air of victory that compounds its power by convincing others. Their poise, assurance and ability increase in direct ratio to the number of selling achievements.

BUILDING YOUR VITAL SELF-IMAGE

There is a seven-step process for building a strong self-image.

1. **Learn to forgive yourself.** It is important not to carry around a guilt complex. Forgive yourself for the little human errors you have made in the past. You have heard that forgiveness is good for the soul. This is certainly true in building a healthy self-image. In this respect, we are not necessarily talking about spiritual forgiveness. We are talking about the forgiveness you give yourself on a daily basis for those little human mistakes that everyone makes from time to time.

Don't dwell on your imperfections. Recognize your good points and be proud of them.

Dr. Leon Teck, the Connecticut psychiatrist, in his book *The Fear of Success* says, "The fear of success can pop up in the most unlikely places." It can be the fear of getting married or being named company president. It can mean fear of winning your weekly tennis game, getting close to a friend, or making an important sale.

The underlying cause, according to Dr. Teck, is that "we were all children once. For a time, we were insignificant. When success finally arrives, we don't quite believe it." Dr. Teck then states the specific reason why most of us don't want to do too well in too many things. He says, "You think you don't deserve it; therefore, you feel guilty about your good fortune. You are afraid of the unearned visibility."

Pamper yourself a little more. You can't be a likable person unless you like yourself. It's almost impossible to like yourself if you cannot discover the way to forgive yourself. The Bible says, "Love thy neighbor as thyself." You can't do a very good job of loving your neighbor if you don't love yourself—can you?

2. **Be able to forgive others.** Don't carry grudges. Remember, you become what you think about. If you carry a grudge, you're likely to become like the person you are carrying the grudge against. The Bible also says, "Forgive us *our* trespasses *as we forgive* those who trespass against *us*." That's saying, "We know we won't be forgiven if we don't forgive."

A man once said to us, "I hate my former partner but he lives 500 miles away—what possible difference could it make if I forgive him since we never meet?" The difference isn't the difference it might make to him—the difference is the difference it makes to you and your life and attitude.

3. **Develop your ability to communicate.** Express how you feel. We have all experienced the situation when we carry something around inside and all of a

sudden decide to express it. We jump all over someone—maybe someone very close to us. However, when it comes out, we feel better and they feel better. It is important to communicate with others, especially those close to you: your spouse, children and friends. Don't carry feelings inside. Let them come out.

Don't be modest in the way you accept compliments. If someone gives you a compliment, thank the person. Communicate how good he or she made you feel.

It is also important to communicate with yourself. In this regard, ask yourself these questions: "When was the last time I was alone? When was the last time I just sat around and thought about my situation?"

Another area of concern is your spiritual communication. If you pray, communicate with God. We are told that in regard to prayer, there is too much communication from us to God—not enough from God to us. Do a lot of praying and remember to let God do some of the "talking."

4. **Build a life model.** In the next chapter we will recommend writing out your life goals. You'll learn to set realistic goals that you can achieve one step at a time. You'll learn how important it is to have a master dream list. *It is important to put in writing the type of person you want to become as well as the things you want to accomplish.*

5. **Use your imagination in a positive manner.** Become an optimist. When you are down in the dumps, imagine the better times ahead. This will give you the drive to meet challenges. People sometimes say, "I just don't have a good imagination." We ask them, "Do you worry very much?" They reply, "I worry all the time." You see, they *have* a good imagination, they're just using it negatively. *Form the habit of*

using your imagination positively. Visualize yourself accomplishing your goals.

One of the great sales personalities of our time is Mary Crowley. Mary has launched thousands of women into selling careers.

Mary believes in the power of expectation. Mary says, "Expect great things to happen. Boldly predict what you are going to do. Be daring and persistent. You may give out—but never give up!" Then she adds, *"Be determined to be somebody because God never made a nobody."*

6. **Compete but don't compare.** You should compete with your friends and associates but you should never compare. "Keeping up with the Joneses" adds unneeded pressures to your selling life. Build your life model: *compare your life with what you ought to be.* Many people are frustrated and have nervous breakdowns because they are comparing themselves with other people. Never compare yourself with others—compete with them.

7. **Be yourself—but be your best self.** It is important to study and learn from other people. It is important to emulate other people, but in the end be yourself. We've heard Dr. Maltz say at our Purdue Institutes, "Be you—because you are the most unique you that God ever made." *Be yourself—but be your best self.*

So, that's the process for building a healthy self-image:

1. Learn to forgive yourself.
2. Be able to forgive others.
3. Develop your ability to communicate.
4. Build a life model.
5. Use your imagination in a positive manner.

6. Compete but don't compare.
7. Be yourself—but be your best self.

Be positive about yourself, your selling job and your future. Be determined to have a strong, healthy self-image.

"Put forth honest, intelligent effort."

BE AWARE OF TWO MENTAL DISEASES

In building your self-image you must be aware of two obstacles or "mental diseases." One is the disease known as "Mumpsimus." Mumpsimus means "a persistent belief in a mistaken idea." If you go back 500 years, almost everyone had common mumpsimus—they believed the world was flat. Today, some people have a mumpsimus about salespeople: "They're selfish, commission-conscious, aggressive, uneducated, etc." You must be careful not to be affected by this disease. It can be prevented by applying the seven processes for building a healthy self-image that we just discussed.

The second disease is known as "Sniop." Sniop isn't a word, it's an acronym. It describes a person who is *S*usceptible to the *N*egative *I*nfluences of *O*ther *P*eople. We are susceptible to the negative input of other people. One time we were in the office of Hubert Noack, a Sales Training Director in Appleton, Wisconsin. He had a sign on his wall that read: "Don't be SNIOPed by someone who has MUMPSIMUS." This is easy to do. This is why it is important to follow the seven-step formula for building a healthy self-image.

"Don't be SNIOPED by someone who has MUMPSIMUS."

To be an effective salesperson, you must develop a strong, healthy self-image. *See yourself at your best.* Visualize yourself reaching your goals. You were born to win. You deserve to win in selling. You will win by building your self-image.

MOTIVATION COMES FROM WITHIN

Ralph Cordiner, during his reign as Chairman of the Board at General Electric, made a significant statement at a sales conference. "We need from every salesperson a determination to undertake a program of self-improvement. Nobody orders a person to develop. Whether you lag behind or move ahead is a matter of personal choice. Self-development is something which takes time, work and sacrifice. Nobody can do it for you. It calls for self-motivation—the kind of motivation that comes from within."

We have found Mr. Cordiner's advice to be sound. It is practical. Live it. You will reach the top rung of the ladder of production honor rolls by staying motivated. Your company's training programs provide content and method. The acid test is, do they get results? *Results call for execution and execution requires motivation—self-motivation.*

Bobby Knight, the fiery Indiana University basketball coach, thinks the will to win is much overplayed. "What success requires is the will to prepare—to stay motivated." We again add to this: "And all motivation is, in reality, self-motivation."

In a previous book, *First Down, Lifetime to Go,* Roger

said, "You can't just talk positive and be a winner, you have to believe it deep inside." *It's not enough to have the will-to-win—you need the will to work-to-win!*

"Spectacular achievements are always preceded by unspectacular preparations."

SIX STEPS TO SELF-MOTIVATION

Motivation is a desire to achieve, a desire to win, a desire to do well, a desire to perform at your best. The well-known Olympic gold medal winner, our good friend Reverend Bob Richards, talks to athletic coaches all over America. Bob asks each group, "What do you think it takes to make a champion athlete?" Some respond that it's coaching. Others say it's talent. Others say it's natural ability. Others say it's being at the right place at the right time. Bob tells us he is convinced the key ingredient in great athletes is desire. Bob believes that when you find athletes with desire, you have individuals who will take coaching. They will use their talent. They'll make their breaks. They will be self-motivated.

How do you motivate yourself and stay motivated for the long haul? Here is a six-step procedure you can follow:

- **Develop self-acceptance.** The starting point is having respect for yourself. As we discussed earlier, it is vital that you have a strong, healthy self-image. To win in selling, think well of yourself.
- **Realize you have the potential for greatness.** When Roger graduated from Annapolis and en-

tered the Navy for four years of active service, most people thought that the inactivity would signal the end of his career. But Roger never doubted his ability not only to *play* pro football but to play *great* pro football. He said, "I was worried about a lot of things when I reported to my first full training camp in July of 1969. I knew people were saying I couldn't make it back after four years, but I had an unbelievably positive attitude."

- **Plan for greatness.** How do you plan for greatness? By *deciding* to do great things, then doing all of the *small* things that add up to greatness. With Roger, it meant running and doing pushups—more than were required. When Ben Hogan was coming back after an auto accident and doctors didn't expect him to walk again, much less play golf, he painfully practiced hour after hour. He went on to become one of America's all-time great golfers—but he also spent more hours *practicing* than any other golfer!
- **Think like successful people think.** Form the habit of asking yourself: "Is this the way a successful salesperson would do it? What would a successful person do with this idea? How would a successful person deal with this? Am I looking and acting like a person who has maximum self-respect?"
- **Act as if it were impossible to fail.** There are two kinds of confidence—quiet confidence and cocky confidence. Cocky confidence inspires a desire in others to see you *fail.* Quiet confidence inspires others to want to see you *succeed!* Roger, "Mr. Clutch" to his teammates, had a quiet confidence on the field that inspired others to believe that, whatever the circumstances, it was still possible to win.

Roger has taken this same quiet confidence with him into thousands of selling situations. It's not only inspiring, but it's believable. People tend to accept you at *your* assessment of yourself.

- **Monitor your results.** Form the habit of measuring and monitoring your sales results. There is great motivation in taking note of the progress you are making. Studying the score causes the sales score to improve.

"Don't settle for second best."

STAYING UP SUMMED UP

Every salesperson's most important customer is himself or herself. Before you can sell anything to anyone, you must sell yourself on your job, your ability, your product and your future.

We referred in an earlier chapter to Rich DeVos who, along with Jay Van Andel, has built one of the biggest and best sales organizations in the world at Amway. Rich believes respect and enthusiasm are vital characteristics for people involved in selling.

Rich says, "Enthusiasm is relatively more important than product knowledge or experience in sales. I am convinced that to be successful, you must be enthusiastic. If you aren't excited about your job or the products you are selling, you can't expect others to be excited either. Enthusiasm stems from the belief that what you are doing is worthwhile and the products you represent are of high quality and they work. And, enthusiasm is contagious. If a person is committed to his or her goals, others will feel it."

Rich goes on to say, "I believe you achieve that which you think you can achieve. I have learned we must respect each individual with whom we come in contact. It takes all persons from one end of the economic spectrum to the other to make the free enterprise system work. We must have respect for ourselves; respect which will work to generate feelings of self-confidence and create a positive image of our job. Our self-concept is an all-important ingredient in achieving success in selling. The salesperson who respects himself or herself and has faith in his or her responsibility will succeed—be it sales or any other endeavor. Those whose aim is low generally hit their target! Those who expect good things to happen usually make them happen. The ingredients are respect, enthusiastic hard work, a commitment to goals and a strong, healthy self-image."

Bob Coode has been selling life insurance in Cleveland for ten years, and he has qualified for the prestigious Million Dollar Round Table ten times. Bob recently admitted to us that successful salespeople often talk to themselves and "sell themselves" all day long. "We do it to overcome the other negative voices," he said. "Our prospects tell us they don't need our product. They hammer at our confidence and challenge our self-esteem all day long. Smart salespeople talk their confidence up. They remind themselves of the obstacles they first had to conquer to win previous sales. They sell themselves on the answers they'll use for the objections they're certain to face. They build a strong case for imagining a successful conclusion because in their conversation with themselves, they are selling their most suspicious listener."

Bob was saying that a strong, healthy self-image precedes and causes almost all of your selling achievements. You are under the influence of your self-image every minute of your selling day. Everything you see, hear or work with creates an impression that produces a result corresponding to the mental picture you first perceived of yourself.

Your self-image first idealizes what self-motivation afterward realizes. Turn on your imagination. Dial to your most desired scene. Spell out a detailed, vivid action shot of yourself as the motivated salesperson you have always wanted to be. It will prove to be one of the most valuable and productive forms of practice you have ever done.

You'll discover yourself being *up* for every selling situation.

STAYING UP REMINDERS

- Upgrading your thinking upgrades your results.
- "Upness" is a product of self-image and self-motivation.
- Self-image can and does change.
- Learn to forgive yourself and others.
- Build a life model.
- Use your imagination in a positive manner.
- Compete but don't compare.
- Be yourself, but be your *best* self.
- Success requires the will to prepare.
- All motivation is in reality self-motivation.
- Develop self-acceptance as a starting point.
- Realize you have the potential for greatness.
- Monitor your results.
- Keep yourself sold on you.

CHAPTER 12

FIVE STEPS TO PROSPEROUS GOAL SETTING AND ACTION PLANNING

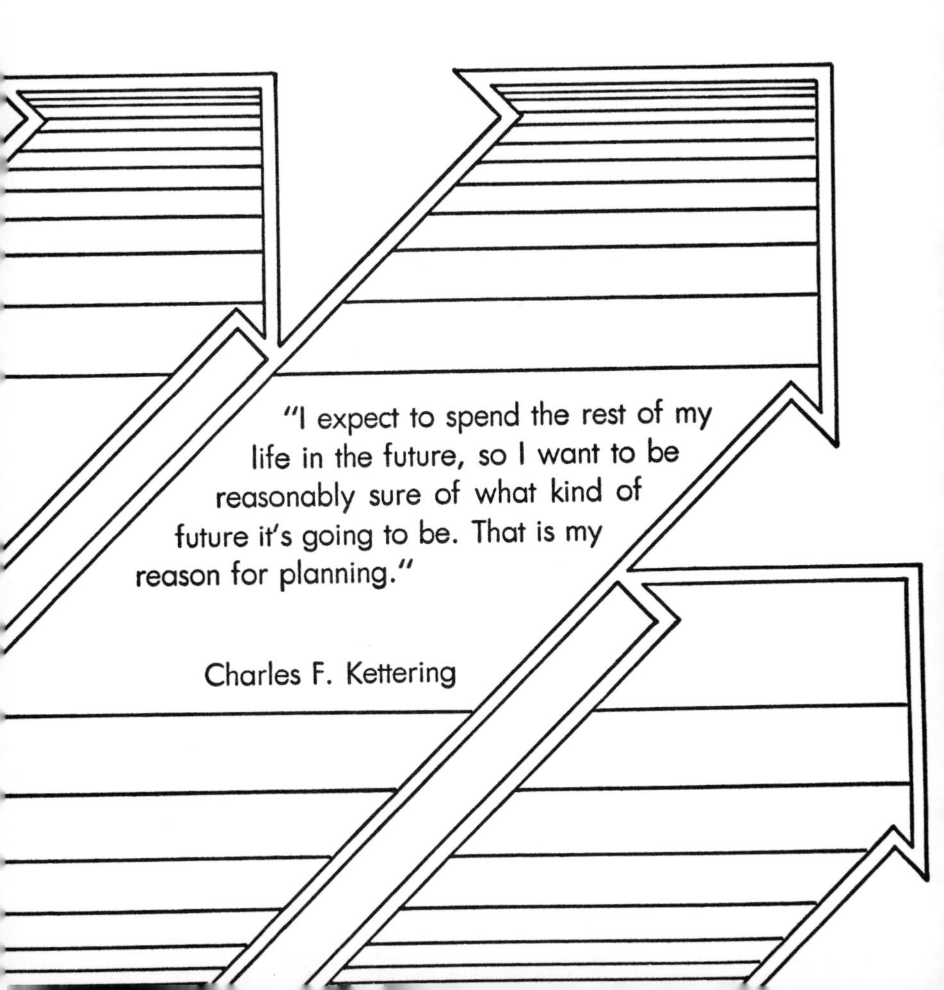

"I expect to spend the rest of my life in the future, so I want to be reasonably sure of what kind of future it's going to be. That is my reason for planning."

Charles F. Kettering

PLAN YOUR FUTURE NOW

The desirable attitude toward your future in selling is summed up in two self-management concepts: goal setting and action planning. When joined together, they form a strong foundation upon which selling success is built.

Experience will teach you that selling success, financial success and happiness are mainly the result of two things:

- persistent effort to develop your personal assets
- setting up and steadfastly pursuing a series of goals for growth

Life doesn't cheat. It doesn't pay in counterfeit coins. It doesn't lock up shop and go home when payday comes. It pays every person exactly what has been earned.

I bargained with Life for a penny,
And Life would pay no more,
However, I begged at evening
When I counted my scanty store;

For Life is a just employer,
He gives you what you ask,

But once you have set the wages,
Why, you must bear the task.

I worked for a menial's hire,
Only to learn, dismayed,
That any wage I had asked of Life,
Life would have gladly paid.

Jessie B. Rittenhouse

The old law that you get what you earn hasn't been suspended.

When you take these truths into your business life and believe in them—when you thoughtfully complete the five-step approach to goal setting and action planning developed in this chapter each year—you've turned a big corner on the high road that will lead you straight to success throughout your selling career.

Earl Nightingale reminds us, "Success is the progressive realization of a worthy idea." Goal setting is determining one's worthy ideal. Action planning is the progressive realization of those ideals.

Goal setting and action planning are as inseparable as night following day, yet equally distinctive. They are the head and tail of the same coin. One says "what" and the other says "how." Together, they say "success."

An individual without goals is like a ship without a captain. The ship may well have the finest equipment and design, yet without a captain to steer and chart its course to a designated port, it goes nowhere—and may even drift aimlessly onto the shoals.

Goal setting establishes your chief aims. It determines your purposes—your worthy ideals. Without such aim, your life will be like an abandoned ship at sea, tossed by the waves of circumstance, often taking the voyage of least resistance.

The key is direction and focus. An individual with growth goals is an individual with determination and drive. Goals for growth animate and invigorate. Your effectiveness and productivity are greatly multiplied when you have singleness of purpose. Tunnel vision is good when your target is clearly sighted.

Goal setting is the initial cause of which success is the final effect.

HOW YOU SET GOALS

Now that you have an understanding of the importance of goal setting, what are some of the criteria to appraise in establishing your chief aims? There are four factors, equally important, in goal setting.

1. Your Goals Must Be Achievable

Why push and strive toward a goal if you know that it is outside of your reach? Properly established goals are attainable only with a maximum effort. They push you to give your optimal level of effort. They have been set realistically high. Vince Lombardi stated, "I firmly believe that any man's finest hour, his greatest fulfillment to all he holds dear, is the moment when he has worked his heart out in a good cause and lies exhausted on the field of battle victorious."

Your goals must push you to your maximum, yet reward you with the satisfying taste of victory when you grasp them—but they *must be attainable.*

As Roger says, "If you're the bottom salesperson on the ladder, a reasonable goal isn't to be the top producer in an office of 100 salespeople in a year. Maybe your first goal should be to make the top twenty—then the top ten.

"If you're a football team and your record is 4 and 8, your goal can't be to make the Superbowl that year—a reasonable goal might be to be 8 and 8.

"The Cowboys always have high goals, but they are attainable. We won a Superbowl one year when we were 4 and 3—it was a long way to go but it was attainable and we knew it. We didn't just have an overall goal—we have goals for each player—they're high goals, measurable goals and yet achievable goals."

2. Your Goals Must Be Believable

"We went into the locker room of a team one year when we were playing in the Superbowl and they had goals right in the locker room—but they were unreasonable. They hadn't been a very strong team the year before but they had exceptionally high goals for the next year that were just unbelievable. Their goals were, in many areas, tougher than ours, and we were a championship team!

"A goal that's not believable will have a negative impact on you."

This is closely related to the first criterion. A goal should reflect realism, not idealism. It must be something you are *convinced* you can reach.

3. Your Goals Must Be Measurable

Think about your favorite athletic event. Would you find it interesting if there were no scoreboard? What makes the game exciting is knowing the score and how much time is remaining. Your goals will become challenging only when they are measurable.

4. Your Goals Must Have Deadlines

Time is your most precious commodity. It can never be replaced. If you are to use your time most productively, your goals must have deadlines. Deadlines bring compulsion and a responsible commitment of action.

"Build a program of self-development."

THE FIVE KEY STEPS TO GOAL SETTING AND ACTION PLANNING

Again, for the sake of emphasis, remember that there are two chief cornerstones that support success. Goal setting sharpens your focus—your plan of action gets you there. In this chapter we will cause you to first evaluate yourself and determine what your life dreams actually are. Next, you will establish a plan of action to achieve your goals. Finally, you will determine the effort required in weekly compartments to achieve these goals.

This must become an annual planning discipline. It is serious business. It requires careful thought. So, begin now—plan the balance of this year and your future now!

Step One: Looking at Me

The first priority on your road to selling success is to realistically evaluate yourslf. There is no substitute for your being completely introduced to your greatest asset: *you*!

Before you can determine where you want to go and

how and when you want to get there, you must first know from where you're starting. The captain of a ship can't chart a course for a distant land without first knowing exactly *where* he or she is *now*. You can't chart a course for the future without knowing where you are, either.

You find where you are by taking personal inventory.

Catalog your needs, interests, strengths and weaknesses. Once you have done this, you can develop ways to meet your needs, satisfy your interests, build on your strengths and strengthen your weaknesses. You're ready to chart your course!

On the pages that follow, we'll conduct a self-analysis in three key areas: business, personal and financial. This exercise will serve as a mirror with which to view yourself.

"The picture is never greater than the artist. You improve the work by first improving the worker."

BUSINESS SELF-ANALYSIS

This proficiency checklist is to serve as a self-inventory of your skills and abilities. Its purpose is to determine the performance/potential gap in your selling. Rate yourself on a scale from 1 to 5 for the following items and then compare your score with the perfect score of 100.

1. Displaying a commanding professional presence	1 2 3 4 5
2. Setting reachable goals with established deadlines	1 2 3 4 5
3. Planning my work the previous day	1 2 3 4 5
4. Prospecting effectiveness	1 2 3 4 5
5. Pre-approach efficiency	1 2 3 4 5
6. Skill in probing for facts	1 2 3 4 5
7. Handling the preparation process	1 2 3 4 5
8. Sales presentation effectiveness	1 2 3 4 5
9. Meeting objections	1 2 3 4 5
10. Closing skill	1 2 3 4 5
11. Obtaining referrals	1 2 3 4 5
12. Use of weekly activity and result report to determine "dollar value" of each selling activity and progress made toward goals	1 2 3 4 5
13. Efficient office administration	1 2 3 4 5
14. Secretarial, telephone, mail services	1 2 3 4 5
15. Letter writing	1 2 3 4 5
16. Staying active in business, civic and church activities	1 2 3 4 5
17. Reading, study and cassettes	1 2 3 4 5
18. Physical fitness program	1 2 3 4 5
19. Managing personal financial affairs	1 2 3 4 5
20. Personal planned self-improvement program	1 2 3 4 5
TOTAL POSSIBLE SCORE	100
MY SCORE	______
Performance/Potential Gap	______

PERSONAL SELF-ANALYSIS

Personal Statistics: Age ____ Height ____ Weight ____

Personal Priority Ranking:

____ career ____ family ____ spiritual

____ social ____ physical ____ knowledge

Greatest personal motivation and interests:

____

____

Personal strengths:

____

____

Personal responsibilities:

____

____

Personal accomplishments of which I am most proud:

____

____

Areas that I must strengthen:

____

____

Personal projects, activities, or hobbies that I plan to initiate:

____

____

Personal habits that I plan to build into my life:

____

____

Planned personal accomplishments for/with my family:

____

____

FINANCIAL SELF-ANALYSIS

(It is essential that you know your family financial position. The NET WORTH of YOU, INC., is the difference between what you own and what you owe.)

ASSETS (what you own)	
Cash:	
Checking Accounts	$________
Savings Accounts	________
U.S. Government Bonds (accrued value)	________
Stocks (market value)	________
Bonds (market value)	________
Life Insurance (cash value)	________
Real Estate—Home (market value) ..	________
Other Real Estate (market value)	________
Automobiles (market value)	________
Personal Property (furniture, jewelry, appliances, furs, etc.)	________
Amounts Owed You	
Other: ________	________
Total Assets	$________
LIABILITIES (what you owe)	
Current Bills (amount owed)	$________
Installment Debt (balance owed)	
Automobile	________
Home Improvement	________
Personal	________
Furniture, Appliance	________
Other: ________	________
Mortgage (balance owed)	________
Other Real Estate (balance owed) ...	________
Other Amounts Owed: ________	________
Total Liabilities	$________
TOTAL ASSETS	$________
TOTAL LIABILITIES .... –	$________
NET WORTH .... =	$________

Step Two: Examining Your Dreams

Your full potential often lies dormant until aroused by your dreams. In the initial step, you took a look forward to the person you can become. You'll see even more.

Remember, "Success is the progressive realization of a worthy ideal." Focus your attention now on what you believe to be life's worthy ideals for you.

In order to do so, allow your mind the freedom of dreaming. What are your life's dreams? What do you have visions of achieving? Lewis Carroll said, "It's a poor sort of memory that only works backwards." *Project yourself mentally into the future.* What would you like to see accomplished in your life?

It is important for a person to dream of what they want to do because, as Homer Rice, the Georgia Tech Athletic Director, says, "People are motivated to do what they themselves decide to do."

On the following pages, you will compile your "Master Dream List." Remember, your only limitations are self-imposed. It is important that you consider everything you will want to do—everything you will want to learn—everything you will want to earn—yes, and everything you will want to become.

You make your dreams—and then your dreams make you.

Dreams are like stars for the seafaring mariner on a dark night. You will use them for direction to safely reach your destination.

Precise yet perceptive is the proverb that states, "Without a vision, the people perish."

BUILDING YOUR MASTER DREAM LIST*

I want to own: ____________________

____

____

I want to know: ____________________

____

____

I want to do: ____________________

____

____

I want to be: ____________________

____

____

I want to earn: ____________________

____

____

I want to learn: ____________________

____

____

*Compliments of Homer Rice, Vice President and Director of Athletics at Georgia Tech.

Step Three: Establishing This Year's Goals

Next, you clarify your objectives. Having established life's chief aims, you must realign your thinking to the present—to this year. *The future is where you dream. Now, this year, is where you live and where you must perform.*

Yearly goals bridge the gap between where you are now and where you want to go in life. They put you on schedule to achieve your life's objectives. Few people know what they want. Still fewer know when they want it.

A financial budget is a key in determining your yearly goals. Before you can set intelligent sales goals, you must first know what your financial needs are. A yearly budget will show you what you must produce, as a *minimum.*

Remember, a controlled inflow, regardless of how great, with an uncontrolled outflow leaves any river dry.

As you establish your personal goals for this year, you will always find it helpful to establish two kinds of goals—minimum and superior.

Your minimum goals are what you must do this year. It is what you will do regardless. *Your minimum goals are committed goals.* They are set realistically high and require a complete dedication to their achievement. There is no room for compromising your minimum goals.

On the other hand, your superior goals are flavored with optimism. These are the things that you would hope to achieve, those things over and above your minimum goals. *Superior goals are bonus goals.*

You will want to give careful thought to your minimum and superior goals. They are small keys that will unlock big futures in selling.

My Budget for This Year (Minimum Income Requirements)	Monthly Average	Annual
Mortgage Payments or Rent		
Household Expenses & Maintenance		
Utilities, Including Fuel		
Food		
Clothing		
Children's School-Related Expenses		
Personal Care, Cleaning, etc. .		
Education, Reading, Dues & Subscriptions		
Entertainment & Recreation, Vacation		
Personal Expenses (Lunch, etc.)		
Auto, Transportation		
Gifts & Contributions		
Medical & Dental, Health Insurance		
Personal Life Insurance, Savings, Investment		
Debt Reduction, Loan Payments		
Taxes		
Business Expenses (Not Reimbursed)		
Miscellaneous		

TOTAL INCOME NEEDED THIS YEAR $________

My Superior Goal $________

THIS YEAR'S SPECIFIC GOALS

KEY SELLING GOALS*	MINIMUM	SUPERIOR
New Calls	________	________
New Customers	________	________
Unit Sales	________	________
Service Calls	________	________
Commission Earnings	$________	$________
Bonus Earnings	$________	$________
Other Income	$________	$________
Total Income	$________	$________

SELF-DEVELOPMENT GOALS*

The selling skills I will develop this year will include the following:

____

____

The knowledge I will acquire this year will be in these areas:

____

____

The habits I will strengthen include the following:

____

____

The most effective way for me to reach and surpass each of the above goals is:

____

____

*Can be further personalized to your particular field.

"Our business in life is to get ahead of ourselves—to break our own records, to outstrip our yesterday by our today, to do the little parts of our work with more force than ever before."

Step Four: Fixing the Action Plan

Briefly, retrace your steps. You have taken an inventory of where you are presently. You have looked at your dreams and seen where you would like to go. You have determined what you must do this year to advance toward achieving your goals.

Now, you take the process one step further. You move one step closer to success. *"What is it that I must do each week in order to accomplish my goals for this year?"*

You have planned your work. Now you must work your plan. When you meet goals on a weekly basis, your year becomes successful. *It is here—with each week's activity and results—that the battle is won.*

Therefore, you must fix a weekly plan of action that will ensure your success. A Weekly Effort Formula becomes indispensable. Obviously, no pat formula can be developed that will be adaptable to every person who enters the field of selling. The activity requirement necessary for success varies according to the nature of your business, your previous experience, your background and your markets. Then, too, this requirement changes as you gain experience, knowledge, skills and confidence.

However, it does serve your best interest if your activity can be measured against a clearly defined standard. A Weekly Effort Formula, when calculated, can be a very helpful self-management tool.

In Frederickton, Canada, George Haynes told us about how much he hates the telephone. "I despise it—but my weekly calculations tell me that I make $45.20 every time I pick it up. This weekly reminder is the only motivation I need to pick up the telephone many times every day."

On the next page, we show you how to set up and live by a Weekly Effort Formula that will show you where your profits lie.

As you look at your Weekly Effort Formula, you will see that it pays to play the odds. The more contacts you make, the more opening interviews you'll get—and the more opening interviews you have, the more closing interviews you'll have. The more closing interviews you have, the more sales you'll make—and the more sales you make, the more commissions you'll earn!

A former associate of ours and a multimillion-dollar producer in Detroit, Bill Mansfield, claims, "The most important factor in selling success is *a firm belief in the law of averages.*" Bill goes on to say, "Top salespeople know that if they are prepared, a certain number of calls will inevitably result in a certain number of interviews—leading to a certain number of sales."

Roger tells how he became a percentage player in football. It was the 1970 season and Los Angeles beat Dallas just as they broke camp. Roger played in the second period and threw a long touchdown pass to Margene Adkins. Later, just as the half was ending, Roger threw an interception.

"Why did you throw the ball?" Coach Landry asked him as he came off the field.

"Wait a second, Coach," Roger said, "I wanted to go for the touchdown."

DEFINITIONS

Pre-approach—a call to arrange an appointment.

Opening interview—a probing, fact-finding interview to determine whether or not you have a prospect. A prospect is one who recognizes a need, has the ability to make a decision, and is salable by you.

Closing interview—the presentation of your recommendation and closing of the sale.

WEEKLY EFFORT FORMULA

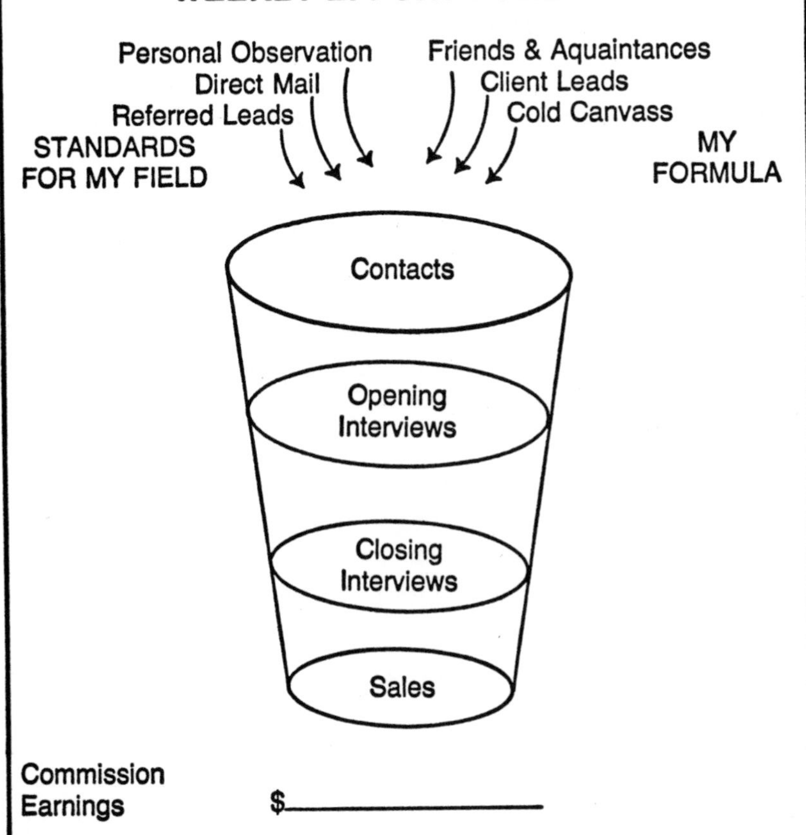

Commission Earnings $________________

HONEST, INTELLIGENT EFFORT IS ALWAYS REWARDED.

"That's not the percentage thing to do," Landry said. "The percentage thing to do is run out the clock and wait for another chance in the second half. Now you've given them the ball and they can score by kicking a field goal."

Learn to play the percentages—go after the big ones, the ones where your chances of making it are good.

The Jones Game Plan of Action

George Jones of Des Moines shared his strategy for setting goals with us.

George reached for his billfold, pulled out a card and told us about his idea. "I review this card daily and revise it quarterly. The card is divided into three sections—my life goals, my goals for this year and the game plan of action that must be taken now in order to reach these goals."

George takes an hour each month to reason the priority goals. "This system has been responsible for me making the Million Dollar Round Table, enjoying better health and staying goal-directed."

This is a simple but powerful idea that has propelled George Jones to a position of leadership in his company. It will do the same for you.

Here is the card George Jones took from his billfold:

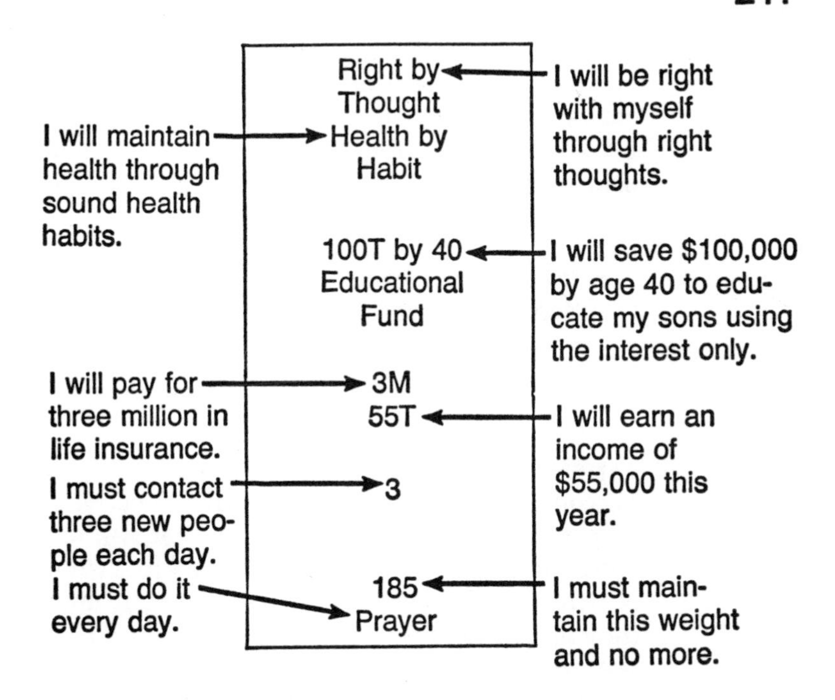

Step Five: Keeping Records to Break Records

You have laid the two chief cornerstones—goal setting and action planning—upon which you will build a successful year. There are no secrets to this kind of strategy—absolutely none. Honest, intelligent effort is always rewarded in selling. It is the law of laws: the law of cause and effect.

It now becomes a matter of (1) staying focused on the priority tasks and (2) measuring your results weekly, because measurement always improves performance.

You need a system of checkups to stay informed of your progress. Just as the stadium scoreboard tells the athlete the score and how much time is left, so will a system of weekly checkups gauge your progress.

Many companies furnish salespeople with a report form for recording weekly activities and results. If yours doesn't, make your own—because it's vital that you be able to constantly monitor your activities. It's easier to get back on course when you're just a little bit off course. If you only check up every six months, it may be too late to reach your goals for the year!

A report form is vital for two reasons:

- It helps you keep abreast of how you're doing against your weekly, monthly, quarterly and annual goals.
- It gives you a data base to help put your next week's plan into writing.

Tyrone Olier took his sales organization to the top of his company with a simple, but quite effective weekly report system. "Each of our associates knows the score, the dollar value of each activity and what must be achieved each week. They know exactly how much they must produce weekly during the balance of the year to meet their annual goals. Each is now sold that *measurement* improves *performance.*"

Like an Olympic athlete who trains for years to win the gold medal and break records, you too must discipline and challenge yourself to pursue your purpose. Records are broken by those who are compelled and driven by their purpose in life. This is your "ownership benefit" in keeping weekly records of your progress. Keeping important records produces consistency—and consistency always produces satisfying results.

GOAL SETTING AND ACTION PLANNING SUMMED UP

"I find the great thing in this world is not so much where you stand as in what direction you are moving. To

reach the port of heaven, we must sail sometimes with the wind and sometimes against it—but we must sail—and not drift, nor lie at anchor."

Oliver Wendell Holmes said that, and it's never been truer than in the field of selling. Heading in the right direction in your sales career requires only that you fix your eyes upon your goal, visualize it with every ounce of your being, and set out toward its achievement.

Become a kind of sponge for information and ideas that will help you on your way. You don't have to waste years in making mistakes in selling that others have made before you. You will be surprised at how quickly you can reach and surpass your goals. But don't be impatient. Know and have faith that what should come to you will come to you in time. Everything in business works on the side of the salesperson who works with nature's laws.

Above all—if you should forget everything else—remember that everything about you, everything you will ever own, know or experience, operates as a result of the law of cause and effect. As Emerson wrote, "Let each learn a prudence of high strain. Let each learn that everything in nature, even dust and feathers, goes by law and never by luck . . . and that what a person sows, he reaps."

That's it—that's all there is to it. Take stock of your present situation, for it is nothing more or less than the result of your past sowing. Then, you decide what you must sow—today and tomorrow and the next day—and in the sowing you know with certainty that having sown you will then reap the rich results . . . the abundant harvest *must* come.

GOAL SETTING AND ACTION PLANNING REMINDERS

- Success can best be defined as the progressive realization of a worthy ideal.
- Goals should be set realistically high. They must be believable.
- The first step in clarifying life goals involves self-analysis.
- Your full potential often lies dormant until aroused by building your master dream list.
- Before you can set intelligent sales goals, you must first establish your financial needs.
- Minimum goals are always committed goals.
- Superior goals are bonus goals.
- A Weekly Effort Formula is essential.
- Discipline yourself to calculate the activity and production results you must make happen each week for the balance of the year to reach your important goals.
- The great thing in selling is not where you stand, but the direction in which you are headed.

CHAPTER 13

THE THIRTEEN WINNING TRAITS OF SUPER SALESPEOPLE

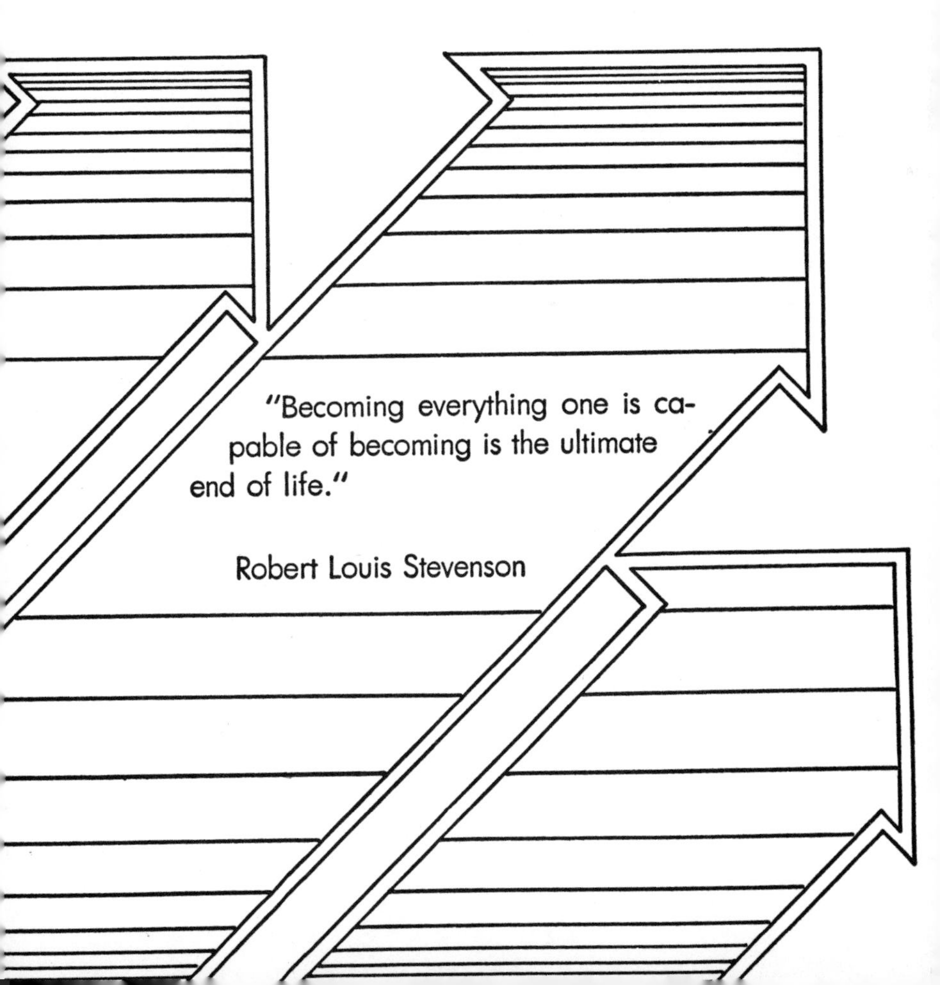

"Becoming everything one is capable of becoming is the ultimate end of life."

Robert Louis Stevenson

WHAT I'VE GOT: WHAT IT TAKES

In the opening chapter, we indicated that many people have a mistaken idea that star performers in selling are born, not made. No doubt you have had an "off day" or two which caused you to have serious doubts about whether you really "measured up" to the role of "super salesperson." Of course, your mythical star salesperson:

- has a magical sales personality
- has a sure-fire sales strategy
- is a mental giant
- is never discouraged
- never fails
- always makes the sale

No real-life individual in sales, no matter how good, can possibly measure up to such a distorted, unrealistic profile.

Every individual in our selling profession carries around a very definite mental picture of "what I've got" and "what it takes" as it relates to being a successful salesperson. Dr. Maxwell Maltz, the recognized authority on self-image psychology, talked to us about this. Dr. Maltz said, "Look around and take a really objective view of the stars in selling. Quickly, you will conclude that they are not really super human. The qualities necessary for success in selling can be developed by anyone. Don't fall into the trap of measuring yourself against a myth!"

"Self-confidence is high on the list of necessary skills," says David Mitchell, Chairman of the Board and Chief Executive Officer for Avon Products, Inc. Mr. Mitchell goes ahead to point out, "This is often an acquired or developed asset. It is gained through experience, and *is constantly reinforced and challenged by both success and failure*. Yes, failure. For the high achiever, disappointment can become a self-induced incentive stimulating the person to reevaluate former concepts and strive toward accomplishing the next goal."

THIRTEEN WINNING TRAITS

Our years of experience have taught us that winners in selling have 13 characteristics in common. As you examine each one, you'll discover that they're traits anyone can develop. It makes no difference how much education or experience you have, or what you have accomplished in your career up to this point. You too can develop and possess these traits.

The 13 winning traits of super salespeople are:

1. **Be and stay committed to goals.**
   Know what you want to achieve. Be totally committed to that goal. View defeat as a temporary thing. It's not so much where you stand, but rather the direction in which you are headed. It's stretching that develops your potential, and it's a complete commitment to realistically high goals that will

cause you to stretch. Measure the progress you are making toward the achievement of your goals. Do this regularly. *Measurement always improves performance.*

2. **Be and stay self-disciplined.**
Self-discipline is developed when you stop doing what you know you should not do, and start doing what you know you should—whether you like it or not. The degree of your success in selling depends on your ability to recognize those few primary activities that make the big difference in producing results. Self-discipline causes you to concentrate on these activities. *It is forming the habit of doing the right things right.* It is having always a sense of urgency.

3. **Be and stay knowledgeable.**
Spectacular results in selling are always preceded by unspectacular preparation. Continually accumulate usable information. It gives you a competitive edge. Have the facts and figures ready before plunging into an interview. *Never let a day pass without having learned something new about your product line or services.* Do your homework. Question people who know. People respect the person who is well informed. Be the best-informed salesperson your prospects ever meet. You'll earn their respect and gain their business.

4. **Be and stay a relationship-builder.**
Build the trust level in all you do. Prospects buy from the individual they trust. Earn the reputation of being 100 percent reliable. *Your success in selling calls for you to be an initiator, an activator, an influencer of attitudes and behaviors.* You function in these roles best by being an effective relationship-builder.

5. **Be and stay self-confident.**
Do this by feeding your mind regularly just as you feed your body. This enables you to accept rejection without too much inner anguish. Use your imagination positively. Remind yourself that you are prepared, poised and persuasive. Your biggest asset is a positive, courageous attitude. This, more than anything else, determines your success in selling. Shakespeare wrote, "Our doubts are traitors, and make us lose the good we oft might win, by fearing to attempt." Confidence is not the absence of fear, it is the conquest of fear. Do the thing you're afraid of and you'll develop the confident, winning feeling.

6. **Be and stay enthusiastic.**
Generate an excitement about what you are selling. It will overcome many shortcomings. Enthusiasm will encourage others to cooperate with you. *Act the way you want to feel.* To be enthusiastic—act enthusiastically.

7. **Be and stay an assistant buyer.**
Prospects are best convinced by reasons they themselves discover. Build the trust level as quickly as possible. Then assist the buyer in recognizing a need and acting upon the solution. Prospects are interested in discussing their business with you only when you indicate by your questions that you intend to show how your proposition will benefit them. *Your aim is always client-building. Customer satisfaction is your stock-in-trade.*

8. **Be and stay perceptive.**
Form the habit of paying attention. Let your "mental radar" work full time. *Deliberately train your eyes to see and your ears to hear.* Develop an

exhaustive observation. It will earn you great dividends.

9. **Be and stay a skillful communicator.**
   You sell with words and expressions. Study both carefully. *You must gain the prospect's understanding and understanding depends on what you say and how you say it.* Express your ideas and recommendations in terms of the self-interest of your prospects. This will cause them to think and act favorably toward you.

10. **Be and stay a perfectionist.**
    Demand excellence of yourself. It attracts and builds credibility. *Don't tolerate mediocrity.* There's no room for compromise among professionals. Stamp your work with excellence.

11. **Be and stay physically fit.**
    Develop the capacity to work hard and long. *Be a self-starter who displays a high continuing level of drive.* As Lombardi said, "Fatigue makes cowards of us all." Diet. Exercise. Run.

12. **Be and stay financially sound.**
    Personal budget-keeping is back in style. It is increasingly essential for you to get the maximum benefit from your selling income and to protect your savings. Do not rely strictly on the instinctive sense of money management. *Get a good handle on your living and business expenses along with your anticipated earnings.* Develop a plan of control over your spending. You will then make progress toward the kind of living which means the most to you.

13. **Be and stay persistent.**
    Always bounce back. In selling, failure means very little if success comes eventually. Resolve to perform what you should; perform without fail that

which you resolve. *Get up when you fall down.* If you get into the game—*stay in!* The secret of success is constancy of purpose.

Back to the strategy that assures victory for you!

The Autobiography of Benjamin Franklin tells us Franklin thought of himself as a very simple man of only ordinary talent. However, like all great individuals, he believed he could achieve success only if he could come upon a strategy that would compel him to obey the essential principles of successful living. Having an imaginative mind, Benjamin Franklin devised a simple but practical strategy that anyone can use. He chose *13* subjects that he felt were important to develop and master. He focused for a week on each subject, which enabled him to go through his entire list four times a year. (Just as we did with our 13 winning traits!) In his final days, Franklin wrote, "This strategy is scientifically sound. Adopt it and you will have taken a sure step toward greatness."

Goethe said, "Before you do something great, you must become something great." Franklin's "focus strategy" moves you toward becoming someone great. *This strategy develops inner motivation. It is this inner motivation that literally moves you toward success!*

IMPROVING YOUR FIELD POSITION

The U.S. Constitution says that we believe that "all men are created equal"—and so they are. But all men and women do not *remain* equal. We firmly believe that, regardless of your "field position" in life now, you can win from where you stand, *if* you begin putting into practice the principles we've been discussing in this book.

We've not put together merely ideas, but workable ideas, ideas that have worked for the three of us, ideas that have worked for thousands of others.

Roger has always said, "Field position of life is important. In football it's great to have ideal field position. As a quarterback it enhanced my chances of moving our team to a touchdown. After the 1972 Superbowl, I kidded Chuck Howley about how he intercepted Bob Griese's pass and made a long run down the sideline, only to fall a little short of the goal line. I told him, 'You could have scored, but you just wanted to give the offense good field position. You wanted your old roommate to be the hero.'

"Well, when God puts us on this earth, he gives some of us good field position and others he doesn't. It's tougher for those who don't have it, but if they still try to do something with their lives, God will reward them some day."

When you look back at Raul Jimenez with a seventh-grade education, trying to make a go of a business in a world full of educated people, you realize that he didn't have very good field position for scoring—yet he now heads a multimillion-dollar-a-year business.

When you look back at W. W. Clements, Chairman of the Board of the Dr Pepper Company, driving a delivery truck in Tuscaloosa, Alabama, you might think he didn't have very good field position—but look at how he scored!

When you look at Carl Joseph, the one-legged football player from Madison High, you might think that he had pretty poor field position—yet he became a football, basketball and track star!

Look at Roger, coming back from the Navy or from surgery—or Tommy John, whose arm was hanging literally by a thread—pretty poor field position, wasn't it? But they went on to win!

Do *you* think *you* have poor field position? You can overcome it from whatever your background, whatever your market, whatever your experience, whatever your past record—*if you want to badly enough!*

You can make it in spite of poor field position—*if* you have made up your mind to succeed.

We want to tell you the greatest sports story of all time.

Charley Paddock had a dream as a little boy. He said, "I want to be a gold medal winner at the Olympics." He went to his coach. "What can I do to be a gold medal winner?" Charley Paddock made the necessary sacrifices. He worked on getting his knees up. He worked on his start. To make the story short, Charley Paddock won the gold medal.

Now listen to it from this point on.

Paddock went around the country saying, "If you've got a dream, if you think you can do something—you can!" A boy in Cleveland, Ohio, came out of the audience and said, "I want to be an Olympic champion too!" Charley Paddock touched the young boy on the shoulder and said, "You can if you'll work, if you'll dream." The young boy was Jesse Owens, who won *four* Olympic gold medals in Germany!

Jesse came back home to Cleveland. Driving down the street in a ticker-tape parade, up came a nine-year-old boy. He put his hands on the side of the car and said, "Gee, Mr. Owens, I would give anything if I could be a champion like you!" Jesse touched this boy's hand and said, "You can if you will work. If you think you can, you can." It was Harrison Dillard who broke Jesse Owens' Olympic record in 1948 and who won another gold medal in 1952.

Harrison Dillard was giving speeches about faith and dreaming and how important it is to life. In Gary, Indiana, the son of a Methodist minister walked up to him and said, "Gee, Mr. Dillard, I would give anything if I could be a champion like you!" It was Lee Calhoun. Lee won the Olympics, breaking Harrison Dillard's record in 1956 and 1960.

Hayes Jones saw a picture of Lee Calhoun. He put it on the wall and said, "I want to be like Lee Calhoun!" He wrote him a letter and Lee wrote him back. He said, "If you will have faith and think that you can, you can." Hayes Jones became an Olympic champion.

Seven Olympic games where one man told another he could—and he did! Where one man had faith and he touched somebody else—they in turn had faith. They are all in the Hall of Fame now. They should call it the "Hall of Inspiration" or the "Hall of Positive Thinking" because that is where it's at. It's the way you think that makes the big difference in sports, in selling and in life.

Here is an unbelievable story. Yet it is so typical of the psychology of a champion and the power of the made-up mind. Bruce Jenner was in Graceland College, Iowa—a little school hardly anyone knew—pretty poor field position. He went down to the Kansas Relays and saw an athlete with a blue USA uniform on. He said, "Boy, I want to become a member of the Olympic team! I want to wear that uniform!" Don't laugh, many of the great performers in history were inspired by the sight of an Olympic uniform. Bruce worked and he made the team. He went to Munich and finished tenth.

While he was there, the magic of the mind began to work. He saw the other athletes. He said, "I can run as fast as they can! I'm as strong as they are! If I put my mind to it and my body in it, I can break the world's record. I can win a gold medal!"

Bruce Jenner came home and wrote down on a piece of paper what he had to do in ten events if he was going to shatter the world record in the decathlon in Montreal four years later.

10.6 in the 100 meter
23′7″ long jump
6′7½″ high jump
49.5 quarter
52′ shot put
162 discus
14.5 hurdles
15′7″ pole vault
215 javelin
4:16 in the 1500 meter

That's what he wrote down on a piece of paper—and that's what he programmed in his mind.

In Eugene, Oregon, in 1975, he hit every mark within a quarter of an inch or a tenth of a second and broke the world's record.

Then he said, "I've got to better myself in six events if I'm going to beat Aveloff of Russia—if I'm going to win the Olympics." Well, he missed—he only bettered himself in five events—he missed the sixth one by a *whole half inch!*

Now here is our question. Would he have accomplished all of this if he had not mentally programmed himself specifically to an exact time and an exact height? Or was the power of the mind the most important thing in that performance—even more important than his field position in Graceland, Iowa?

The answer is rather obvious.

Mary Kay Ash, founder of Mary Kay Cosmetics and the leader of one of the most dynamic sales organizations in America today, talked to us about this matter of attitude. Mary Kay said, "I believe most people never even begin to tap their full potential because of their lack of faith in their own abilities. God placed within us tremendous ability—and unfortunately most of us die with music still unplayed. It is said that only 10 percent of the potential we have is ever really tapped. As a potential salesperson or possibly someone already in the sales field, the first thing is to believe in yourself and your product. After that, you can and you will convey the same belief to your prospects and customers."

THE MOST MOTIVATIONAL

Every field of human endeavor is led by a relatively small percentage of the people in it. The sales field is no exception. Historically, it has divided itself into two groups: (1) those who lead rich, rewarding and interesting lives and (2) those who live average and largely unrewarding lives.

One time we were talking about these two groups with Bob Richards, the former Olympic champion. The discussion centered on this question: "What is the strongest motivational thought a salesperson can carry with himself or herself?" Think about it for a minute. You are determined to join the top group of salespeople who know more, do more and have more. A successful career is made up of successful days. Now, again, **"What is the strongest motivational thought a salesperson can carry with himself or herself?"**

Well, we discussed this at some length. Here are a few of the thoughts that surfaced near the top of our list:

- Honest, intelligent effort is always rewarded.
- It's not where you stand, it's the direction in which you are headed.
- If you can get in the game—stay in.
- You can alter your performance by altering your mental attitude.
- Get up when you fall down.
- When it's dark enough, you can see the stars.

Finally, we reached unanimous agreement. We concluded that the strongest motivational thought of all was this one:

GOD IS WITH ME

Carry this thought with you and watch the change it will make in your life. You were born to win. God is with you and wants you to have an abundant life.

This leads to our wish for you. It's the same for you as it is for our associates, our families and ourselves. Our wish is that the God who programmed you to win—the God who computerized you to succeed—the God who made it possible for you to conquer death itself—that God will be with you this day and every day throughout your selling career.

All the best to you always!

INDEX

A

Accomplishment, term, 53
Achievements, spectacular, 20–21
Action planning (*see* Goal setting, action planning)
Activity, term, 53
Aerobics, 31, 32
Alertness, 58
Appointment, gain, 92–93
Appointment book, 195
Appreciation, show, 178–181
Approach, objectives, 74, 103
Authority to buy, 87–88, 98
Automobile, 198

B

"Box Time" theory, 55
Buying decision:
  acting, 74
  approve proposition, 74
  discipline, 73
  help them make, 76
  how buyer buys, 73–74
  no one wants to be sold, 75
  possible solution to problem, 74
  recognize need, 74
  reminders, 76–77
  see and listen to salesperson, 74
  steps in selling, 74–75
    approach, 74
    closing, 75
    pre-approach, 74
    presenting, 74–75
    probing, 74

Buying decision (*cont'd*):
  success habits, 72–73
    living right, 73
    selling right, 72–73
    studying right, 73
    thinking right, 72
    working right, 72
  want-creator, 75
Buying motive, dominant, 108–110

C

Calendar, daily planning, 55
Call reluctance, 91–92, 99
Cancer treatment, 30
Center-of-influence strategy, 63
Closing:
  act of hesitation, 165
  ask for questions, 162
  asking them to buy, 170
  ask your questions, 162
  assuming, 166
  buying signs, 165–166
  consciousness, 159–161
  deal with decision-makers, 159
  emotion, 168–169
  emulate pros, 165
  entire selling process, 157–158
  facial expressions, 165
  gauge prospect's pace, 163
  impending event, 167
  inducement, 169–170
  language you must learn, 164
  minor point, 166–167
  motivation, 75
  physical action, 167–168
  prospect's attention, 165

Closing (*cont'd*):
questions, 171–172
ask yourself these, 171–172
assist buyer with, 171
reminders, 174
rules of selling, 158
silence, 170–171
stimulate action, 162–163
strategy, 161–163
summarize, 162
summed up, 173–174
tone of voice, 165
when to stop selling, 164–165
words and questions, 165
your personality, 158
Cold canvass, 64–65
Company:
identify with, 184
information, 83–84, 98
Complaints, handle fast, 182–183
Confidence, 26–27, 27–28, 73, 208–209, 250
Contact, initial, 81–100
(*see also* Pre-approach)
Conversations, unnecessary, 193

D

Daily planning calendar, 55
Deadlines, 56, 195, 197, 227
Decisions:
buying
(*see* Buying decision)
pre-approach, 81–82
who makes, 87–88
Delegation, 199
Dictating, 198
Direct mail strategy, 64
Discipline, self-, 20, 71, 73
Disease, 30, 31

E

Educators, 52
Effectiveness, 196–197
Endless chain, 62–63
Endorsement, 84
Energy, 32, 33
Exercise program, 31–32
Expectation, success, 26–27

F

Facts, finding, 107
Family life, 35–36
Financial manager, 29–30
Fitness, physical, 30–33
Follow-through:
be best-informed, 182
consistent reliability, 182
handle complaints fast, 182–183
initial sales value, 177
reminders, 187
serve what you sell, 182
serving better, 183–184
be positive, 183
give more than you get, 184
strive for stability, 183
think of helping others, 183
value relationships, 183
show appreciation, 178–181
for an interview, 181
manners and actions, 181
never forget customer, 181
order received, 179–180
seek opportunities, 181
send prospects, 181
supply leads, 181
thanks for referrals, 181
those who assist you, 180–181
summed up, 185–186
you are firm, 184–185
Four-minute barrier, 89–90

G

Generators, 52
Getting in, 85, 98–99
Goals, time management, 195
Goal setting, action planning:
aims, purposes, 220
examining your dreams, 229, 233
fixing action plan, 237–241
goals, 220–221, 227
achievable, 220–221
believable, 227
deadlines, 227
measurable, 227
how, 220
keeping records, 241–242

Goal setting, action planning (*cont'd*):
limitations self-imposed, 129
looking at me, 228–229
reminders, 244
summed up, 242–243
this year's goals, 234

H

Habits, 52–53, 54–55, 71–73
Honesty, 28–29

I

Individual, influence of, 184
Information for presentation, 107
Initial contact, 81–100
(*see also* Pre-approach)
Integrity, 37
Interceptors, 51–52
Interruptions, 56
Introduction, 84

J

Junior associate strategy, 64

K

Knowledge, 34

L

Learning is listening, 105–107
Listening, 84, 93–94, 105–107
Living right, 73

M

Made-up mind, 19–47
Malignancies, 30
Management, time, 191–202
(*see also* Time)
Meetings, unplanned, 193
Mind:
made-up, 19–47
upness, 205
(*see also* Upness)
where sale is made, 105
Momentum, 197
Moral values, 28–29
Motivation:
comes from within, 214–215
impossible to fail, 216–217
monitor results, 217
plan for greatness, 216
potential for greatness, 215–216
self-acceptance, 215
think like successful people, 216
Motive, buying, 108–110

N

Need, 74, 104, 111
Needs-satisfier, 75

O

Objections:
always assert, 138
answering now, 142
anticipate, 140–141
ask prospect to repeat, 144
attitude toward, 138–139
be assistant buyer, 149–150
classifying, 139
example or story, 146–147
hear prospect out, 143
ignore, 141–142
insincere, 151
isolating, 145–146
not answers to all, 149
permission to answer later, 142
reminders, 154
restating, 144–145
six step strategy, 142–148
stay in control, 137
stimulating action, 147–148
summary, 151–153
when to answer, 140
why, 139–140
Observing, 57, 62
Odds, playing, 25–26
Opportunity, 21–22
Organization, lack, 193

P

Paperwork, 193, 199
Paying attention, 57–58, 63

Physical fitness, 30–33
Planning, action
(*see* Goal setting, action planning)
Planning and prospecting:
educators, 52
generators, 52
interceptors, 51–52
planning, 53–56, 65–67
daily planning calendar, 55
deadlines set, 56
desired results, 56
important things first, 56
interruptions, 56
productivity, 56
results, 56
same hour, same place, 54
"Self-Organization Day," 55
prospecting, 57–65, 65–67
alertness, 58
center-of-influence, 63
cold canvass, 64–65
direct mail, 64
endless chain, 62–63
junior associate, 64
observe, 57, 62
paying attention, 57–58, 62
"referred lead," 63
tickler system, 59–61
reminders, 66–67
summed up, 65–66
suppliers, 51
Positive feelings, 91, 183
Pre-approach:
aim, 74
authority to buy, 87–88, 98
call reluctance, 91–92
decision-maker, 88
doing something now, 86
"do's" and "don'ts," 90
endorsement, 84
final result wanted, 85
focus on rewards, 91, 99
four-minute barrier, 89–90
gain appointment, 92–93
get in, 85, 98–99
information, 83–84, 98
about prospect, 83, 98
about prospect's company, 83–84, 98
introduction, 84
Pre-approach (*cont'd*):
learn your lines, 89
listen to, 84
most people are nice, 92, 99
objectives of planning, 83–84
object of your call, 93
positive feelings, 91
prepare technically, 91
preparing, 82
read, 84
reminders, 99–100
right contact, 85
sell prospect on listening, 93–94
series of decisions, 81–82
start at top, 88
talk with, 84
telephone, 94–97, 99
basic strategies, 95–96, 99
making contact, 94–95
recommended times, 96–97, 99
Preparation, achievements, 20–21
Presentation:
arouse interest, 118
ask for order, 123, 128
be assistant buyer, 127
company reputation, 121–122
create desire, 119–120
credibility, 127
demonstrate, 127
emotion and logic, 127
established strategy, 124
gain buyer's confidence, 120–122
gain instant attention, 116–118
gain understanding, 126
get prospect involved, 124
guarantee, 121
impact words, 125–126
key buyer benefits, 122–123
love of excellence, 130
motivate to action, 122–124
never interrupt, 127
objections, 137–154
(*see also* Objections)
objective, 74–75
only the best, 128–130
personalize, 124
powerful expressions, 128
prospect sells self, 127
prospect's language, 121

Presentation (*cont'd*):
prospect's questions, 123
prospect's self-interest, 124
reminders, 132–133
reputation of salesperson, 129
research, 121
review, 124
simple, 121
stop-look-listen, 126–127
summarize strategically, 127
summed up, 130–132
testimonials, 120–121
Priorities, 195, 196
Probing:
advantages, 104–105
dominant buying motive, 108–110
finding facts, 107
good listeners, 107
how much you care, 106
learning is listening, 105–107
mind of prospect, 105
need, 74, 104, 111
objectives, 74, 104, 111
solution, 74, 104, 111
where sale is made, 105
Productivity, 56
Prospect:
information, 83, 98
sell on listening, 93–94
Prospecting
(*see* Planning and prospecting)

Q

"Quiet hour," 199
Quitters, 42

R

Reading, 34–35, 84, 198
Recorder, 198
Referrals, thanks for, 181
Relationships, value, 183
Reliability, consistent, 182
Results, defining, 56, 85
Rewards, focus on, 91, 99

S

Salesmanship, importance, 22–25
Salesperson, super, 247–258
Scheduling, poor, 194
(*see also* Time)
Secretary, 195, 198
Self-confidence, 26–27, 27–28, 73, 208–209, 250
Self-discipline, 20, 71, 73
Self-image:
building strong, 209–213
ability to communicate, 210–211
be best self, 212
build life model, 211
compete, don't compare, 212
forgive others, 210
forgive yourself, 209–210
positive use of imagination, 211–212
changes, 206–208
mistaken idea, 213, 214
negative influences, 213, 214
obstacles, 213–214
self-confidence, 208–209
what it is, 206
you will be true to it, 206
Self-motivation, 214–217
Self-Organization Day, 55
Selling:
principles, 22–25
process, 74–75
right, 72–73
Serving better, 183–184, 185
Solution, 74, 104, 111
Specialists, 198
Spiritual life, 37–38
Stability, strive for, 183
Studying right, 73
Succeeding, 20
Success:
five habits, 72–73
give impression, 27–28
Super salesperson, 247–258
Suppliers, 51
Systems, 195

T

Talking, 84
Telephone, pre-approach, 94–97, 99
Telephone numbers, 199
Thanks, 179, 181
Thinking right, 72

Tickler system, 59–61
Time:
common problems, 193–194
consciousness, 195
deadlines, 56, 195, 197
"fire-fighting," 194
give yourself a raise, 193
194
high-payoff activities, 196
high-quality vs. low-quality, 194–199
how important, 200
invest it wisely, 200
lack of organization, 193
making calls, 193
management tools, 195
momentum, 197
more, if you plan, 191
no shows, 193
planning priorities, 196
poor scheduling, 194
procrastination, 194
productive, 193
reminders, 201–202
sense of urgency, 197
staying effective, 196–197
summed up, 200–201
"time savers," 198–199
unplanned meetings, 193
working *smarter*, 193
Times, telephoning, 96–97, 99
Training, 20
Traits:
assistant buyer, 250
commitment to goals, 248–249
enthusiasm, 250
financial soundness, 251
knowledgeability, 249
perceptiveness, 250–251
Traits (*cont'd*):
perfectionism, 251
persistence, 251
physical fitness, 251
relationship-builder, 249
self-confidence, 250
self-discipline, 249
skillful communication, 251
winning, 248–252

U

Upness:
defined, 205
goal setting, 220–221
mind, 205
motivation, 214–217
(see also Motivation)
reminders, 219–220
self-image, 206–214
(*see also* Self-image)
staying up, 217–219
Urgency, sense of, 197

W

Waiting time, 198
Want-creator, 75
Winners, 42
Winning:
learned habit, 21
odds player, 25–26
self-discipline, 20
training, 20
traits, 248–252
(*see also* Traits)
Working right, 72